THE LANGUAGE OF
POST-MODERN ARCHITECTURE

VENTURI, SCOTT BROWN AND ASSOCIATES, *National Gallery Extension*, London, 1991: 'heteromorphic contextualism'

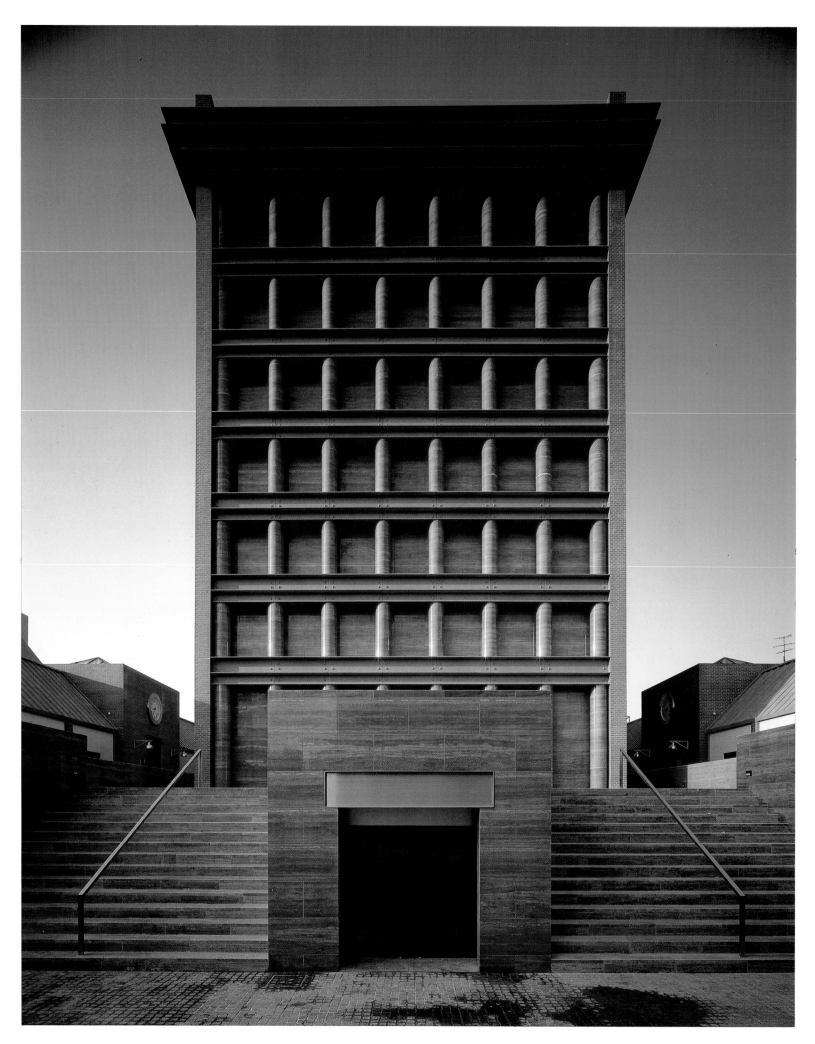

ALDO ROSSI, *Hotel Il Palazzo*, Fukuoka, 1990: 'Post-Modern Classicism'

HANS HOLLEIN, *Haas Haus* interior, Vienna, 1990: 'the interior public realm

KISHO KUROKAWA, *Museum of Contemporary Art*, Hiroshima, 1988: 'symbiosis of past, present and future'

THE LANGUAGE OF
POST-MODERN ARCHITECTURE
THE SIXTH EDITION

CHARLES JENCKS

ANTOINE PREDOCK, *Fine Arts Center, Arizona State University*, Tempe, 1987-89: 'small-block planning'

RIZZOLI
NEW YORK

Jacket front: ANTOINE PREDOCK, *Fine Arts Center, Arizona State University*, Tempe, 1987-89 (Timothy Hursley)
Jacket back: ARATA ISOZAKI, *Disney Building*, Lake Buena Vista, Florida, 1989-91 (Charles Jencks)

To Maggie

First published in the United States of America in 1991 by
RIZZOLI INTERNATIONAL PUBLICATIONS, INC
300 Park Avenue South, New York, NY 10010

Published in Great Britain in 1991 by
ACADEMY EDITIONS
an imprint of the Academy Group Ltd, 7 Holland Street, London W8 4NA

Sixth revised enlarged edition
First edition 1977 Second edition 1978 Third edition 1981 Fourth edition 1984 Fifth edition 1987

Library of Congress Cataloging-in-Publication Data

Jencks, Charles.
The language of post-modern architecture / Charles Jencks — 6th rev. ed.
204 p 30.5x25.2cm
Includes bibliographical references.
ISBN 0-8478-1359-2
1. Architecture. Postmodern. I. Title.
N A682.P67J38 1991 724'. 6—dc20
91-4526 CIP

Printed and bound in Singapore

CONTENTS

INTRODUCTION
Death for Rebirth

Now that Post-Modern architecture has triumphed around the world, many people have declared it dead. This, the fate of all successful movements, is something to be celebrated. Born in a fit of love, they grow to maturity all too quickly, are vulgarised, mass-produced and finally assigned to the scrap-heap of history. The same thing happened to Modernism, as the reader will shortly discover, so it is no surprise that those who arrived first at the morgue to certify the new Post-Modern corpse – and see it stayed buried – were none other than the Neo-Modernists. This occurred in 1982, and the participants at this convivial wake brought along doctored photographs of Michael Graves' Portland Building blowing up, as if to reassure themselves of the truth.

By 1986 – ironically, just when many of the world's largest architectural practices were shifting to a Post-Modern mode – the Italian magazine *Modo* announced with an air of revelation that the style was old hat. Not to be outdone at late discovery was the President of the Royal Institute of British Architects who, in 1989, attacked the genre as 'bimbo architecture' and declared for the Year 2000: 'we simply cannot go to the Millennium Ball wearing the threadbare rags of Post-Modernism'. Out of fashion? If ever there were proof of a movement's continued vitality it was these obituaries and attacks, for who is going to waste time flogging a dead style? As if to underline this, the President promptly apologised for his flagellation of the anti-chic and asked a major Post-Modern architect for forgiveness. Such are the vicissitudes of the Style Wars. But there is more than style at stake.

Inevitably, the life and death of an architectural movement, like civilisation, is based on a biological metaphor: but this is only somewhat relevant to anything as complex as an architectural language. Columns and curtain walls come and go irrespective of cultural health. However, many people felt liberated from the dogma and strictures of Modernism when, along with Peter Blake and other architectural medics, I took its failing pulse in the 1970s. As John Summerson later wrote of these diagnoses – 'in the 1980s it has become fashionable to declare the Modern Movement dead. As a serious statement this is arguable, but it is an interesting idea – perhaps the first really inspiring new idea since the Movement was born. It is, anyway, liberating'.

The notion of death frees one from the tyranny of the prevailing orthodoxy and since Modernism had a virtual stranglehold on the profession and academies from the late 1930s to the 1970s, many architects and much of the public were exhilarated. Modern Architecture was no longer a necessity and the idea of the *Zeitgeist* and technological determinism – or, indeed, any determinism – was

1 KISHO KUROKAWA, *Museum of Contemporary Art*, Hiroshima, 1988. By clothing ambiguously a traditional shape (the pitched roof evokes the Edo storehouse) in a futuristic material and then giving it somewhat western mouldings, Kurokawa blends past, present and future in a complete synthesis.

discredited. Architecture could again be based on context, mood, culture, ornament, or almost whatever mattered to the architect and client. And, it has to be added today, the 'death of Post-Modernism' produced a similar relief, for that also loosened the bonds of professional doctrine and tyrannical fashion, and increased freedom of choice.

Pluralism versus Monism

Thankfully, today no single orthodoxy dominates Western society: neither the Pre-Modernism advocated by Prince Charles, the Neo-Modernism advocated by his adversary the President of the RIBA, nor the Post-Modernism caught in a cross-fire between the two camps. If anything reigns it is pluralism – and that 'ism' is incapable of ruling since it depends on fostering choice. There is a paradox here because pluralism is *the* Post-Modern ideology above all others. How can this condition exist without the triumph of the Post-Modern style? Because, as even the remaining Modernists now grant, we live in a post-modern era, the information age where plural cultures compete and there is simply no dominant cultural style or ethos. Or if, say, Deconstruction is fashionable in 1989, it is declared *passé* in two years – the average age of an architectural movement in the global village.

In the pre-industrial past Traditional culture was the leading way of thought; during the industrial age Modernism became the most important *episteme;* while in the post-industrial period none of these competing cultures – High, Low, Traditional, Mass, Pop, Ethnic or Other – speaks for the majority of urban dwellers. Most of the time in the huge megalopolis we are all minorities – yes, even those who have cornered what used to be called 'the ruling taste', the Establishment. This can be alienating, and many people deplore the competition of language games and values, and the retreat into a previous orthodoxy, whether Modern or Traditional. But those with a Post-Modern sensibility enjoy the diversity, and know why it is necessary and positive.

What is at stake in this situation, what constitutes the new world view? Fundamentally it is the growing understanding that pluralism creates meaning; or put negatively in the cool terms of information theory, that 'where there is no difference, there is no information'. Variety of style and habitation generates meaning, because significance is generated by a field of tensions, or an oppositional system. Just one of these many systems will be explained below, but they are concerned with more than style, much more. Any architecture signifies values and supports a way of life; and these are relational matters, as much as is any aesthetic.

Traditionalists and Modernists have one thing in common: they tend to dislike pluralism and suppress it. Consider Le Corbusier's injunctions: 'The "styles" are a lie . . . Our own epoch is determining, day by day, its own style' – that is, a single one based on industrialisation and the Machine Aesthetic. Or compare this monism with Prince Charles' norms of harmonisation. When he attacked the original scheme for extending London's National Gallery, he rephrased the Modernist's plea for consistency: 'I would understand better this type of High-Tech approach if you demolished the whole of Trafalgar Square and started again with a single architect for the entire layout, but what is proposed is like a monstrous carbuncle on the face of a much-loved and elegant friend.' The implication, with its heavy irony, is that a whole lot of aesthetically unified carbuncles would be acceptable.

The norm of stylistic harmony is upheld by architects the Prince favours – Quinlan Terry and Leon Krier – as much as it is by Late- and Neo-Modernists. Lloyds' of London, the Hong Kong Bank, the Arab Institute or little-red-fire-engine pavilions at the Parc de la Villette in Paris are all confined to a unity of material, time and mood – whatever their style. And this despite the fact that they are equivalent in size to a traditional village. When the Classical unities become this dominant, when large chunks of the environment housing thousands of people are built at a stroke in the same manner, one can speak of a totalising impulse still prevalent with the Traditionalists and traditional avant-garde. *Plus ça change, plus c'est la même intégration.*

The Post-Modern Paradigm

This is not true of Post-Modern urbanism. Large developments, such as the decade of building in Berlin under IBA, mix various architects, styles, ages and uses of buildings – sometime even on the same street. While common urban typologies such as the perimeter block are adopted, and some aesthetic rules of the game are imposed, various architects are also encouraged to produce difference, using oppositions within these frameworks. By the late 1970s, this became a norm which was demonstrated in the 1980 Venice Biennale: its *Strada Novissimma* was composed as a system of differences. Soon thereafter, Rob Krier and the Berlin planners under IBA adopted the policy of hiring multiple architects for a district, and combined this strategy with infill building and rehabilitation. By the mid 1980s, the policy had disseminated to developers – Broadgate in London, Battery Park City in New York, the Faneuil Hall complex in Boston and downtown Frankfurt were typical commercial versions of the idea. What had started in 1961, when the first shot of Post-Modernism was fired by Jane Jacobs in her book the *Death and Life of Great American Cities,* had now become a mini-orthodoxy. At least one quarter of all mega-developers saw the point of diversity: mixed ages, mixed uses and complexity made economic as well as aesthetic sense.

It's fascinating that the 'Jacobite manifesto' should fit in so well with the larger Post-Modern paradigm which was growing at the time, and that she should appreciate the fact: such self-awareness is rare. If one steps back from urbanism and architecture and looks at philosophy, literature and science, one finds the same general points emerging in the sixties: the interest in interconnection and symbiosis which characterise ecology; the preoccupation with diversity and difference which typify Post-Modern philosophy and politics; and the understanding of interrelated variables on which the new 'sciences of complexity' are built. At the end of her book, in a chapter called 'The Kind of Problem a City Is', Jacobs shows that urban questions are not particularly ones of 'simplicity', nor 'disorganised complexity' – both of which characterised Modern science from Newton to the development of statistics. Rather, a city is a *problem of organised complexity* like those with which the life sciences deal.

All the key Post-Modern sciences are rooted in this new *episteme* – ecology,

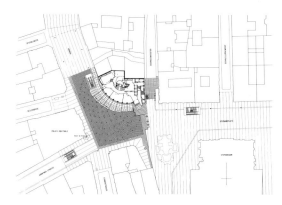

2, 2a HANS HOLLEIN, *Haas-Haus*, St Stevens Square, Vienna, 1988-90. This infill building of mixed use – shops, offices, restaurants, interior piazza etc – completes a corner site next to a medieval cathedral and meditates between the four different styles of the adjacent buildings (Gothic, Baroque, turn of the century, 1950s Modern). Responding to the complex and contradictory urban pressures, it transforms the pale green building to its left into a stepped square motif, then into a Modern curtain wall, then into a curved cylinder that recalls an ancient fortification that stood here. This shape also contains the space with the cathedral and turns the corner as the building then takes up the grammar of the back street. A Post-Modern chameleon building, like James Stirling's Tate Addition (1980-87), it also has a Classical temple and Modern cantilever on the roof. Like Kurokawa, Hollein refers to this time-building as a 'symbiosis' of past, present and future.

ethology, biology, holography, the cognitive sciences, psycholinguistics, semiology, chaos theory, neural nets, and so on. Almost all of these deal with feedback, non-linear equations and sudden self-organising phenomena, whereas the Modern sciences, as Jacobs argues, deal with dual- or multi-variable statistical issues. The 'sciences of simplicity' – Newton's laws of gravity and the workings of the solar system are the prototypes – established the Modern paradigm, while the sciences of complexity – Noam Chomsky's ideas of deep structure, or Ilya Prigogine's of self-organisation are the archetypes – created the Post-Modern *episteme*. So we have an implicit consensus, or an overlap of thought patterns and heuristic models centering on pluralism and complexity. Organised complexity as idea, fact and style typifies the urbanism of Jane Jacobs, the architecture of Robert Venturi and the literature of Umberto Eco – which is why these disparate manifestations help sum up the Post-Modern paradigm. Indeed, Venturi's *Complexity and Contradiction in Architecture,* 1966 is considered, after Jacobs' book, the second major treatise to start defining Post-Modern architecture.

What is Post-Modern Architecture?

Post-Modern architecture is obviously concerned with more than *pluralism* and *complexity*, although these two key words begin to locate its centre. To suggest the wealth of concepts involved in its definition, I will briefly summarise and emphasise some of the essential definers.

The primary strategy architects have created to articulate the pluralism of culture is that of *double-coding*: mixing their own professional tastes and technical skills with those of their ultimate clients – the inhabitants. Double-coding exists at many levels and has done so in several periods: it may be an ancient temple which mixes abstract geometry and representational sculpture, high and low art. It may be the Post-Modern Classicism of James Stirling that contrasts monumental and high-tech codes; or vernacular and commercial codes, as in the case of Charles Moore. The dualities invariably contrast the local with the contemporary – hence the label Post-*Modern*. But whatever the combination, it is the concept of coding itself which is essential to this growing tradition.

Modern architects simply, and somewhat naively, perceived and constructed the meanings they cared about in architecture. This could be successful or disastrous, as I point out in the first two sections of this book. By contrast, Post-Modernists are keenly aware that architecture is a *language* perceived through codes, and that codes and therefore actual seeing differs somewhat in every culture. Hence the complex relation of the architect to the client – again partly explicable by an emergent science of complexity, semiotics: the theory of signs. This theory forms the background for Part Two, and is one of the crucial ways in which Post-Modern thought differs from its predecessor; but this book is about a growing tradition of architecture, not its intellectual foundations. I have tried to give just enough theory here to explain the main concepts of architectural semiotics and drive home the point that, for Post-Modernists, the perceptual codes of the users are just as important as those of the architects – another reason for double-coding. Modernists and Traditionalists, by contrast, focus on the producers.

3 DUAL CODING, *Temple of Artemis* at Corcyra, early 6th century BC. The typical Greek pediment shows the mixture of meanings, popular and élite, which could be read by different groups of people, on different levels. Here the running Gorgon, Medusa, with her snakes, and the rampant lion-panthers, and the various acts of murder are all represented dramatically in strong colour. This representational art literally breaks the abstract geometry at the top, but elsewhere harmony and implicit metaphor reign. Human proportions, visual refinements and a pure architecture of syntactic elements also have their place. Two different languages, each with its own integrity and audience.

There is more to Post-Modern architecture than its conception as a multi-level language. If one were to list the defining characteristics they would extend far beyond the four or five stylistic categories that historians usually apply to a period – for instance, the four that Hitchcock and Johnson found in the International Style in 1932. Anthony Blunt, in a polemical analysis, *Some Uses and Misuses of the Terms Baroque and Rococo as Applied to Architecture,* finds the historian cannot work with fewer than ten definers. It could be worse. In my own attempt to classify Late, Neo and Post-Modern architecture, I found at least thirty important design ideas, ideological definers and stylistic preoccupations – and there are obviously more. Architectural movements are as complex to define as bird species are for the taxonomist, and demand the synthesising of many characteristics into a whole. The historian classifies overlapping sets of definers by family resemblances, as the philosopher Wittgenstein put it – and this is partly a global, and partly an inductive judgement.

The characteristics of the Post-Modern come from its attempt to cut across the spectrum of tastes with a variety of styles: thus it seeks a *radical eclecticism,* or a multiple-coding, as well as the double logic I have already mentioned. Readers will find subsections devoted to this, as well as the other key definers: *historicism, contextualism,* the new *complex post-modern space, metaphor* and *abstract representation.* The motives extend beyond this to the search for a *relevant ornament,* a *contextual symbolism,* an *anthropomorphism* – in short, to the search for a *suitable content* to represent.

There are indeed more than thirty norms and forms which define the movement, and these will be explored in the pages following Part Two. For other writers, the situation is somewhat simpler. In *The Doubles of Post-Modernism,* 1980, the architect Robert Stern supports a 'traditional post-modernism' which is concerned with *historical continuity* and, like this book, the 'struggle for cultural coherence that is not falsely monolithic': that is, one based on architectural 'form as communicating sign' which a wide public can understand. Elsewhere he mentions as essential an intense concern for 'ornament', 'context', and 'historical allusion'.

Paolo Portoghesi, in *Postmodern, The Architecture of a Postindustrial Society,* 1982, not only places emphasis on the *information society,* but again on the idea of *historical continuity* and the role of *city typologies* in sustaining this. Thus Stern and Portoghesi, through their writing, architecture and exhibitions, have led the movement towards the historicism to which much of the public – sadly – reduces it. While their work often has a creative integrity, the genre which follows it is frequently commercialised cliché.

The agenda is much larger and more important than the superficial facadism to which giant commercial commissions and the Disney Corporation have bent it. But there also *is* this weakness to a certain strain of the tradition. 'Disneyworld Postmodernism', discussed in a later section, and the kitsch versions of the genre, are the main reasons critics pronounce the movement dead while it still moves. It is true, however, that the other traditions show the same problems of over-production; and these are *systemic* as I pointed out in the first edition of this book. The commercial and production viruses which contaminated Modern Architecture

are now attacking its child. 'Fast-Food-Mega-Build' – to give it as horrible a name as I can – corrupts all movements, and as long as architecture is produced on the run, in too great volume, it will suffer these problems of over-production. They are, once again, diseases of success.

Heinrich Klotz, in *The History of Postmodern Architecture* (Germany 1984, USA 1988) offers a slightly different focus than that given here. He takes up the communicational aspect that all writers stress and bends it towards 'narrative content'. Form does not just follow function, in his definition of Post-Modern architecture, but 'fiction'. The concern for *Meaning in Architecture* (the subject of a book George Baird and I edited in 1969) becomes the central preoccupation for Klotz, and this very wide concern allows him to include many architects – Rem Koolhaas, John Hejduk and Richard Meier – who I (and no doubt they themselves) would be much happier to see in some other slot, perhaps marked 'Late-' or 'Neo-Modernist'. The three of them, as other New Moderns, have been attacking Post-Modernism since at least 1982.

Nonetheless, Heinrich Klotz is right to show the ambiguity of these practitioners – who all *revise, ironise,* and *distort* abstract Modernism – and in these weak senses are 'post'. But defining the movement by the single category 'fiction' or 'allusion and association', as he does elsewhere, is much too loose. All architecture has some representational and allusive meaning, even if it is to a previous abstraction or tradition of non-meaning (as in Hannes Meyer's work). So, otherwise exemplary as history, Klotz's definition of the subject is at once too wide, in its inclusion of Neo-Modernists, and too narrow, in its reduction to 'fiction'. We simply cannot escape the multiple definition of a plural movement – which is why the reader will here find six main strands of Post-Modernism and several key definers.

All this dispute over categories and the intentions of a movement may sound academic, or irrelevant to architectural practice – but it is not. Differences of meaning create divergences in evolution – as we have seen in the Prince of Wales' recent battle, first with the Modernists, then with the Post-Modernists.

The Failure of Prince Charles' Crusade

In 1984, on the 150th anniversary of the RIBA, Prince Charles launched what he later termed a 'crusade' – against the heathens, nihilists, abstractionists and all those who were building an anti-Christian, materialistic architecture in Britain. Character-istically, in this Holy War, he copied the example of Post-Modernists and my own use of metaphors to attack the sterile malapropisms of Mies van der Rohe and those who prefer abstract sculpture to significance. Mies' proposed skyscraper for Central London he vilified and destroyed as a 'glass stump'. Other verbal missiles stopped the 'monstrous carbuncle' designed for the National Gallery, James Stirling's '1930s wireless' put forward also for Central London, and the 'prison camp' proposed by Sir Philip Dowson and Arups for London's Paternoster site. As visual metaphors these exocets were wide of the mark, but as Royal bombs they were very effective. The Prince, surrounded by a coterie of Traditionalists and with TV and the newspapers egging him on, could not resist the temptation to sink the designs and reputations of England's finest professionals. He claimed in a *Sunday Times*

4,4a

5,5a

4, 4a JAMES STIRLING and MICHAEL WILFORD, *Number One Poultry Scheme*, London 1987, revised 1988, 1989. Attacked by Prince Charles as an 'old 1930s wireless', this is actually a sensitive response to a complex triangular site. It looks like everything but an old radio set: it partly alludes to the Classical masonry *and* Modern glass buildings. It also adopts a medium block size between the scale of adjacent large office blocks and the tiny medieval blocks and streets. If built this Post-Modern Classical infill would provide a *res publica* and open space – at the base and on the roof – in an area which sorely needs both. After the building's third trial, the highest court in the land, the House of Lords, finally gave its approval in March 1991.

article in 1989 that he did not have any real power, but the truth was that he did have great power to destroy.

The pity of all this is even greater. Prince Charles' misdirected crusade embodies a lot of common sense and has a following even among Modernists. Indeed, everybody who watches television knew by 1980 that tower blocks were out, that abstract Modernism was usually boring, and that rapacious development was the main cause of city deconstruction. James Stirling and Sandy Wilson – two of the Prince's victims – had been saying such things for fifteen years; they were the clichés of the average professional. Furthermore, many architects were inclining towards pluralism and ready to accept the partial validity of his three Cs: Community Architecture, Classicism and Conservation. One will find these three mini-movements discussed and partly defended here, years before he jumped on the Post-Modern bandwagon – only to squash it. Ninety per cent of what Prince Charles advocates is beneficent, has been said before, and gains general assent; the problem is with the other ten per cent.

By attacking such humane and respected architects as Philip Dowson for being 'inhuman', by censoring his design for the St Paul's area as 'a prison camp' and calling it 'watered-down Classicism' and 'half-hearted'; by intervening to influence developers and manipulate a democratic process, he has sent two very clear messages to the architectural profession: that he holds their values in contempt, and that he is prepared to act undemocratically.

The pity, again, is that he usually favours such things as participation in design and an open process of choosing architects. But encouraging developers from America, Japan and Britain to come, cap in hand, to his country estate Highgrove to present their schemes behind closed doors – and trim them to a Classicist *cut* – is no way for a Prince to behave. That's the style of the Old Boys' Network. And this from a Prince who has supported community architecture and minorities. Of monarchy he has even said, 'It can be an elective institution. After all, if people don't want it, they won't have it'.

This is rather how most architects felt by September 1989, the date of the Prince's one-sided book and television film *Vision of Britain,* with its accompanying exhibition at the Victoria and Albert Museum. Before this, many in the design community, including me, felt that the Royal intervention had at least publicity and populism to recommend it. While architecture was becoming ever more topical in other countries, the popular press in Britain had not really taken it up before 1984; so the Prince could gain a certain credibility over time simply by being the pretext for provoking public debate.

Vision of Britain changed all that. While a popular success in viewing and rating terms, it was not a hit with journalists, critics, architects or the Establishment. A characteristic opinion, by a respected historian and writer on country houses – Mark Girouard – spoke for the informed minority. The Prince's tastes were too predictably limited; like 'Pavlov's dog', Girouard wrote, 'when he sees a pitched roof, a chimney stack, a pediment, a column or a sash window, he wags his tail; when he sees concrete, or is deprived of his bowl of ornament, he barks'. This was devastating, coming from a writer both eminent in the field and one who shares

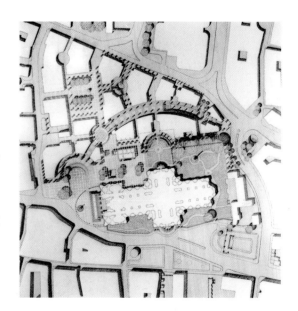

5,5a PHILIP DOWSON & ARUP ASSOCIATES, *Paternoster Square Competition Proposal,* London, 1987 revised 1989. The Post-Modern Classical scheme which won a competition and then was revised after public consultation was torpedoed by Prince Charles' two interventions. Actually the proposal he supported behind the scenes, through the newspaper *The Evening Standard* and in private meetings, took many of its design ideas and massing from the previous Arup proposal. This scheme lowers the scale near St Paul's, creates a series of glimpsed views of the cathedral, provides a public arcade at the back and uses a medium block size typology – so does John Simpsons'.

much in terms of values and background with the Prince.

Such opinions were confirmed at the 'Official Debate' I had the misfortune to chair at the V & A near the close of the exhibition. It degenerated into name-calling, and showed very clearly the kind of climate which the Prince's attack had created in Britain. On my right, Lucinda Lambton and Leon Krier were pitted against Martin Pawley and Sandy Wilson sitting to the left. Once the debate started, I couldn't help remembering the origins of 'left- and right-wing' – categories architecturally determined by the seating positions of the two opposing camps in the Estates General at the time of the French Revolution.

I don't remember who threw the first parallel that night at the V & A. In any case, Prince Charles was compared to Pol Pot, then a Modernist to Honecker, then the Prince of Wales to Stalin, then a Modernist to Ceaucescu, then the Prince to Hitler, then . . . I should have declared the meeting closed at that point, for the next two hours brought little light and much blood.

The only real conclusion was the vote at the end of the evening, which showed that the audience of over three hundred generally approved of the Prince's intervention, but questioned his taste, and disliked his tactics. By an overwhelming majority they supported his focusing of public opinion on architecture; but by a vote of two to one they rejected his stylistic preferences, and by two and a half to one they disapproved of his methods of influencing planning decisions.

No doubt in supporting the Traditionalists, and, later, the ecological movement, the Prince has found two issues worth promoting. Furthermore, his creation of a summer school for training craftsmen and architects in the traditional virtues, and his commissioning Leon Krier and others to design part of a town in Dorchester are very positive moves of his crusade. But because of the overkill and his vindictive attacks over a period of six years, he has polarised and frightened his dreaded enemy to the point where – irony upon irony – it has now become unified and gained a credibility and purpose it previously lacked. Neo-Modernism has been turned into a professional mainstream by these attacks. It is not only the Old Cold War that thrives on demonology.

The RIBA, with its Neo-Mod President leading ranks of Born-Again Modernists; youthful designers, whipped up into paroxysms of Royal-loathing by Martin Pawley crying 'Hitler, Pol Pot, Stalin'; and the average professional, confused in the crossfire – all reflect the impact of the Prince's crusade. Oh, melancholic and misdirected Prince, if you really want to change Britain then change the hearts and minds of those who lead it: insults merely entrench and enhance your enemy.

Trumpet

What has all this tempest in a Royal-Isle to do with Post-Modernism? First of all, it has taken media attention away from Post-Modernism, which is a good thing, just at the point in the 1980s when it was becoming a major approach for most firms around the world. That decade, in retrospect, shows the simultaneous growth of at least three separate movements: Traditional, Modern and Post-Modern. The building boom in the West and the growth of pluralism have meant that, paradoxically, all sides have been winning the Style Wars. Usually in architectural history, different approaches wax and wane in opposition. But every now and then, when the economic and cultural conditions are right, there is a sudden, mutual flowering of different traditions, just as in evolutionary history there can be a simultaneous explosion of new species – all prospering for a time. This can be conceived, visually, as the expanding end of a trumpet.

We are entering a new period of world communications where literally hundreds of styles and ways of life will thrive simultaneously, cheek-by-jowl. They may not appreciate or understand each other. But tolerance, a respect for difference, an enjoyment of variety are *the* attitudes suited to the information age, and pluralism is its philosophy. Post-Modern writers such as David Lodge have insisted on the truths of dialogue and 'dialogic'; urbanists such as Jane Jacobs have shown the economic and social benefits which flow from a varied city fabric; and semioticians such as Umberto Eco have shown how a plural field of discourse creates the precondition for meaning. Such philosophies, major ideas and practices are now in the air, if not dominant. We are well into the post-modern era whether or not the Post-Modern Movement enjoys widespread favour in any particular place.

My own preference is that it remain one voice among many – that it not dominate a city or culture. When it does, at Disneyworld, the results are, to say the least, unfortunate and, hard to believe, even Modernist. True Post-Modernists really do believe in a field of tensions, in the necessity for Traditional and Modern approaches to flourish, in order to sustain all of their meanings. And so, opposed to the reigning ideologies of Prince Charles and the President of the RIBA, they do not want a crusade, or victory over the enemy. They realise the enemy is themselves in another mood and cultural situation, and that the system of oppositions must be supported as an end in itself. No difference? – no richness, no meaning.

* * *

This layer-cake of a book, after first appearing in 1977, now has its sixth addition and edition. It does not make for easy digestion, but the successive layers do have one virtue. They show, to a degree, what the Post-Modern Movement looked like at several different stages: when it was young in the early seventies, searching for a pluralist style; when in the late seventies it became adolescent and more eclectic; when, in the mid-eighties, it reached middle age as Post-Modern Classicism; and what it looks like now in its second birth – varied still, and still doubly-coded. Writing history in stages makes an untidy story, but it has the advantage over reconsidered history of showing the choices open at different moments, and how events were perceived at the time. It also leads to ironies which may perplex the reader: three architects who were criticised for being Modern abstractionists in 1976, and the First Edition – James Stirling, Arata Isozaki and Ricardo Bofill – had become the leading Post-Modernists in 1977 and the second and subsequent editions. Several such switches in direction can be detected and they underscore the point about Post-Modernist double-coding: often the best practitioners were former Modernists.

I first used the term Post-Modern in writings and lectures in 1975. This was not the origin of the phrase – which apparently extends way back to 1870 and the English painter John Watkins Chapman, who used it to mean 'more Modern than Modern' (ie Post-Impressionism). The term and some of its overtones were picked up around 1910 and then, later in the 1930s, by the historian Arnold Toynbee and others. But its first consequential uses were not until the 1960s and in the literary world; here, except for the writings of Leslie Fiedler, it was used negatively but infrequently. It wasn't until 1971, and the literary critic Ihab Hassan's *POSTmodernISM: A Paracritical Bibliography,* that one finds a really positive use of the term. Surprisingly, Hassan uses it to mean what I and other critics will mean by Late- or Ultra-Modernism – that is the Modernism of extreme Avant-Gardism, Deconstruction, silence and Minimalism. My own first uses – 'The Rise of Post-Modern Architecture' were published in a book in 1975 and the London journal, *AAQ,* and the positive reaction to these articles and lectures surprised me. My audience was, in a sense, more Post- than I. In any case, these early stirrings translated into the first edition of this book, which then went into many translations – some legal and others (as in Czechoslovakia, China, South Korea and Taiwan) paralegal. The Movement took off. By the late 1970s the concept was taken up, in the sense I had used it, by the literary and art worlds; but then, in 1979, because of Jean-Francois Lyotard's *La condition postmoderne,* it was translated closer to Hassan's sense. Back and forth the definition and our general understanding of it has gone, while Hassan himself has come closer to my, Umberto Eco's and John Barth's usage: see his collection *The Postmodern Turn* (1987, the Ohio State Press). The phrase now has two contradictory uses (the *Doubles of Post-Modernism,* as Robert Stern wrote in 1980). One may deplore or support this ambiguity, but there is no alternative term enjoying widespread usage which summarises the set of meanings that I, Eco and so many others now give to the phrase. It has caught on and stuck – first to the architectural movement outlined in this book, then to other art and literary movements.

'The Post Modern House' was written in 1945 as an article by the Harvard Professor Joseph Hudnut, but the term was used only in the title and without the conceptualisation of a movement. Later uses by architects occurred infrequently – in 1964 concerning a Philip Johnson building, in 1967 by Nikolaus Pevsner, in 1975 in conversation between Peter Eisenman and Robert Stern – but my articles and book started the 'named' movement. Needless to say, the movement itself existed well before Stern, I or others theorised it.

Aside from my own *What is Post-Modernism?,* 1986, and *Post-Modernism – The New Classicism in Art and Architecture,* 1987, the major books on architecture are Paolo Portoghesi's *Postmodern, The Architecture of a Postindustrial Society,* 1982, and Heinrich Klotz's *Moderne und Postmoderne, Architektur der Gegenwart 1960-1980* (German 1984, English 1988).

The two best general books on the term and concept are Wolfgang Welsch's *Unsere Postmodern Moderne,* 1988, and Margaret Rose's *The Post-Modern and The Post-Industrial – A Critical Analysis* (Cambridge University Press, to appear 1991).

5b ARATA ISOZAKI, *Disney Building,* Lake Buena Vista, Florida, 1989-91. The Florida headquarters building for Disney shows that this corporation can actually produce a convincing and deep architecture that is nevertheless light-hearted. A collage of pinks, reds and greens as well as images – nuclear power station, Aldo Rossi's *House of the Dead,* Mickey Mouse ears – this building pulls it all together with the central cone, a walk-through sun dial. This time-theme is underscored in various ways, especially by the interior symbolism and spatial differences. The Post-Modern goal of representing high and low taste cultures without debasing them is here realised.

PART ONE
The Death of Modern Architecture

Happily, we can date the death of Modern Architecture to a precise moment in time. Unlike the legal death of a person, which is becoming a complex affair of brain waves versus heartbeats, Modern Architecture went out with a bang. That many people didn't notice, and no one was seen to mourn, does not make the sudden extinction any less of a fact, and that many designers are still trying to administer the kiss of life does not mean that it has been miraculously resurrected. No, it expired finally and completely in 1972, after having been flogged to death remorselessly for ten years by critics such as Jane Jacobs; and the fact that many so-called Modern architects still go around practising a trade as if it were alive can be taken as one of the great curiosities of our age (like the British monarchy giving life-prolonging drugs to 'The Royal Company of Archers' or 'The Extra Women of the Bedchamber').

Modern Architecture died in St Louis, Missouri on July 15, 1972 at 3.32 pm (or thereabouts) when the infamous Pruitt-Igoe scheme, or rather several of its slab blocks, were given the final *coup de grace* by dynamite. Previously it had been vandalised, mutilated and defaced by its black inhabitants, and although millions of dollars were pumped back, trying to keep it alive (fixing the broken elevators, repairing smashed windows, repainting), it was finally put out of its misery. Boom, boom, boom.

Without doubt, the ruins should be kept, the remains should have a preservation order slapped on them, so that we keep a live memory of this failure in planning and architecture. Like the folly or artificial ruin – constructed on the estate of an eighteenth-century English eccentric to provide him with instructive reminders of former vanities and glories – we should learn to value and protect our former disasters. As Oscar Wilde said, 'experience is the name we give to our mistakes', and there is a certain health in leaving them judiciously scattered around the landscape as continual lessons.

Pruitt-Igoe was constructed according to the most progressive ideals of CIAM (the Congress of International Modern Architects) and it won an award from the American Institute of Architects when it was designed in 1951. It consisted of elegant slab blocks fourteen storeys high with rational 'streets in the air' (which were safe from cars, but as it turned out, not safe from crime); 'sun, space and greenery', which Le Corbusier called the 'three essential joys of urbanism' (instead of conventional streets, gardens and semi-private space, which he banished). It had a separation of pedestrian and vehicular traffic, the provision of play space, and local amenities such as laundries, crèches and gossip centres – all rational

6 MINORU YAMASAKI, *Pruitt-Igoe Housing*, St Louis, 1952-55. Several slab blocks of this scheme were blown up in 1972 after they were continuously vandalised. The crime rate was higher than in other developments, and Oscar Newman attributed this, in his book *Defensible Space*, to the long corridors, anonymity and lack of controlled semi-private space. Another factor: it was designed in a purist language at variance with the architectural codes of the inhabitants.

substitutes for traditional patterns. Moreover, its Purist style, its clean, salubrious hospital metaphor, was meant to instil, by good example, corresponding virtues in the inhabitants. Good form was to lead to good content, or at least good conduct; the intelligent planning of abstract space was to promote healthy behaviour.

Alas, such simplistic ideas, taken over from the philosophies of Rationalism, Behaviourism and Pragmatism proved as irrational as the philosophies themselves. Modern Architecture, as the son of the Enlightenment, was an heir to its congenital naiveties, too great and awe-inspiring to warrant refutation in a book on mere building. I will concentrate here, in this first part, on the demise of a very small branch of a big bad tree; but to be fair it should be pointed out that Modern Architecture is the offshoot of Modern Painting and the Modern Movements in all the arts. Like rational schooling, rational health and rational design of women's bloomers, it has the faults of an age trying to re-invent itself totally on rational grounds.

These shortcomings are now well known, thanks to the writings of Ivan Illich, Jacques Ellul, E F Schumacher, Michael Oakshott and Hannah Arendt, and the overall misconceptions of Rationalism will not be dwelt upon. They are assumed for my purposes. Rather than a deep extended attack on Modern Architecture, showing how its ills relate very closely to the prevailing philosophies of the modern age, I will attempt a caricature, a polemic. The virtue of this genre (as well as its vice) is its license to cut through the large generalities with a certain abandon and enjoyment, overlooking all the exceptions and subtleties of the argument. Caricature is of course not the whole truth. Daumier's drawings didn't really show what nineteenth-century poverty was about, but rather gave a highly selective view of some truths. Let us then romp through the desolation of Modern Architecture and the destruction of our cities, like some Martian tourist out on an earthbound excursion, visiting the archaeological sites with a superior disinterest, bemused by the sad but instructive mistakes of a former architectural civilisation. After all, since it is fairly dead, we might as well pick over the corpse.

Crisis in architecture

In 1974 Malcolm MacEwen wrote a book of the above title which summarised the English view of what was wrong with the Modern Movement (capitalised, like all world religions), and what we should do about it. His summary was masterful, but his prescriptions were wildly off the mark: the remedy was to overhaul a tiny institutional body, the Royal Institute of British Architects, by changing a style here and a heart there — as if these sorts of things would make the *multiple causes* of the crisis go away. Well, let me make use of his effective analysis, not his solution, taking as a typical grotesque of Modern Architecture one building type: modern hotels.

The new Penta Hotel in London has 914 bedrooms, which is almost nine times the average large hotel of fifty years ago, and it is 'themed' (a word of decorators) in the International Style and a mode which could be called Vasarely-Airport-Lounge-Moderne. There are about twenty of these leviathans near each other, on the way to the London Airport (it is known in the trade as 'Hotellandia'), and they create a disruption in scale and city life which amounts to the occupation of an

7 RICHARD SEIFERT, *Penta Hotel*, London, 1972. The English government subsidised these kinds of hotels in the late sixties to cope with the tourist boom. Twenty or so, with about 500 bedrooms, sprang up on the main route in from the airport. On the outside they are uptight International Style; on the inside Lapidus Ersatz. (R Seifert & Partners).

invading army – a role tourists tend to fulfil.

These newly formed battalions with their noble-phoney names include The Churchill (500 bedrooms, named after Sir Winston and themed in the Pompeian-Palladian style by way of Robert Adam); the Imperial Hotel (720 bedrooms, International outside, fibreglass Julius Caesar inside); and the Park Tower (300 bedrooms, themed in Corn-on-the-Cob and various sunburst motifs inside).

A recurring aspect of these hotels, built between 1969 and 1973, is that they provide very modern services, such as air-conditioning, themed in old-world styles which vary from Rococo, Gothic, Second Empire, to a combination of all three styles together. The formula of ancient style and modern plumbing has proved inexorably successful in our consumer society, and this Ersatz has been the major commercial challenge to classical Modern Architecture. But in one important way, in terms of architectural *production*, Ersatz and Modern Architecture contribute equally to alienation and what MacEwen calls 'the crisis'.

8 I have tried to untangle the different causes of this situation, at least eleven in number, and show how they operate in the two modern modes of architectural production (listed in the two right hand columns of the diagram).

For contrast, the first column on the left refers to the old system of *private* architectural production (operating largely before World War I) where an architect knew his client personally, probably shared his values and aesthetic code. An extreme example of this is Lord Burlington's Chiswick Villa, an unusual situation where the architect was the builder (or contractor), client and user all at once. Hence there was no disparity between his rather élite and esoteric code (a spare, intellectual version of the Palladian language) and his way of life. The same identity

8 'CRISIS IN ARCHITECTURE' a diagram of three systems of architectural production. The left column shows the implications of the old, private system of production, while the right columns show the two modern systems. Critics of Modern Architecture have emphasised several of these eleven causes of the crisis, but clearly the causes are multiple and work as a system tied into the economic sphere. The question is: how many variables must be changed for the system to change?

9 SAUSALITO BAY BOAT HOUSES, 1960. Like the Hand-made Houses of California, these boat houses depend on the oldest form of architectural production – *self-build*. Each one is tailor-made by the inhabitant in a different style, and you find cheek-by-jowl, a Swiss chalet boat house and a converted caravan, or here, the Venturi style next to the A-frame Fuller style.

	SYSTEM 1 - PRIVATE private client is architect user	SYSTEM 2 - PUBLIC public client and architect users differ	SYSTEM 3 - DEVELOPER developer client and architect users differ
1 ECONOMIC SPHERE	Mini-Capitalist (restricted money)	Welfare-State Capitalist (lacks money)	Monopoly-Capitalist (has money)
2 MOTIVATION	aesthetic inhabit ideological use	solve user's problem housing	make make money money to use
3 RECENT IDEOLOGY	Too various to list	progress, efficiency, large scale, anti-history Brutalism, etc.	Same as System 2 plus pragmatic
4 RELATION TO PLACE	local client user architect in place	remote users move architects to place	remote and absent changing clients draughtsmanship
5 CLIENTS RELATION TO ARCHITECT	Expert friend same partners small screen	Anonymous Doctor changing designers large team	Hired Servant doesn't know designers or users
6 SIZE OF PROJECT	"small"	"some large"	"too big"
7 SIZE/TYPE OF ARCHITECTS OFFICE	small partnership	large centralised	large centralised
8 METHOD OF DESIGN	slow, responsive innovative expensive	impersonal, anonymous, conservative, low cost	quick, cheap and proven formulae
9 ACCOUNTABILITY	to client-user	to local council and bureaucracy	to stockholders developers and board
10 TYPES OF BUILDING	houses, museums, universities etc.	housing and infrastructure	shopping centres hotels, offices, factories, etc.
11 STYLE	multiple	impersonal safe, contemporary vandal-proofed	pragmatic cliche and bombastic

10 PENTA RESTAURANT interior with its royal, fibreglass cartouche *Dieu-et-mon-droit*. Actually Holiday Inns, the biggest multinational in hotels, prefabricates these fibreglass symbols and then sends them out to some of their 1,700 concessions. The multinationals have been instrumental in standardising world taste and creating a world 'consumption community'. The National Biscuit Company foresees the goal of two billion biscuit munchers eating their standard average cookie.

11 DISNEYLAND, opened in 1955 as a dream of Walt Disney, started the new form of ride-through parks where people are put on a continuously moving assembly line and then shunted past 'experiences'. Sometimes the ride is effortless and you aren't aware of the mechanisms. At other times long queues form and you are ushered into people pens. Multinationals such as Pepsi, Ford, General Electric and Gulf have heavily invested in Disney Enterprises.

exists today, although on a more modest scale and as a relative rarity – the 'Handmade Houses' which are built outside urban centres in America, or the boat house community in Sausalito, in San Francisco Bay, where each boat house is built 9 by the inhabitant in a different, personalised style. These self-built houses testify to the close correspondence there can be between meaning and form when architectural production is at a small scale and controlled by the inhabitant.

Other factors which influenced this type of production in the past include the *mini-capitalist economy* where money was restricted. The architect or speculative builder designed relatively *small* parts of the city at one go; he worked *slowly*, responding to well-established needs, and he was *accountable* to the client, who was invariably the user of the building as well. All these factors, and more that are shown in the diagram, combined to produce an architecture understood by the client and in a language shared by others.

The second and third columns refer to the way most architecture is produced today and show why it is out of scale with historic cities, and alienating to both architects and society. First, in the economic sphere, it is either produced for a public welfare agency which lacks the money necessary to carry out the socialist intentions of the architects, or it is funded by a capitalist agency whose monopoly creates gigantic investments and correspondingly gigantic buildings. For instance, the Penta Hotel is owned by the European Hotel Corporation, a consortium of five airlines and five international banks. These ten corporations together create a monolith which by financial definition must appeal to mass taste, at a middle-class 10 level. There is nothing inherently inferior about this taste culture; it is rather the economic imperatives determining the size and predictability of the result which have coerced the architecture into becoming so relentlessly pretentious and uptight.

Secondly, in this type of production, the architect's motivation is either to solve a problem, or in the case of the developer's architect, to make money. Why the latter motivation doesn't produce effective architecture as it did in the past remains a mystery, (unless it is connected with the compelling pressures of predictable taste). But it is quite clear why 'problems' don't produce architecture. They produce instead 'rational' solutions to over-simplified questions in a chaste style.

Yet the greatest cause of alienation is the *size* of today's projects: the hotels, garages, shopping centres and housing estates which are 'too big' – like the architectural offices which produce them. How big is too big? Obviously there is no easy answer to this, and we await the detailed study of different building types. But the equation can be formulated in general, and it might be called 'the Ivan Illich Law of Diminishing Architecture' (parallel to his discoveries of counter-productive growth in other fields). It could be stated as follows: 'For any building type there is an upper limit to the number of people who can be served before the quality of the environment falls.' The service of the large London hotels has fallen because of staff shortages and absenteeism, and the quality of tourism has declined because the tourists are treated as so many cattle to be shunted from one ambience to the next in a smooth and continuous flow. Programmed, continuously-rolling pleasure, the shunting of people into queues, pens and moving lines, a process which was

11 perfected by Walt Disney, has now been applied to all areas of mass tourism, resulting in the controlled bland experience. What started as a search for adventure has ended in total predictability. Excessive growth and rationalism have contradicted the very goals that the institution of tourism and planned travel was set up to deliver.

The same is true of large architectural offices. Here design suffers because no one has control over the whole job from beginning to end, and because the building has to be produced quickly and efficiently according to proven formulae (the rationalisation of taste into clichés based on statistical averages of style and theme). Furthermore, with large buildings such as the Penta, the architecture has to be produced for a client whom no one in the office knows (that is, the ten corporations), and who is, in any case, not the user of the building.

In short, buildings today are nasty, brutal and too big because they are produced for profit by absentee developers, for absentee landlords for absent users whose taste is assumed as clichéd.

There is, then, not one cause of the crisis in architecture, but a *system of causes*; and clearly to change just the style or ideology of the architects, as is proposed by many critics, isn't going to change the whole situation. No amount of disaffection for the International Style or Brutalism, for high-rise, bureaucracy, capitalism, gigantism, or whatever else is the latest scapegoat is going to change things suddenly and produce a humane environment. It would seem we have to change the whole system of architectural production at once, all eleven causes together. And yet perhaps such a radical move is not necessary. Perhaps some causes are redundant, some are more important than others, and we only have to change a combination of a few. For instance, if large architectural offices were divided into small teams, given a certain financial and design control, and put in close relation to the ultimate users of the building, this might be enough. Who knows? Experiments must be tried with different variables. All that can be said at this point is that the situation has systemic causes which have to be varied as a structure if deep changes are to be made. I will pursue only two causes of the crisis: the way the Modern Movement has impoverished architectural language on the level of form; and has itself suffered an impoverishment on the level of content, the social goals for which it actually built.

Univalent form

For the general aspect of an architecture created around one (or a few) simplified values, I will use the term 'univalence'. No doubt in terms of expression the architecture of Mies van der Rohe and his followers is the most univalent formal system we have, because it makes use of few materials and a single, right-angled geometry. Characteristically this reduced style was justified as rational (when it was uneconomic), and universal (when it fitted only a few functions). The glass-and-steel box has become the single most used form in Modern Architecture, and it signifies throughout the world 'office building'.

Yet in the hands of Mies and his disciples this impoverished system has become fetishised to the point where it overwhelms all other concerns, just as the leather

12 MIES VAN DER ROHE, *Seagram Building*, New York, 1958. Corner detail and plan. The plane of I-beams is extended out a few inches from the column line so that the corner is clearly articulated with angles of steel. The interior curtains now can only be raised to pre-selected, harmonious positions. Mies kept full-scale I-beam details by his desk to get the proportions just so. He thought this member was the modern equivalent of the Doric column, but as Herbert Read once said: 'In the back of every dying civilisation sticks a bloody Doric column.'

boot dominates the shoe fetishist and distracts him from larger concerns. Are I-beams and plate glass appropriate to housing? That is a question Mies would dismiss as irrelevant. The whole question of appropriateness, 'decorum', which every architect from Vitruvius to Lutyens has debated, is now rendered obsolete by Mies' universal grammar and universal contempt for place and function. (He considered function as ephemeral, or so provisional as to be unimportant.)

His first, classic use of the curtain wall was on housing, not for an office – and obviously not for functional or communicational reasons, but because he was obsessed by perfecting certain formal problems. In this case, Mies concentrated on the proportion of the I-beam to panel, set-back, glass area, supporting columns and articulating lines. He kept full-scale details of these members close to his draughting board so he would never lose sight of his loved ones.

A larger question thus didn't arise: what if housing looked like offices, or what if the two functions were indistinguishable? Clearly the net result would be to diminish and compromise both functions by equating them: working and living would become interchangeable on the most banal, literal level, and the particular virtue of each obscured. The psychic overtones to these two different activities would remain unexplored, accidental, truncated.

Another masterpiece of the Modern Movement, the Chicago Civic Center, designed by a follower of Mies, also shows these confusions in communication. The long horizontal spans and dark corten steel express 'office building', 'power', 'purity', and the variations in surface express 'mechanical equipment'; but these primitive (and occasionally mistaken) meanings don't take us very far. On the most literal level the building does not communicate its important civic function; nor, more importantly, the social and psychological meanings of this very significant building task (a meeting place for the citizens of Chicago).

How could an architect justify such inarticulate building? The answer lies in terms of an ideology which celebrates process, which symbolises only the changes in technology and building material. The Modern Movement fetishised the means of production, and Mies, in one of those rare cryptic aphorisms that is too delirious to let pass, gave expression to this fetish: 'I see in industrialisation the central problem of building in our time. If we succeed in carrying out this industrialisation, the social, economic, technical and also artistic problems will be readily solved.' (1924)[2]

What about the theological and gastronomic 'problems'? The bizarre confusion to which this can lead is shown by Mies himself in the Illinois Institute of Technology campus in Chicago, a large enough collection of varied functions for us to regard it as a microcosm of his surrealist world.

Basically, he has used his universal grammar of steel I-beams along with an infill of beige brick and glass to speak about all the important functions: housing, assembly, classrooms, student union, shops, chapel, and so forth. If we look at a series of these buildings in turn we can see how confusing his language is, both literally and metaphorically.

A characteristic rectangular shape might be deciphered as a teaching block where students churn out one similar idea after another on an assembly line – because the factory metaphor suggests this interpretation. The only recognisable

13 C F MURPHEY, *Chicago Civic Center*, 1964. In terms of Mies' curtain wall this solution shows the horizontal emphasis – long spans and under-played verticals in brown, specially-rusted steel. Except for the Picasso sculpture and flags out front, you would not recognise the civic importance of this building, nor the various political functions that occur within. (Hedrich-Blessing)

14 MIES VAN DER ROHE, *Siegel Building, IIT*, Chicago, 1947. Is this an astrophysical research lab? The whole campus is in the 'universal' aesthetic of steel, glass and beige brick, except for the most important building. (*See* 18)

14 sign in the building, the lattice-work disc at the top, suggests that the students are budding astrophysicists; but of course Mies cannot claim credit for this bit of literalism. Someone else added it, destroying the purity of his fundamental utterance. What he can claim credit for, and what has exercised great architectural debate (a debate between two English deans, Sir Leslie Martin and Lord Llewelyn-

15 Davies), is his solving of the *problem* of the corner. These two schoolmen disputed, with medieval precision and inconsequentiality, whether the corner symbolised 'endlessness', or 'closedness' like a Renaissance pilaster. The fact that it could symbolise both or neither, depending on the code of the viewer, or the fact that larger questions of factory symbolism and semantic confusion were at stake – such questions were never raised.

Not so far away from this disputatious corner is another architectural

16 conundrum, designed in Mies' universal language of confusion. Here we can see all sorts of conventional cues which give the game away: a rectangular form of cathedral, a central nave structure with two side aisles expressed in the eastern front. The religious nature of this building is heightened by a regular bay system of piers; it's true there are no pointed arches, but there are clerestory windows on both aisle and nave elevations. Finally, to confirm our reading that this *is* the campus cathedral, we see the brick campanile, the bell tower that dominates the basilica.

In fact, this is the boiler house, a solecism of such stunning wit that it can't be

17 truly appreciated until we see the actual chapel, which looks like a boiler house. This is an unassuming box in industrial materials, sandwiched balefully between dormitory slabs with a searchlight attached – in short, signs which confirm a reading of prosaic utility.

Finally, we come to the most important position on campus, the central area, where there is a temple constructed in a homogeneous material that distinguishes

18 it from the other factories. This temple is raised on a plinth, it has a magnificent colonnade of major and minor orders, and a grandiose stairway of white marble

15 THE INFAMOUS IIT CORNER of the previous building. The corner looked like a full *visual* stop to Leslie Martin, yet Llewelyn-Davies argued it looked 'endless' because it was stepped back with two I-beams and an L-beam. The fact that the whole building signified 'factory', when it was for teaching, was typically overlooked in this fetish for details and esoteric meaning.

16 MIES VAN DER ROHE, *IIT Cathedral/Boiler House*, Chicago, 1947. The traditional form of a basilica with central nave and two side aisles. There are even clerestory lights, a regular bay system and campanile to show that this is the cathedral.

17 MIES VAN DER ROHE, *IIT Boiler House/Church*. A dumb box placed to either side of high-rise buildings, which are in the same vernacular. Blank on three sides and lit by a searchlight – clearly this is the boiler house.

planes miraculously hovering in space, as if the local god has ultimately worked his magic. It must be the President's house, or at very least, the Administration Centre. Actually it is where the architects work – what else could it be?

So we see the factory is a classroom, the cathedral is a boiler house, the boiler house is a chapel, and the President's temple is the School of Architecture. Thus Mies is saying that the boiler house is more important than the chapel, and that architects rule, as pagan gods, over the lot. Of course Mies didn't intend these propositions, but his commitment to reductive formal values inadvertently betrays them.

Univalent formalists and inadvertent symbolists

Lest we think Mies is a special case, or somehow uncharacteristic of Modern architects in general, let us look at similar examples which stem from the reaction against his particular language: the formalist reaction in America and the Team Ten critique in Europe both turned against the Miesian approach in the sixties.

Frank Lloyd Wright's last work, the Marin County Civic Center, is characteristic 19 of the formalist architecture. The building is based on the endless repetition of various patterns (and their transformation), which are uncertain in their overtones – in this case the baby-blue and golden baubles reminiscent of a Helena Rubenstein ambience, and superimposed arches associated with a Roman aqueduct. The arches belie their compression function and hang, with gilded struts, in tension. A golden minaret-totem-pole, which also has Aztec and Mayan associations, crowns the site of this city centre (which is missing only its city). In defence one can applaud its compelling, surrealist image, justifiable in terms of its kitsch extravagance, but not much more. Like the Chicago Civic Center already mentioned, it doesn't tell us anything very profound about the role of government (escapism?) or citizens' relation to it.

If we look at the work of I M Pei, Ulrich Franzen, Philip Johnson or Skidmore, 20 Owings and Merrill, the leading American architects, we find the same erratic signification – always a striking form, a reduced but potent image, with unintended

18 MIES VAN DER ROHE. *IIT President's Temple/School of Architecture*, Chicago, 1962. The black temple hovers miraculously from a giant order of steel trusses and a minor order of I-beams. The white horizontal steps also break the law of gravity. The building occupies a major point on the campus, as the President's house should. (John Winter)

19 FRANK LLOYD WRIGHT. *Marin County Civic Center*, San Rafael, California, 1959-64. The great *Pont du Gard* made out of cardboard, gilt and golden bauble, surmounted by an Aztec minaret, with interior bowling alleys of space and a baby-blue, opaline roof with cookie-cutter hemi-circles. An excellent piece of Kitsch modern, unfortunately unintended.

20 I M PEI, *Christian Science Church Center*, Boston, 1973. Very hard-edge Le Corbusier – in fact, Chandigarh done with precision concrete. From the air you can appreciate the fact that this centre is laid out like a giant phallus which culminates, appropriately, in a fountain. Ledoux designed a phallus-planned building as a brothel, but there is no further indication here that some elaborate message is intended.

21 meanings. For instance, Gordon Bunshaft's museum for the Hirschhorn Collection, the only collection of modern art on the Mall in Washington, is in the very powerful form of a white masonry cylinder. This simplified shape, ultimately stemming from the eighteenth-century 'Modernists', Boullée and Ledoux, was meant to communicate power, awe, harmony and the sublime. And so it does. But, as *Time* magazine and other journals pointed out, it symbolises more accurately a concrete bunker, a Normandy pillbox, with its battered walls, impenetrable heaviness, and 360 degree machine-gun slit. Bunshaft is inadvertently saying 'keep modern art from the public in this fortified stronghold and shoot 'em down if they dare approach'. So many cues, in such a popular code, reinforce this meaning and make it obvious to everyone not retrained in the architects' code. It might have been a multivalent statement of this meaning had the architect really intended it and combined the pillbox image with further cues of an ironic nature. But, as with the unintended witticisms of Mrs Malaprop, all credit for humour must go to the subconscious.

22, 23   Aldo Rossi and the Italian Rationalists try very sympathetically to continue the classical patterns of Italian cities, designing neutral buildings which have a 'zero degree' of historical association; but their work invariably recalls the Fascist architecture of the thirties – despite countless disclaimers. The semantic overtones are again erratic, and focus on such oppressive meanings, because the building is oversimplified and monotonous. Serious critics and apologists for them, such as Manfredo Tafuri, find themselves evading the obvious in their attempt to justify such buildings with elaborate, esoteric interpretation.[3]

This disparity between popular and elitist codes can be found everywhere in the Modern Movement, especially among the most highly acclaimed architects, such as
24 James Stirling, Arata Isozaki, Ricardo Bofill and Herman Hertzberger. The better the Modern architect, the less he can control obvious meanings. Hertzberger's Old Age Home is, on a sophisticated level, the delightful casbah he intended, with many small-scale places and a closely grained urban fabric where the individual is psychologically hidden and protected by the nooks and crannies. As an abstract piece of form it communicates humanism, care, intricacy and delicacy. That is the Chinese puzzle quality of the various interlocked elements, and spaces acquire these meanings by analogy. Yet such subtle analogy is hardly enough when more potent, metaphorical meanings have run amok. For what are the obvious associations of this Old Age Home? Each room looks like a black coffin placed between white crosses (in fact a veritable war cemetery of white crosses). Despite his humanism, the architect is inadvertently saying that old age, in our society, is rather fatal.

Ah well, these 'slips-of-the-metaphor' are committed more and more by the top Modernists, and they can even be made by architects who see architecture as a language – by Peter and Alison Smithson. It is interesting that, like other apologists for the Modern Movement since 1850, they justify their work in terms of the linguistic analogy, and look to previous languages of architecture for their lesson. They say of the city of Bath: 'it's unique . . . for its remarkable cohesion, for *a form*
25 *language understood by all . . . contributed by all*'.[4] Their analysis of this Georgian city of light and dark stonework shows it to have a wide relevant language, a consistent

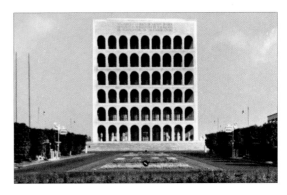

21 GORDON BUNSHAFT and SOM, *Hirschhorn Museum*, Washington DC, 1973. Symbolism at its most inadvertent – a concrete pillbox meant to protect art from the people? A marble doughnut? (Hirschhorn Museum)

22 ALDO ROSSI, *The Gallaratese Neighbourhood*, Milan, 1969-71. A long portico of repeated piers is surmounted by endlessly recurring rectangular windows. The interior corridors are also barren funnels of emptiness. Because the forms are 'empty' some critics have assumed they are above historical associations; but the signs are conventional and the meanings are quite well established in Italy.

23 GUERRINI, LAPADULA and ROMANO, *Palace of Italian Civilisation*, EUR, Rome, 1942. Deflowered Classicism and endlessly repeated blank forms. This is the architecture of control, and some future study may show how it depends on boring redundancy for its coercion.

language, from humble details such as street grilles, to grand gestures such as porticoes. These porticoes the Smithsons characterise as metaphors for large doors, and pediments as metaphors for cheaper doors – in short, they are acutely aware of the way architectural language depends on *traditional* symbolism.

This makes their own anti-traditionalism all the more poignant and bizarre; but the Smithsons, as veritable descendants of the Romantic age, must 'make it new' each time to avoid the stigma of conventionality. Thereby, of course, they successfully avoid communicating, for all developed languages must contain a high degree of conventional usage, if only to make innovations and deviations from the norm more correctly understood.

When speaking about a possible Modern language, Peter Smithson comes down firmly like a 1920s Modernist in support of a machine aesthetic: '. . . for the machine-supported present-day cities only a live, cool, highly controlled, rather impersonal architectural language can deepen that base-connection, make it resonate with culture as a whole.'[5]

The fallacies of this position are well known, yet many architects today are still committed to such notions because of their training in processes of production, and their ideology of progress. They still believe in a *Zeitgeist* and one determined by machinery and technology – so buildings they produce symbolise these now somewhat old-fashioned demons.

The great irony is, however, that they also believe in providing essentially humanist values of 'place, identity, personality, home-coming', (I am quoting from several Team Ten sources, values which the Smithsons share). How can you communicate these meanings if you use a new language based on the machine metaphor? It would be very hard, practically impossible, and the Smithsons haven't yet pulled off this miracle. Their Robin Hood Gardens, in the East End of London, 26 simply does not do the trick.

Robin Hood Gardens is not a modern version of the Bath Crescent, in spite of the large urban gesture and V-shaped plan. It does not accentuate the identity of each house, although Smithson admires Bath for being 'unmistakably a collection of

24 HERMAN HERTZBERGER, *Old Age Home*, Amsterdam, 1975. An intricate puzzle of small-scaled elements, a human scale in the details. But this is multiplied to vast proportions. The incessant symbolism of white crosses containing black coffins is equally unpremeditated and unfortunate.

25 JOHN WOOD II, *Royal Crescent*, Bath, 1767-80. One of the first examples of housing treated as a palace – the coliseum was another model. Although making a grand urban gesture, the individual houses still have an identity, marked by vertical separation and several variations in articulation (chimneys, fire walls, fences). The Smithsons are acutely aware of this symbolism, which makes their failure to provide its equivalent all the more poignant. (Bath City Council)

26 ALISON and PETER SMITHSON, *Robin Hood Gardens*, London, 1968-72. Unrelieved concrete (except for curtains), popularly identified now with the image of an industrial *process*. The variations of vertical fins are not strong enough to identify each apartment. The packed-in scale gives the feeling of a dense human wall.

27 separate houses'. It suppresses this in favour of visual syncopation, a partially
28 randomised set of vertical fins, and horizontal continuity – the notion of a
communal street deck. These 'streets in the air' have, surprisingly, all the faults
which the Smithsons had recognised in other similar schemes. They are under-
used; the collective entries are paltry and a few have been vandalised. Indeed, they
are dark, smelly, dank passageways. Little sense of place, few collective facilities and
fewer 'identifying elements', which the architects had reasonably said were needed
in Modern buildings.

The Smithsons claim they have provided a sense of place: 'On the garden side
the building is unified. It is an urban place, a part of the definition of a city, provided
it does not become a repetitive pattern which organises a homogeneous space.'[6] Indeed
the space isn't homogeneous, it has kinks and an artificial mound near the centre.
But these deviations from the norm and the subtle cues of visual separation are
hardly strong enough to override the repetitive pattern and homogeneous
material. These signify more strongly 'council housing', 'anonymity', 'the authorities
didn't have enough money to use wood, stucco, etc' – in short, they signify 'social
deprivation'. The Smithsons' laudable intentions of providing a community building
on the scale of the Bath Crescent and offering the same degree of individual
expression and identity in an architectural language understood by all – these
positive aims are denied by the built form.

Such contradictions between statement and result have reached impressive
proportions in Modern Architecture, and one can now speak of a 'credibility gap'
that parallels the loss of trust in politicians. The root causes of this are, I believe,
based on the nature of architecture as a language. It is *radically schizophrenic* by necessity,
partly rooted in tradition, in the past – indeed in everyone's childhood experience
of crawling around on flat floors and perceiving such normal architectural elements
as vertical doors. And it is partly rooted in a fast-changing society, with its new
functional tasks, new materials, new technologies and ideologies. On the one hand,
architecture is as slow-changing as spoken language (we can still understand
Renaissance English); and, on the other, as fast-changing and esoteric as modern art
and science.

Put another way, we learn from the beginning the cultural signs which make any
urban place particular to a social group, an economic class and real, historical
people; whereas Modern architects spend their time unlearning all these particular
signs in an attempt to design for universal man, or Mythic Modern Man. This 3-M
monster of course doesn't exist, except as a historical fiction – the creation of
modern novelists, sociologists and idealistic planners. Mr Triple-M is no doubt a
logical necessity for architects and others who want to generalise a statistical
average. Tom Wolfe has criticised novelists for writing about such non-existing
creatures, and the same points could be scored against architects.[7] They try to
provide Modern Man with a mythic consciousness, with consistent patterns
reminiscent of tribal societies, refined in their purity, full of tasteful 'unity in variety',
and other such geometric harmonies; when in fact Modern Man doesn't exist, and
what he would want if he did would be realistic social signs. Signs of status, history,
29, 30 commerce, comfort, ethnic domain, signs of being neighbourly (though also a bit

27, 28 SMITHSONS, *Robin Hood Gardens*, street in the air, and
collective entry. The long empty streets in the air don't have
the life or facilities of the traditional street. The entry ways, one
of which has been burned, are dark and anonymous, serving
too many families. The scheme has many of the problems
which Oscar Newman traced to a lack of defensible space.
Here architectural critic Paul Goldberger mimes a mugger's
threatening gesture – commonplace in these corridors.

better off than the Joneses). Modern architects aren't trained in these codes, they don't know how to get close to this reality, and so they go on providing a mythic integration of community (often now a projection of middle-class values).

Too bad: society can go on without architects, personalise housing estates or blow them up, or hire interior decorators. It doesn't matter (except in Russia); there are always other realistic professions who are ready to move in.

In any case, before we finish with this Modern Architecture-Bashing (a form of sadism which is getting far too easy), we should mention one dilemma architects face (which isn't entirely of their own making), because it has an effect on the language they use.

Univalent content

Let us now examine the major commissions, the most prevalent building types which have engaged the skill of architects in this century. A certain disinterest is needed here, because the truths are hard and the solutions not forthcoming. Many will deny or gloss over the social realities behind architecture because they are so trivial and depressing and of no one's desire, no one's fault. The major mistake architects made in this century, on this score, is perhaps to have been born at all.

Let us nevertheless look at the major monuments of Modern Architecture and the social tasks for which they were built. Here we will find a strange but unnoticed deflection of the Modern architect's *role as a social utopian*, for we will see that he has actually built for the reigning powers of an established, commercial society; and this surreptitious liaison has taken its toll, as illicit love affairs will. The Modern Movement of architecture, conceived in the 1850s as a call to morality, and in the 1920s (in its Heroic period) as a call to social transformation, found itself unwittingly compromised, first by practice and then by acceptance.[8] These architects wished to give up their subservient role as 'tailors' to society and what they regarded as 'a corrupt ruling taste', and become instead 'doctors', leaders, prophets, or at least midwives, to a new social order. But for what order did they build?

1 Monopolies and big business: Some of the accepted classics of Modern Architecture were built for clients who today are multinational corporations. Peter Behrens' Berlin Turbine Factory was for the General Electric of its day, AEG. This building of 1909 is often considered the first great work of European Modern Architecture because of its pure volumetric expression, its clear clean use of glass and steel, almost the curtain wall, and its refinement of utilitarian products – the beginning of industrial design. Further landmarks of architecture, those that modified the language slightly, were Frank Lloyd Wright's curvilinear poetry of pyrex tubing and streamlined brick, built for a large wax company; Gordon Bunshaft's classic solution for the office tower, two pure slabs set at right angles, one on top of the other, erected for the multinational based on soap; Mies van der Rohe's dark, Rolls-Royce solution to the curtain wall built for the Seagram's Whiskey giant; Eero Saarinen's walk-through bird-of-prey built for TWA; and numerous refinements of the curtain wall built by the large offices, such as Skidmore, Owings and Merrill, for soft drink companies, tobacco chains, interna-

29, 30 LAS VEGAS and EXETER CATHEDRAL CLOSE, two different kinds of social manifestations in which the architecture lends itself to direct symbolic expression. Regardless of our views of either social group, it has to be said that Modern architects have disregarded this level of symbolic detail and particularity. Most cities contain ethnic diversity, but what large development incorporates the Chinese restaurant, the front of the local butcher? Architects have been too removed from this level of detail, and will be until they are retrained as anthropologists or journalists to understand social reality.

tional banks and oil companies. How should one express the power and concentration of capital, the mercantile function, the exploitation of markets? These building tasks would be the monuments of our time, because they bring in the extra money for architecture; and yet their potential role as social paragons is without credibility.

2 International exhibitions, World Fairs: Another genealogy of Modern Architecture is traced from the Crystal Palace of 1851 to the Theme Pavilion at

33 Osaka 1970. This line of descent has a series of technical triumphs to its credit, resulting in the new language of lattice structures, the open girders of Eiffel, the pin-jointed parabolas of industrial sheds, the translucent and geometric domes of Buckminster Fuller, and the soaring tents of Otto Frei (these tents always soar in architectural criticism). Indeed these triumphs did a great deal to aestheticise the experience of architecture; historians and critics skipped lightly over the content of the structures, their propagandist role; and focused instead on their spatial and

34 optical qualities. The mass media followed suit. Overlooked was the blatant nationalism and ersatz ambience which constituted ninety per cent of the World Fairs. Why? Because this ignored content was so obviously hedonistic and lacking in subtlety, and because there was no great understanding of how this blatant content works in mass culture, nor how it is occasionally humorous, creative and provocative.

3 Factories and engineering feats: From Walter Gropius' Fagus Factory, 1911, to Le Corbusier's 'home as a machine for living in', 1922, we have the birth and establishment of the major metaphor for Modern Architecture: the factory. Housing was conceived in this image, and the Nazis were not altogether wrong in

35 attacking the first international manifesto of this metaphor, the *Weissenhof Siedlungen*, 1927, for its inappropriateness. Why should houses adopt the imagery of the mass production line and the white purity of the hospital?

More recent mass housing in England, for instance that in London, or Milton Keynes, has followed this pervasive twentieth-century metaphor. That no one asked to live in a factory did not occur to the doctor-Modern-architect, because he was out to cure the disease of modern cities, no matter how distasteful the medicine. Indeed, better if it tasted like castor oil and caused convulsions, because then the transformation of bourgeois society was more likely to be complete, the patient would reform his petty acquisitive drives and become a good collectivised citizen.

Such metaphors for housing have been rejected almost everywhere they've been applied, (exceptions occur in Germany and Switzerland), but they have taken hold in appropriate areas: stadia, sports grounds, aircraft hangars, and all the large-span structures traditionally associated with engineering. Here the poetry of

36 process is exhilarating without being wildly inappropriate or surreal, and we can claim the single, unmitigated triumph of Modern Architecture on the level of content.

4 Consumer temples and churches of distraction: Someone from an alien culture would be amazed to see, if he took a quick helicopter trip over any of our sprawling cities, that urban man worshipped at institutions devoted to

31 PETER BEHRENS, *AEG Factory*, Berlin, 1909. Often regarded as one of the first great modern buildings, the fountainhead too of industrial design, this work set the factory as the major metaphor for subsequent building. Here the marriage was made between big business, 'good design', and the functional style. This union was eagerly sought for at the time by the German *Werkbund*, and it bore multinational fruit sixty years later. (Bauhaus Archive)

32 FRANK LLOYD WRIGHT, *Johnson Wax Building*, Racine, Wisconsin, 1938. Columns taper downwards and are supported on brass shoes. Everything takes up the curve theme in this 'total work of art'. The idea of a unified corporate image became standard by the fifties for such multinationals as the CBS, IBM, Olivetti, etc. (US Information Service)

33 KENZO TANGE, *Theme Pavilion, EXPO 70*, Osaka, 1970. A megastructure carrying various services was finally built after being contemplated by the avant-garde for ten years. World Fairs often allow such grandiose and creative ideas to be realised, and have therefore played an important role in the evolution of Modern Architecture. (Masao Arai)

34 The CAMBODIAN PAVILION, Osaka, 1970. Designed with the advice of Prince Norodom Sihanouk, this typically nationalist pavilion echoes Khmer architecture and Angkor Wat. Most World's Fair architecture has an air of pastiche about it which could offend convinced nationalists, but it conforms to mass standards of propriety. This manifestation is overlooked by serious critics and remains undiscussed. (Japan Information Service)

35 PATRICK HODGKINSON, *Foundling Estate*, London, 1973. Long lines of housing with greenhouse living-rooms are stacked on the diagonal. The grand public entrance, the largest of its kind in Great Britain, looks as if it leads to a ceremonial space, at least a stadium, but it actually culminates in an empty plaza. The Futurist styling and semantic confusion are again a consequence of the Modern Movement's rejection of rhetoric and a theory of communication.

36 KENZO TANGE, *National Gymnasia for the Olympic Games*, Tokyo, 1964. Two buildings in subtle counterpoint are placed on a podium. The concrete masts, which hold the hyperbolic curves, end in the conventional Japanese 'slant' which has become something of a cliché. The gentle curves and structural expression are also traditional signs.

commercial gods. Modern architects haven't altogether mastered this territory of Disneyland and ride-through parks, of Kings Road and Sunset Strip, but they are beginning to try, and we can already count the triumphs. The exquisite technological jewels of Hans Hollein, the boutiques and candle shops, and high-gloss 37 mausolea given over to selling religious relics for the wedding finger. So much design talent and mystery expended on such small shops would convince an outsider that he had at last stumbled on the true faith of this civilisation. And when he came to see the same medals worshipped in the large hotels, constructed in the theological material of mirrorplate, his interpretation would be confirmed. The culture idolises tinsel, personal adornment, private jewellery. The more adept 38 Modern architects become at embellishing buildings (and of course they are working at a distinct disadvantage, having previously equated 'ornament' and 'crime'), the more the anomaly appears. A jewel is a jewel; it is not a fitting object for great architecture. The banality of content will not go away.

Architecture obviously reflects what a society holds important, what it values both spiritually and in terms of cash. In the pre-industrial past the major areas for expression were the temple, the church, the palace, agora, meeting house, country house and city hall; while in the present, extra money is spent on hotels, restaurants and all those commercial building types I have mentioned. Public housing and buildings expressing the local community or the public realm suffer the cutbacks. Buildings representing consumer values generate the investment. As Galbraith says of American capitalism, it results in private wealth and public squalor.

Several Modern architects, and even a few Post-Modernists, in a desperate attempt to cheer themselves up, have decided that since this is an inevitable situation, it must also have its good points. Commercial tasks are more democratic than the previous aristocratic and religious ones; 'Main Street is almost all right' according to Robert Venturi.

When these commercial design tasks first emerged into consciousness, about the turn of this century, they were celebrated by the Futurist, Sant' Elia, with a glee

and moralising tone that were later to become common. He contrasted the new building tasks, given over to commerce and energy, with the previous ones devoted to worship – the nineteenth-century dynamo versus the thirteenth-century Virgin:

> The formidable antithesis between the modern world and the old is determined by all those things that formerly did not exist . . . we have lost our predilection for the monumental, the heavy, the static, and we have enriched our sensibility with a *taste for the light, the practical, the ephemeral and the swift*. We no longer feel ourselves to be the men of the cathedrals, the palaces and the tribunes. We are the men of the great hotels, the railway stations, the immense streets, colossal ports, covered markets, luminous arcades, straight roads and beneficial demolitions.[9]

In short these embrace the social activities of a middle-class tourist wandering from railway station to hotel along wide super-highways dotted with bulldozed sites and lit by glowing neon signs. With slight modifications, Sant' Elia could be describing the glitter of Las Vegas, or, less fashionably, the main street of Warsaw. Whatever the country, whatever the economic system, such secular building tasks are the important ones today, and so much Modern art and architecture tries to celebrate this fact. 'The heroism of everyday life', that notion shared by Picasso, Léger and Le Corbusier in the twenties, was a philosophy which tried to place banal objects on a pedestal formerly reserved for special symbols of veneration. The fountain pen, the filing cabinet, the steel girder and the typewriter were the new icons. Mayakovsky and the Russian Constructivists took art into the streets and even performed one grand symphony of sirens and steam whistles, while waving coloured flags on top of factory roofs. The hope of these artists and architects was to reform society on a new class and functional basis: substitute power stations for cathedrals, technocrats for aristocrats. A new, heroic, democratic society would emerge, led by a powerful race of pagan supermen, the avant-garde, the technicians and captains of industry, the enlightened scientists and teams of experts. What a dream!

Indeed, the managerial revolution did occur, and socialist revolutions happened in a few countries; but the dream was taken over by Madison Avenue (and its equivalents), and the 'heroic object of everyday use' became the 'new, revolutionary detergent'. Societies kept on worshipping at their old altars, with diminishing faith, and tried to incorporate the new values at the same time. The result? Ersatz culture, a caricature of the past and future at once, a surreal fantasy dreamed up neither by the avant-garde, nor the traditionalists, and abhorrent to both of them.

With the triumph of consumer society in the West and bureaucratic state capitalism in the East, our unfortunate Modern architect was left without much uplifting social content to symbolise. If architecture has to concentrate its efforts on symbolising a way of life and the public realm, it's in a bit of a fix when these things lose their credibility. There's nothing much the architect can do about this except protest as a citizen, and design dissenting buildings that express the complex situation. He can communicate missing values and ironically criticise the ones he dislikes. But to do that he must make use of the language of the local culture, otherwise his message falls on deaf ears, or is distorted to fit this local language.

37 HANS HOLLEIN, *Jewellery Shop*, Vienna, 1975. Hollein uses voluptuous, shiny marble to set off the polished mechanical equipment. The contrast of circle and fissure, of skin-like marble and glistening gold lips folding over each other, is explicitly ironic and sexual. Tight space is cut up to loosen the customer's libido even further. Perhaps only a Viennese could have brought off this mixture of commerce and sensuality.

38 JOHN PORTMAN, *Bonaventure Hotel*, model, Los Angeles, 1976. Portman has revived the nineteenth-century tradition of the grand hotel – at least the cost part of this tradition – with lavish Regency Hyatts in several American cities. He gives the exteriors an absolute geometric image, parts of which in mirrorplate flash reflections like overblown jewels. The planning is reminiscent of the megalomaniacal schemes of Boullée.

.vi.   .Vij.   .VIij.   .ix.   .x.

Thuscana   Dorica   Jonica   Corinthia   Composita

PART TWO
The Modes of Architectural Communication

Monsieur Jourdain, Molière's *Bourgeois Gentilhomme*, was rather surprised to discover that he had been speaking prose for forty years – 'without knowing anything about it'. Modern architects might suffer a similar shock, or doubt that they've been speaking anything as elevated as prose. To look at the environment is to agree with their doubt. We see a babble of tongues, a free-for-all of personal idiolects, not the
39   Classical language of the Doric, Ionic and Corinthian Orders. Where there once were rules of architectural grammar, we now have a mutual diatribe between speculative builders; where there once was a gentle discourse between the Houses of Parliament and Westminster Abbey, there is now across the Thames, the Shell
40   Building shouting at the Hayward Gallery, which grunts back at a stammering and giggling Festival Hall. It's all confusion and strife, and yet this invective is still language even if it's not very comprehensible or persuasive. There *are* various analogies architecture shares with language and if we use the terms loosely, we can speak of architectural 'words', 'phrases', 'syntax', and 'semantics'.[10] I will discuss several of these analogies in turn, showing how they can be more consciously used as communicational means, starting with the mode most commonly disregarded in Modern Architecture.

Metaphor

People invariably see one building in terms of another, or in terms of a similar object; in short, as a metaphor. The more unfamiliar a Modern building is, the more

39 The FIVE ORDERS: Tuscan, Doric, Ionic, Corinthian and Composite from Sebastiano Serlio's *The Book of Architecture*, 1611.

40 The SOUTH BANK, London, 1976. With large chunks devoted to different functions: *left to right:* The Queen Elizabeth Hall, Royal Festival Hall and Shell Tower carry on their distinctive form of garbled conversation. Each chunk sends out a single, if muted, message that it is an 'important' monument of some unspecified kind.

41 CONCRETE GRILLES, now the sign of parking garage, were first used on offices in America in the late fifties. They work here to carry the external loads and mask the cars. While the 'cheese grater' is now no longer perceived as a metaphor, the precast grille is on rare occasions still used for offices. Whether it signifies garage or office depends on the frequency of usage within a society.

42 KISHO KUROKAWA, *Nakagin Capsule Building*, Tokyo, 1972. 140 boxes were driven to the site and lifted on to the two concrete cores. Each habitable room has built-in bathroom, stereo tape deck, calculators and other amenities for the businessman. The metaphor of stacking rooms like bricks or sugar cubes has re-emerged every five years or so ever since Walter Gropius proposed it in 1922. The overtones are ambiguous: to some they have always suggested regimentation, to others the unity in variety of the Italian hill town. (Tomio Ohashi)

they will compare it metaphorically to what they know. This matching of one experience to another is a property of all thought, particularly that which is creative. Thus, when pre-cast concrete grilles were first used on buildings in the late fifties, they were seen as 'cheese-graters', 'beehives', 'chain-link fences'; while ten years later, when they became the norm in a certain building type, they were seen in functional terms: 'this looks like a parking garage'. From metaphor to cliché, 41 from neologism through constant usage to architectural **sign**, this is the continual route travelled by new and successful forms and technics.

Typical negative metaphors used by the public and by critics such as Lewis Mumford to condemn Modern Architecture were 'cardboard box', 'shoe-box', 'egg-crate', 'filing cabinet', 'grid-paper'. These comparisons were sought not only for their pejorative, mechanistic overtones, but also because they were strongly **coded** in a culture which had become sensitised to the spectre of 1984. This obvious point has some curious implications, as we shall see.

One implication became apparent when I was visiting Japan and the architect Kisho Kurokawa. We went to see his new apartment tower in Tokyo, made from 42 stacked shipping containers, which had a most unusual overall shape. They looked like stacked sugar cubes, or even more, like superimposed washing machines, because the white cubes all had round windows in their centres. When I said this metaphor had unfortunate overtones for living, Kurokawa evinced surprise. 'They aren't washing machines, they're bird cages. You see, in Japan we build concrete-box bird nests with round holes and place them in the trees. I've built these bird nests for itinerant businessmen who visit Tokyo, for bachelors who fly in every so often with their birds.' A witty answer, perhaps made up on the spot, but one which underscored very nicely a difference in our visual codes.

A well-known visual illusion brings this out even more: the famous 'duck-rabbit 43 figure', which will be seen first one way then the other. Since we all have well learned visual codes for *both* animals, and even probably now a code for the hybrid monster with two heads, we can see it three ways. One view may predominate, according to either the strength of the code or according to the direction from which we see the figure at first. To get further readings ('bellows' or 'keyhole' etc) is harder because these codes are less strong for this figure, they map less well than the primary ones – at least in our culture. The general point then is *that code re-strictions based on learning and culture guide a reading, and that there are multiple codes, some of which may be in conflict across subcultures.* In very general terms, there are two large subcultures: one with the Modern code based on the training and ideology of Modern architects, and another with the traditional code based on everyone's experience of normalised architectural elements. As I have already mentioned, there are very basic reasons why these codes may be at odds and architecture may be radically schizophrenic, both in its creation and interpretation. Since some buildings incorporate various codes, they can be seen as mixed metaphors, and with opposing meanings: eg the 'harmonious, well-proportioned pure volume' of the Modern architect can become the 'shoe-box' or 'filing cabinet' to the public.

One Modern building, the Sydney Opera House, has provoked a superabun- 45 dance of metaphorical responses, both in the popular and professional press. The reasons are, again, that the forms are both unfamiliar to architecture and reminiscent of other visual objects. Most of the metaphors are organic: thus the architect, Jorn Utzon, showed how the shells of the building related to the surface of a sphere (like 'orange segments') and the wings of a bird in flight. They also relate, obviously, to white sea shells, and it is this metaphor, plus the comparison to the white sails bobbing around in Sydney Harbour, that have become journalistic clichés. This raises another obvious point with unexpected implications: the interpretation of architectural metaphor is more elastic and dependent on *local* codes than the interpretation of metaphor in spoken or written language.

Some critics have pointed out that the superimposed shells resemble the growth of a flower over time – the unfolding of petals; while architectural students of Australia caricatured this same aspect as 'turtles making love'. From several points of view, the violent aspect of broken and smashed up shapes is apparent – 'a traffic accident with no survivors'; while again these same views elicit possible organic metaphors – 'fish swallowing each other'. Reinforcing this interpretation are the shiny, scaly elements of the tiled surface which are apparent up close. But the most extraordinary metaphor, and the one which Australians apply with a certain bemused affection, is 'scrum of nuns'. All those shells leaning over, confronting each other in two main directions, resemble the head-dresses and cowls of two opposed monastic orders, and the wildly unlikely idea that this could be a scrimmage of mother superiors dominates the possibilities. 'Wit' has been defined as 'the unlikely copulation of ideas together', and the more unlikely *but* successful the union, the more it will strike the viewer and stay in his mind. A witty building is one which permits us to make extraordinary but convincing associations.

The question obviously arises of how appropriate these metaphors are to the building's function and its symbolic role. Concentrating on this aspect and momentarily disregarding other things such as cost (the Australians spent something like twenty times the original estimate for their mixed metaphor), we might come to the following conclusion. On the one hand the organic metaphors

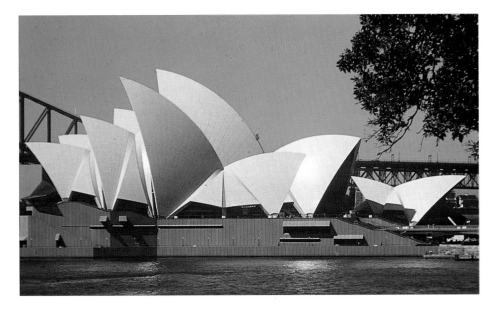

43 The DUCK-RABBIT ILLUSION, read from left to right by duck hunters and from right to left by frequenters of the Playboy Club. Since this illusion is so well known we can now see it as a new animal with two heads. But note: you can only read it one way at a time depending on the code you choose to adopt. (E H Gombrich, *Art and Illusion*)

44 CARTOON presented by students when Queen Elizabeth officially opened the building. (From *Architecture in Australia*)

45 JORN UTZON, *Sydney Opera House*, Australia, 1957-74. A mixed metaphor: the shells have symbolised flowers unfolding, sailboats in the harbour, fish swallowing each other and now, because of the local code, high cost. As with the Eiffel Tower, ambiguous meanings have finally transcended all possible functional considerations and the building has become simply a national symbol. This rare class of sign, like a Rorschach test, provokes response which focuses interest on the responder, not the sign. It could be called the 'enigmatic sign', because, like the ocean, it happily receives projected meanings from everyone. (New South Wales Government Office, London)

46 KONSTANTIN MELNIKOV, *Russakov Club*, Moscow, 1928. The wedge shape plus rectangular flytower became established as the 'word' for auditorium in the language of Modern Architecture because of this building. The shapes follow, more or less, the volumes needed for the functions.

47 ROBERT VENTURI, *The Duck versus Decorated Shed*. Venturi would prefer more decorated sheds, because he contends they communicate effectively, and modern architects have for too long only designed 'ducks'. The duck is, in semiotic terms an iconic sign, because the signifier (form) has certain aspects in common with the signified (content). The decorated shed depends on learned meanings – writing or decoration – which are *symbolic* signs.

48 SECURITY MARINE BANK, Wisconsin, c1971. The *symbolic* shed, one part communication of status and security, the other part function. Commercial pressures today naturally dissociate signifier and signified in this way, a destructive tendency for architectural symbolism which depends on a resonance of meaning. (Wayne Attoe)

are very appropriate to a cultural centre: images which suggest growth are particularly apt for meanings of creativity. The building flies, sails, splashes, curves up and unfolds like an animated vegetable. Fine. Perhaps if the building were renamed The Australian Cultural Centre (not the Sydney Opera House) and justified as a symbol of Australia's liberation from Anglo-Saxon dependence (the overriding influence of Britain and America), then its interpretation might be clearer. We could then see these extraordinary metaphors in their most positive light, as symbols of Australia's break with colonial conformity and provinciality.

But doubts arise. We know the building was designed by a European (not an Australian) as an *opera* house – and one that works neither economically nor functionally in the manner it was conceived. Since such knowledge is an integral part of the code with which we interpret the building, our judgement cannot avoid being contaminated by this knowledge. It's rather like looking at the duck-rabbit figure: our perception is bent and shaped by codes based on previous experience. It is virtually impossible to perceive the building without knowing about the notorious 'Sydney Opera House Case', the firing of the architect, the cost, and so forth. So these local, specific meanings also become symbolised in the 'extravagant' shells.

Several Modernists criticised the Opera House for other reasons: as a piece of literal communication the building tells you little and dissimulates much. You can't pick out the various theatres, restaurants and exhibition halls beneath the shells, which is why it has been so annoying to certain architects brought up in the tradition of expressive functionalism. They expect to see each function given a clear and separate volume, which ideally speaking, is an outline of the function – such as the auditorium. They would have designed the building as a series of boxy 46 fly towers and wedge shapes (the conventionalised 'word' for auditorium in Modern Architecture). The building violates this code, as Classical architecture often did, by obscuring actual functions behind overall patterns. The debate then becomes whether such obscurantism is justified by the wit and appropriateness of the organic metaphor. I think it is, but others would deny this.

Perhaps one of them would be Robert Venturi, who also starts from the position that architecture should be looked at as communication, but comes to different conclusions from mine. He contends that buildings should look like 'decorated sheds, not ducks'. The decorated shed is a simple enclosure with signs 47 attached like a billboard, or the application of conventional ornament, such as a 48 pediment symbolising entry; whereas a duck, for him, is a building in the shape of its function (a bird-shaped building selling duck decoys), or a Modern building where the construction, structure and volume become the decoration. Clearly the Sydney Opera House is a duck for Venturi, and he wishes to underplay this form of expression because he thinks it has been overdone by the Modern Movement. I would disagree with this historical judgement, and take even greater exception to the attitudes implied behind it.

Venturi, like the typical Modernist that he wishes to supplant, is adopting the tactic of exclusive inversion. He is cutting out a whole area of architectural communication, duck buildings (technically speaking **iconic** signs), in order to make his preferred mode, decorated sheds (**symbolic** signs) that much more potent. Thus we are being asked to follow an exclusive, simplistic path. Clearly we need all the modes of communication at our disposal, not one or two; and it's the Modernist commitment to architectural street-fighting that leads to such oversimplification, not a balanced theory of signification.

In any case, the Sydney Opera House does pose some difficult problems as a duck, because of its lack of a shared, public symbolism – a point Venturi's extreme position brings out. While the organic metaphors are suitable analogues for a culture centre, they are not reinforced by conventional signs which spring from the Australian vernacular, and therefore they have an erratic signification. Rather, they emanate from the widespread formalist movement of Modern architects, a movement which might be more appropriately termed surrealist. Like a Magritte painting – the apple which expands to fill a whole room – the meaning is striking but enigmatic and ultimately evasive. What precisely is Utzon trying to say, beyond the primitive and exciting? Why, besides creativity, all the sails, shells, flowers, fish and nuns? Clearly our emotions are being heightened as an end in itself, and there is no exact goal towards which all these meanings converge. They float around our mind to pick up connections where they will, like a luxuriant dream following overindulgence.

They do however prove a general point about communication: the more the metaphors, the greater the drama, and the more they are slightly suggestive, the greater the mystery. A mixed metaphor is strong, as every student of Shakespeare knows, but a suggested one is powerful. In architecture, to name a metaphor is
49 often to kill it, like analysing jokes. When hot dog stands are in the shape of hot dogs, then little work is left to the imagination, and all other metaphors are suppressed: they can't even suggest hamburgers. Yet even this kind of univalent metaphor, the Pop architecture of Los Angeles, has its imaginative and communicative side. For one thing, the customary scale and context are violently distorted, so
50 the ordinary object, for instance the doughnut, takes on a series of possible meanings not usually associated with this item of food. When it's blown up to thirty feet and built out of wood and sits on a small building, it becomes the Magritte object that has taken over the house from the occupants. Partly hostile and menacing, it is nevertheless a symbol of sugary breakfasts and *Gemütlichkeit*.

Secondly, an architecture made up from such signs communicates unambiguously to those moving fifty miles per hour through the city. In contrast with so much Modern building, these iconic signs speak with exactitude and humour about their function. Their literalism, however infantile, articulates factual truths which Mies' work obscures, and there is a certain general pleasure (which doesn't escape children) in perceiving a sequence of them. Contrary to Venturi, we need more ducks; Modern architects haven't propagated enough.

One who tried was Eero Saarinen. Immediately after he selected Utzon's Opera House as the winner of the competition, he returned to America and designed his
51 own version of the curvilinear, shell building. The TWA terminal in New York is an icon of a bird, and by extension, of aeroplane flight. In the details and merging of circulation lines, of passenger exits and crossways, it is a particularly clever working

49 HOT DOG STAND, Los Angeles, c1938. Reinforced with additional signs such as oozing mustard, 'Tail-o-the-pup' etc. This architecture would appear to be unambiguous, yet at the Architectural Association in London it is classified in the slide library as a 'hamburger stand'. Once again, visual codes are mainly local.

50 HENRY J GOODWIN, *Big Donut Drive-in*, Los Angeles, 1954. Originally there were ten of these giants, now there are, alas, three. The doughnuts sold are big.

out of this metaphor. A supporting strut is mapped to a bird's leg, the rain-spout becomes an ominous beak, an interior bridge covered in blood-red carpet becomes, I suppose, the pulmonary artery. Here the imaginative meanings add up in an appropriate and calculated way, pointing towards a common metaphor of flight – the mutual interaction of these meanings produces a multivalent work of architecture, a true symbolic architecture.

The most effective use of *suggested* metaphor that I can think of in Modern Architecture is Le Corbusier's chapel at Ronchamp which, because of its 52 suggestiveness is a good candidate for the first Post-Modern building. It has been compared to all sorts of things, varying from the white houses of Mykonos to Swiss cheese. Part of its power is this suggestiveness – to mean many different things at once, to set the mind off on a wild goose chase where it actually catches the goose, 53-58 among other animals. For instance a duck (once again this famous character of Modern Architecture) is vaguely suggested in the south elevation; but so also are a ship and, appropriately, praying hands. The visual codes, which here take in both elitist and popular meanings, are working mostly on an unconscious level, unlike the hot dog stand. We read the metaphors immediately without bothering to name or draw them (as done here) and clearly the skill of the artist is dependent on his ability to call up our rich storehouse of visual images without our being aware of his intention. Perhaps it is also a somewhat unconscious process for him. Le Corbusier only admitted to two metaphors, both of which are esoteric: the 'visual acoustics' of the curving walls which shape the four horizons as if they were 'sounds' (responding in antiphony), and the 'crab shell' form of the roof. But the building has many more metaphors than this, so many that it is over-coded, saturated with possible interpretations. This explains why critics such as Pevsner and Stirling have found the building so upsetting, and others have found it so enigmatic. It seems to suggest precise ritualistic meanings, it looks like the temple of some very complicated sect which reached a high degree of metaphysical sophistication; whereas we *know* it is simply a pilgrimage chapel created by someone who believed in a natural religion, a pantheism.

51 EERO SAARINEN, *TWA Building*, New York, 1962. Designed after Saarinen judged the Sydney Opera House competition. Here the concrete shells are clearly recognisable as a metaphor of flight, although there are other animals suggested. (TWA)

52 LE CORBUSIER, *Ronchamp Chapel*, France, 1955. View north. The building is over-coded with visual metaphors, and none of them is very explicit, so that the chapel always seems about to tell us something which we just can't place. The effect can be compared to having a word on the tip of your tongue which you can't quite remember. But the ambiguity can be dramatic rather than frustrating – you search your memory for possible clues.

53-58 METAPHORS of *Ronchamp*, drawn by Hillel Schocken in a seminar on architectural semiotics at the Architectural Association. The mapping is amazingly literal when compared to the actual views.

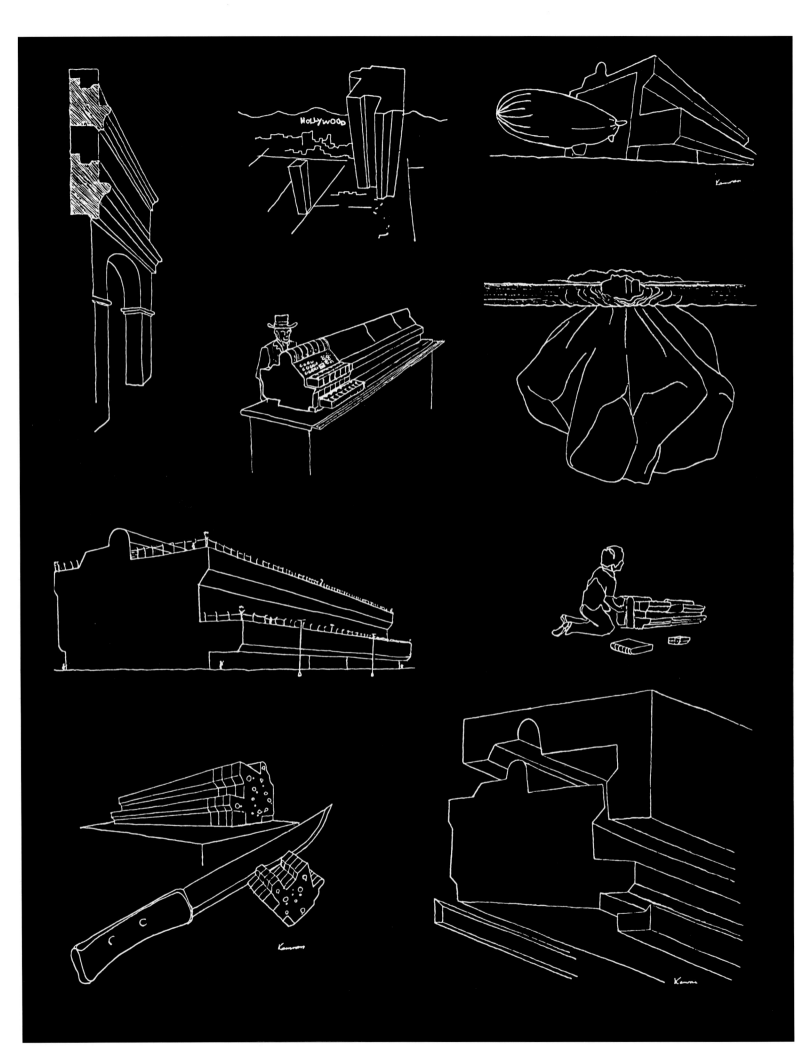

Put another way, Ronchamp has all the fascination of the discovery of a new archaic language; we stumble upon this Rosetta stone, this fragment of a lost civilisation, and every attempt to decode its surface yields another coherent meaning which we know does not refer to any precise social practice, as it appears to. Le Corbusier has so overcoded his building with metaphor, and so precisely related part to part, that the meanings seem as if they had been fixed by countless generations engaged in ritual: something as rich as the delicate patterns of Islam, the exact iconography of Shinto, is suggested. How frustrating, how enjoyable it is to experience this game of signification, which we know rests mostly on imaginative brilliance.

Another recent building which crystallises a series of metaphors through its unusual shape is Cesar Pelli's Pacific Design Center in Los Angeles – known locally as 'the Blue Whale'. Opposed to Ronchamp and TWA, it makes use of rectilinear forms and a curtain wall of three different types of glass, but these familiar elements nonetheless call up unfamiliar associations because of their peculiar treatment: 'iceberg', 'cash register', 'aircraft hangar', and most appropriately 'extruded architectural moulding' (it's a centre for interior decorators and designers).

These metaphors can be mapped quite literally in terms of outline shape and section; not so the 'Blue Whale' image which relates only in terms of colour and mass. And yet this is the favoured nickname. Why? Because there happens to be a local restaurant whose doorway is a large blue whale's mouth, and the building is recognised as a leviathan in its small-scaled neighbourhood swallowing up all the little fish (in this case the diminutive decorators' shops). In other words, two local pertinent codes, the large scale and the connection with the local restaurant, take precedence over the more plausible metaphors of the building, the aircraft hangar or moulding – a good example of the way architecture is even more at the mercy of the perceiver than, say, poetry.

Architecture as a language is much more malleable than the spoken language, and subject to the transformations of short-lived codes. While a building may stand three hundred years, the way people regard and use it may change every decade. It would be perverse to rewrite Shakespearean sonnets, change love poetry to hate letters, read comedy as tragedy; but it is perfectly acceptable to hang washing on decorative balustrades, convert a church into a concert hall, and use a building every day while never looking at it (actually the norm). Architecture is often experienced inattentively or with the greatest prejudice of mood and will – exactly opposite to the way one is supposed to experience a symphony or work of art.[11] One implication of this for architecture is that, among other things, the architect must over-code his buildings, using a redundancy of popular signs and metaphors, if his work is to communicate as intended and survive the transformation of fast-changing codes.

Surprisingly, many Modern architects deny this most potent metaphorical level of meaning. They find it nonfunctional and personal, literary and vague, certainly not something they can consciously control and use appropriately. Instead they concentrate on the supposedly rational aspects of design – the cost and function, as they narrowly define them. The result is that their inadvertent metaphors take

59 PDC metaphors seen in a seminar on architectural semiotics, UCLA, 1976, drawn by Kamran. The metaphors were voted on by the class and placed in the following order of plausibility: 1 aircraft hangar, 2 extrusion or architectural moulding, 3 station or terminal building, 4 model of a building, 5 warehouse, 6 blue iceberg, 7 prison, 8 a child's building-blocks or puzzle. The fact that so many metaphors turned out to be actual building types (eg 'station or terminal') shows that the PDC recalls other architecture quite strongly.

60 CESAR PELLI, *Pacific Design Center*, Los Angeles, 1976. A long, high building which looks like an extruded moulding, among other things, because its section is projected throughout the building and on the end elevations. This metaphor is appropriate to its function, since the building displays the mouldings of interior designers (among other products). Its blue exterior, in translucent, transparent and reflective glass, gives it a startling presence in Los Angeles; and because of its size, it is known as 'The Blue Whale'.

61 MANUFACTURERS HANOVER TRUST, New York, 1970. This kind of building on Park Avenue and elsewhere is often satirised by cartoonists such as Steinburg and Kovarsky, who will represent it as grid paper, bank account statement, or any number of economic graphs which rise and fall.

metaphorical revenge and kick them in the behind: their buildings end up looking like metaphors of function and economics, and are condemned as such. The situation is bound to change, however, as both social research and architectural semiotics demonstrate the interpersonal, shared response to metaphor. This is much more predictable and controllable than architects have thought; and since metaphor plays a predominant role in the public's acceptance or rejection of buildings, one can bet that architects will see the point, if only for their own prosperity. Metaphor, seen through conventional visual codes, differs from group to group; but it can be coherently, if not precisely, delineated for all these groups in a society.

61

Words

Underlying much of what I have been saying so far is the notion of cliché – the fact that the architectural language, like the spoken one, must use known units of meaning. To make the linguistic analogy more complete, we could call these units architectural 'words'. There are dictionaries of architecture which define the meanings of these words: doors, windows, columns, partitions, cantilevers, and so forth. Obviously these repeated elements are a necessity of architectural practice. The building industry standardises countless products and the architectural office repeats its favourite details in building after building over many years.

As in language, yesterday's creative metaphor becomes today's tired usage, a conventional word. I have mentioned that the wedge shape became a sign of the auditorium, and that concrete grilles – the cheese-grater metaphor – became, largely, the sign of a parking garage ('office' is the secondary usage). Yet, there is a crucial difference between the 'words' of architecture and of speech. Consider the case of the column. A column on a building is one thing, the Nelson Column in Trafalgar Square another, the column smoke-stack at Battersea Power Station in London a third, and Adolf Loos' entry for the Chicago Tribune Column a fourth. If the column is a 'word', then the word has become a phrase, a sentence and, finally, a whole novel. Clearly architectural words are more elastic and polymorphous than

62-66

62-66 The COLUMN as a 'WORD', seen in different contexts, changes its meaning. At ST MARTIN-IN-THE-FIELDS, London, 1726, it is seen on a portico with other columns of the same order clearly signifying 'colonnade', 'entrance', 'public building' as well as historical associations. NELSON'S COLUMN, Trafalgar Square, 1860, shifts the semantic overtones towards commemoration, 'victory', 'politics', 'standing alone' etc. The COLUMN-SMOKESTACKS at BATTERSEA POWER STATION, London, 1929-55, have entirely different associations because of their syntactic properties. They are placed above a massive base on four corners (incidentally, this is now *the* sign of power station), and so the building looks, from another perspective, like an overturned table. Smoke belches out the top – which has no capital or entablature – so the 'fluted columns have been violated'. Adolf Loos' CHICAGO TRIBUNE COLUMN, a competition entry for a newspaper, was a double pun on the word column ('newspaper column', 'tribune', the name of the newspaper). Loos felt that the Doric Order was a most basic statement of architectural order and therefore fitting for a monument. Finally, the KENTON COUNTY WATER TOWER, Ohio, 1955, again shows the polyvalent aspect of this vertical shape, how it can be used on elevator shafts, chimneys, rocket launchers and oil derricks. Because of the column's positive associations with antiquity, it is often used as a disguise for new, prosaic functions.

those of spoken or written language, and are more based on their physical context and the code of the viewer for their specific sense. To determine what 'Nelson's Column' means you have to analyse the social-physical context ('Trafalgar Square as a centre for political rallies'), the semantic overtones of Nelson ('naval victories', 'historical figure', etc), the syntactic markers ('standing alone', 'surrounded by open space and fountains'), and the historical connotations of column ('use on temples', 'Three Orders', 'phallic symbol', etc). Such an analysis is beyond the scope of this book, but an initial attempt has been made at analysing the column in general, which shows how fruitful this can be.[12] We can make a componential analysis of architectural elements and find out which are, for any culture, distinctive units.

Modern architects have not always faced up to the implications of clichés, or traditional words. They have, by and large, tried to avoid the re-use of **symbolic signs** (the technical term for meaning set by conventional usage) because they felt these historical elements signified lack of creativity. For Frank Lloyd Wright and Walter Gropius, the use of historical elements even signified lack of integrity and character. An architect who used the symbolic sign was probably insincere and certainly snobbish – the Classical orders were a kind of pretentious Latin, not the everyday vernacular of industrial building and sober utility. From these latter building tasks, a universal language, they hoped, could be constructed, a sort of Esperanto of cross-cultural usage based on functional types. These signs would be **indexical** (either directly indicating their use, like arrows, linear corridors), or else **iconic**, in which case the form would be a diagram of its function (a structurally-shaped bridge, or even Venturi's duck). Modern architectural words would be limited to these types of signs.

However, the problem with this approach is that most architectural words are symbolic signs; certainly those that are most potent and persuasive are the ones which are learned and conventional, not 'natural'. The **symbolic** sign dominates the **indexical** and **iconic**, and even these latter depend somewhat on knowledge and convention for their correct interpretation. There was thus a devastating theoretical mistake at the very core of the Modern language. It couldn't work the

67, 68 LE CORBUSIER, *Pessac Housing*, before and after, 1925 and 1969. Ground floors were walled up, pitched roofs were added, the ribbon windows were divided up, terraces were turned into extra bedrooms, and a great number of signs which connoted 'security', 'home', 'ownership', were placed all over the exterior, thus effectively destroying the Purist language. (Architectural Association, Philippe Boudon)

69 The ETON HOUSE, *Ideal Home Exhibition,* London, 1974. The facial metaphor is often present at the Ideal Home Exhibition, with two or three examples strictly symmetrical about the front door ('mouth'). Various signs of status are tacked on (such as the fibreglass Adam detailing), but the snobbism is more apparent than real: it is not meant to convince the neighbours that you sent your son to Eton, but simply to distinguish the building from 'council housing'. This is perhaps the strongest social motivation, the distinction between 'us' and 'them' (those 'controlled' by the government). Hence the Ideal Home styles are relatively permissive, including Swiss Chalet and American Ranch House. In fact for 1976, the Ideal British Home was Colonial, an unforeseen consequence of 1776.

way the architects hoped because no living language can: they are mostly based on learned conventions, on **symbolic** signs, not ones which can be understood directly, without training.

A good example of architects' mistaken attitude towards the symbolic sign is their treatment of the pitched roof, which conventionally signifies 'home' in Northern countries. The Modern architect disregarded this custom for functional and aesthetic reasons, to create roof gardens, more space, rectilinear form (Walter Gropius gave six rational reasons for designing flat roofs). Not surprisingly these flat-top buildings were regarded as alien, as insecure, even unfinished and 'without a head'. The houses had been decapitated. Many of the inhabitants of Le Corbusier's Pessac felt his stark white cubical forms lacked a proper sense of shelter and protection, so they shortened the ribbon windows, added shutters and more window mullions; they articulated the blank white surfaces with window boxes, cornices and eaves; and some put on the old Bordeaux sign of protection, the pitched roof. In short, they *systematically misunderstood* his Purist language and systematically redesigned it to incorporate their conventional signs of home. Ironically, at the end of his life Le Corbusier acknowledged the legitimacy of the people distorting his message when he said of the changes at Pessac: 'Life is right, the architect wrong.'

In spite of the many flat-roofed housing estates today, certain unreconstructed people still go on in their incorrigible way thinking that pitched roofs mean shelter and psychological protection. Many studies have shown this, and a major building society in England, recognising the fact, has taken as its symbol an archetypal couple walking arm in arm under a pitched-roof umbrella. Since this sign exists, and since repeated usage will create the **symbolic** sign, the architect might change his attitude towards these conventions. He might regard them as powerful meanings to be used normally in a straightforward way, if only to catch the attention of an audience he wants to convert and send unusual meanings.

If one wants to change a culture's taste and behaviour, as do Modern architects, then first one has to speak the accepted language. If the language and message are changed at the same time, then both will be systematically misunderstood and reinterpreted to fit the conventional categories, the habitual patterns of life. This is precisely what has happened with Modern housing estates. Pruitt-Igoe and Pessac are the two most celebrated examples. A more promising approach for the Modern architect, or social interventionist, would be to study the *popular* house in all its variety and see how it signifies a different way of life for different taste cultures and ethnic groups.

Broadly speaking, these groups are classified in socio-economic terms by sociologists and market researchers, even though there is a lot of overlap and borrowing between groups, and there are other forces at work.[13] The class influence on taste is only one of several influences. It seems to me more exact to speak of semiotic groups than class-based taste cultures, because those groups which share preferences of **meaning** have a life and continuity of their own, which is only lightly coloured by socio-economic background. Basically, semiotic groups are in different universes of signification and have different views of the good life. I will mention three versions of the popular house which spring from these different groups.

1 The ideal of many working-class families is to buy a detached, small house, a bungalow roughly similar to others in an area they know. The values expressed in these houses are security, ownership, separation (a free-standing building), and a kind of conservative anonymity (represented by conforming more or less to the norm of the area). Levittown in America, and the Ideal Home Exhibition in Britain, as well as most buildings in both countries, cater to this semiotic group. It could be called conservative or conformist, sensible or petit-bourgeois, depending on which values are stressed and who is doing the valuing, because all these aspects are very clearly signified in the language. The archetype is a two-storey house with a central doorway, a symmetrical displacement of windows on either side, a chimney and pitched roof – all of which vaguely resembles a face with two eyes (top windows), nose (entrance portico) and mouth (doorway).

The band of planting in front of the house could be the shirt collar or moustache, symbolic 'moat', or 'forest', depending on what other signs are stressed. Since this group often wants to signal its new-found independence, meanings tend to support the old Anglo-Saxon maxim, 'every man's home is his castle' – and the castle may be defended by a picket fence or garden gnomes. There is a stately avenue winding to the front door – the curved pathway; past sylvan forests – bushes.

2 The next semiotic group tends to take the previous values for granted, since it hasn't just left what is regarded as the teeming city. In America this group might be called middle-class fastidious, since the clipped lawns and status signs of colonial provenance (nearly always false) harangue the passer-by like some Bicentennial orator in a fit of nationalism. Indeed, cleanliness and caution, hard work and discretion, prosperity and sobriety – all the images of WASP success – are there to brand this as the ultimate bourgeois dream. The only problem with this classification is that the appeal of these values reaches much further than the middle class.

For instance, the reigning style of movie star houses, those of Beverly Hills and Bel Air which sell from a quarter of a million dollars to three million, fall in this category. The movie stars clearly aren't middle-class, even if their tastes look it and they've come from this background. Are they slumming, or have they just adopted a previously existing semiotic tradition and then amplified it? Often they are called the 'aristocracy of America', because their values and way of life have become the standard of emulation for the mass of America. Films, and countless sightseeing bus trips going past the stars' houses (a minor industry since 1922), have made these buildings the most influential on popular taste. They tend to be in one of six styles: 1 Southern Mansion, 2 Old English, 3 New England Colonial, 4 French Provincial/Regency, 5 Spanish Colonial, or 6 Contemporary/Colonial Hybrid. These are also the six reigning styles of the popular suburban house. A close investigation will reveal that most of these houses are Ersatz. That is, few of them are serious, scholarly revivals, there is almost no pretence to historical accuracy or serious eclecticism. The styles are notional, signs of status and historical roots – but signs to remind you of the past, not convince you that the building is living in the present.

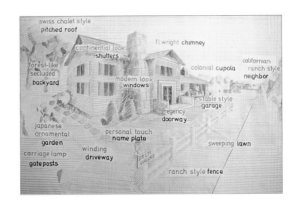

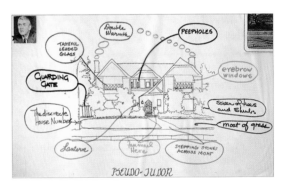

70 KEVIN FISHER, *English Popular House Analysis*, 1976. This synthesis of several reigning trends in the market shows how eclectic and permissive the popular English house is becoming. A pastiche of Japanese, American and English, modern and traditional, urban and rural. Few architects would dare use such a language because of its impurity, so the market remains open to the speculators. It is of course possible to use any language to send any message.

71, 72 JIMMY STEWART'S *House*, Beverly Hills, c1940. A very fastidious mixture of Tudor and Japanese architecture with Swiss accents. The clarity of outline, the black and white alternatives, the very studied informality of massing and planting send out a clear message. Such houses, often exposed in films, have confirmed if not created our image of the American Dream House. Similar examples can be found outside every major city from Boston to Los Angeles, and since the norm is so invariable it almost constitutes a 'language without speech'. Put another way, one could say the language does the talking and the designer is a mouthpiece of this language. (Carol Barkin and Stephanie Vaughan)

3 Another semiotic group distinguishes itself from the previous one by inverting these signs and values. A studied casualness is preferred to fastidiousness, a kind of seedy, unselfconscious comfort is preferred to blatant order and rectitude. The down-at-the-heels aristocrat and the intellectual, the drop-out and left wing socialite all unite against what they take to be the vulgarity of the previous group's 'good taste'. Even the Modern architect unites with them on this score.

Thus we find the emphasis on nature and **naturalness**, the building isolated and hidden in the actual woods (as opposed to bushes), which are not manicured to near perfection. They are allowed to grow almost freely, just cut back at certain points to reveal a gable here, a roof there, as if by felicitous chance. In fact, it is our old friend the picturesque tradition, the celebration of the carefully careless and studied accident, in a variety of new clothes. These may be the white Modern Architecture of the 1920s (Le Style Corbu has actually become a popular status-badge when handled by Richard Meier), the stick-and-shed style of the 1960s, or the House and Garden style of the last seventy years, represented on a collective level by such resorts and communities as Portmeirion and Port Grimaud.

Portmeirion is a misplaced Italian hill town set on the lush Welsh coast, surrounded by two miles of rhododendron and other exotic overgrowth. Every vista is carefully composed as a landscape, each path wanders perfectly around every rock outcrop, each bush and flower relates miraculously to near and far buildings, and space ebbs and flows like water into small contained pools and dramatic, open cascades. *Trompe l'oeil*, phoney windows, buildings shrunken to five-sixths of their normal size, eye traps, calculated naiveties, whimsical conceits (a sailboat is turned into concrete, and thence into a retaining wall) – this sort of easy-going wit has proven popular with writers and tourists. The builder, Sir Clough William-Ellis, has cannibalised old buildings and preserved parts of them in his new confections.

This care for the old and traditional is very apparent and one may take it as a characteristic sign of this semiotic group. The ancient is valued not so much for itself, but as a sign of continuity between generations and a connection with the past. While the first guess is that such values and understatements appeal only to élite tastes, this does not turn out to be true. For instance, 100,000 visitors come to Portmeirion every year, this sophisticated version of Disneyland; and millions visit country houses in England, mostly because of their rich historical associations.

These three semiotic groups, the conservative, the fastidious and the 'natural', hardly exhaust the plurality of taste cultures which exist in any large city. In America, there is also the Main Street tradition, which Robert Venturi and Denise Scott Brown have analysed as a series of signs, and England has its counterpart in the High Street.

Venturi, Scott Brown and their team have been instrumental in calling attention to this wide area of symbolism, and have put on an exhibition 'Signs and Symbols of American Life', which has presented some of the images that make up a popular language. Their own design, where possible, incorporates these signs, usually in an ironic and esoteric way. While many critics deplore their work as unnecessarily banal, or ugly, or condescending – that is, anything but popular – their deadpan

74

73

75

76

77

73 PORTMEIRION, *view up Battery Square and Pantheon*, showing seaside architecture and Italian campanile. This stage-set architecture has, not surprisingly, been used in several films and commercials. This was the first creation of a formula that was later applied, in a cheapened version, to communities such as Port Grimaud, and ride-through parks such as Disneyland.

74 RICHARD MEIER, *Douglas House*, Harbor Springs, Michigan, 1971-73. The villa in nature, enclosed, protected, and yet standing out as a man-made element. This Italian tradition, taken over equally by Le Corbusier and the upper classes, contrasts the raw and the cooked, the untouched and the finished. Here Meier uses a Corbusian syntax to represent the interior space, which is layered both horizontally and vertically through four storeys. (Ezra Stoller)

75 ROBERT VENTURI, DENISE SCOTT BROWN and TEAM, *The Street*, section from an exhibition 'Signs of Life: Symbols in the American City', Renwick Gallery, Washington DC, 1976. Public buildings, state capitols, courts in a classicising style are mixed with the commercial vernacular. This exhibition documented popular symbolism in three major areas: the house, the main street and the commercial strip. The 'lessons' that these designers drew favoured symbolic instead of sculptural architecture, 'decorated sheds' instead of 'ducks'. (Smithsonian Institution, Washington DC)

76, 77 VENTURI and RAUCH, *Tucker House*, Katonah, New York, 1975. The exterior exaggerates elements of the popular code the overhanging eaves and picture window – while the interior uses the white, planar International Style as a backdrop for Kitsch and other objects. Actually, the fireplace with its round mirror is a miniature of the house, a very witty comment on the traditional idea of aedicules, miniature models and dolls' houses. (Stephen Shore)

approach is not necessarily a bad thing. After all, an architect may use a language without sending the customary messages, and if he wants to signify 'the ugly and ordinary' with this language he has a perfect right to do so. The Venturis justify their approach as social criticism: they want to express, in a gentle way, a mixed appreciation for the American Way of Life. Grudging respect, not total acceptance. They don't share all the values of a consumer society, but they want to speak to this society, even if partially in dissent. Also their sensibility is, through and through, Modernist, their training has been in the language of Le Corbusier and Louis Kahn, so they cannot use popular signs in a relaxed and exuberant way – on a level with the Las Vegas sign artists whom they admire. But how could they? It takes years, perhaps a generation, to master the unselfconscious and conscious use of a new language, and so these architects are, to use a phrase borrowed from the Futurists, 'the primitives of a new sensibility'.

We may expect to see the next generation of architects using the new hybrid language with confidence. It will look more like Art Nouveau than the International Style, incorporating the rich frame of reference of the former, its wide metaphorical reach, its written signs and vulgarity, its symbolic signs and clichés – the full gamut of architectural expression.

Syntax

Another aspect architecture shares with language is more mundane than metaphors and words. A building has to stand up and be put together according to certain rules, or methods of joinery. The laws of gravity and geometry dictate such things as an up and down, a roof and floor and various storeys in between, just as the laws of sound and speech formation dictate certain vowels, consonants and ways of speaking them. These compelling forces create what could be called a syntax of architecture – that is, the rules for combining the various words of door, window, wall, and so forth. Most doors, for instance, follow the syntactical rule 78 requiring a floor, necessarily flat, on both sides. What happens when this rule is constantly broken? The fun-house at the Amusement Park – which takes advantage of the fact that the nervous system unconsciously knows the syntactical rules and enjoys having them broken from time to time. Delirious word-salads, the speech of schizophrenics and poetry, all distort conventional grammar. It is obviously one of the defining characteristics of all sign systems used aesthetically. They call attention to the language itself by misuse, exaggeration, repetition, and all the devices of rhetorical skill.

Michael Graves speaks about 'foregrounding' the elements of architecture by turning them on their side, extending them out from their usual, functional context and painting them like a Juan Gris Cubist composition. His houses are poetic distortions of a Cubist syntax, whose only fault, in terms of communication, is in the choice of a limited syntax and under-coding. You need a reader's guide to 80 appreciate the fact that a blue balustrade is a column lying down. The Handmade Houses of the West Coast use a much more accessible syntax in a similar way. 79 Shingles, wood siding, different types of standard windows tipped on their sides, placed at the corner of the building, roofs pitching at odd angles, logs used without

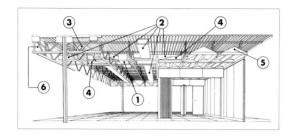

78 EZRA EHRENKRANTZ, *SCSD (Schools Construction System Development)*, California, 1960s. The syntax of architecture obviously relates to functional concerns, as this drawing shows. Six major elements: 1 mixing boxes, 2 rigid ducts, 3 flexible ducts, 4 outlets, 5 lighting, 6 roof plenum, show the air-conditioning requirements. These were combined with roof, floor and a partition system to give a flexible syntax that could be changed in several ways. (Drawing by Mary Banham from *The Architecture of the Well-tempered Environment* by Reyner Banham)

79 HANDMADE HOUSE, West Coast, c1970. Traditional wooden construction and ready-made windows and doors are displaced from their usual syntactic position to, again, call attention to themselves: 'The Window Building' (from *Handmade Houses, A Guide to the Woodbutcher's Art*, by Art Boericke and Barry Shapiro, 1973. The owner and place are not identified)

80 MICHAEL GRAVES, *Benacerraf House addition*, Princeton, 1969. A Cubist syntax is used to call attention to itself. This heightening of our perception of doors, stairways, balustrades and views from a terrace is complex and masterful. It is so rich here that one forgets to ask what the functions are (actually an open terrace above, and a playroom and breakfast room below). Note how the structure, sometimes unnecessary, is pulled away from the wall. Railings and cut-out wall planes also serve to define a net of rectilinear space. The front balustrade is, conceptually, a column lying on its side – a play on syntactical meaning, as is the whole addition. (Laurin McCracken)

finishing – these syntactical tricks have a richer resonance of meaning, except, of course, for those trained in synthetic cubism. Again, it is a matter of coding and richness of coding which is at stake, not an absolute difference in meaning.

The syntax of architecture has preoccupied the Modern Movement to the point of obsession, which is one reason it will not be emphasised here. Starting with nineteenth-century theorists, Viollet-le-Duc, Semper and Choisy, this interest in structure and syntax took over from a variety of concerns. Architecture suddenly was reduced to its constructional process, the way it was put together. Louis Kahn wrote about THE FORM of building as if it were the Architectural Saviour which would rescue him from all other obligations

Carrying on this reduced tradition, Peter Eisenman produces beautiful syntactic knots which dazzle the eye, confuse the mind, and ultimately signify *for him* the process that generated them. How enticing; how banal. The spirit of process is supposed to lift you heavenwards so you overlook the prosaic assumptions. Once again, as with Mies, the analogy of beautifully consistent form is meant to stand for the missing values, transport the mind above ordinary concerns. But this Architectural Ascension is not quite miraculous enough; there is no lift-off, that is, syntactically speaking. Semantically (a mode of communication Eisenman disdains), his buildings convey the sharp white light of rationality and the virtues of geometrical organisation: the exciting 'bridges to cross', surprising punched-out 'holes of space', the framed 'vistas', the Chinese puzzle of structure. So far as one can recognise these semantic meanings and connect them with other associations (Protestantism, the white architecture of the twenties), then these buildings have a wider meaning. In other words, the pure realm of syntax is only relevant perceptually when it is incorporated into semantic fields.

Semantics

In the nineteenth century, when different styles of architecture were being revived, there was a fairly coherent doctrine of semantics which explained which style to use on which building type. An architect would pick the Doric Order for use on a bank because the Order and the banking function had certain overtones in common: sobriety, impersonality, masculinity and rationality (a bank was meant to look tough enough to discourage robbers, and sensible enough to encourage depositors). Not only were these semantic properties set by comparison, by looking at the Orders in opposition to each other and other styles, but so were a host of syntactic aspects: the size of the Doric capital, the column's relation to other columns, and its proportion to the cornice, frieze and base. Since these forms and relationships were used coherently, people felt able to pass judgement on their *suitability*. They could tell what the building signified, and they could read a slight change in emphasis, a variation of proportion, as a change in meaning.

Of course, this is to idealise the situation, as only a small part of the community could make these distinctions. But at least *some* could, and this community (echoing the root-word 'communication') kept the architect responsive to the whole enjoyable game of signification. He knew that if the semantic system were violently overthrown or became too complicated, his communication would be reduced to

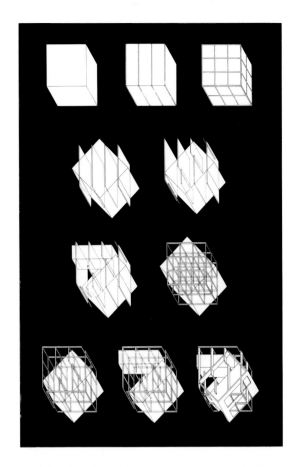

81, 82 PETER EISENMAN, *House III* for Robert Miller, Lakeville, Connecticut, 1971. Several of the drawings which generated the house show the main oppositions between two grids at 45 degrees (step 6), a conceptual cage of boxed space (step 7), a column grid (step 3), and wall planes in 'shear' (step 5). Bridges and open volumes unite and divide the room functions. The facades 'mark' some interior transformations – if you look at them with the diagrams in your hand and think for a long time. This architecture, like nineteenth-century programme music, demands a complementary text in order to be fully understood.

83 J C LOUDON, *How to Dress a Utilitarian Cottage*, sketches from Loudon's *Encyclopaedia*. A basic cube with hipped roof is transformed with verandah and terrace, with trellis, a castellated Gothic jacket, monastic habit and Elizabethan front. The style is chosen according to the owner's role and place of residence.

primitive gestures. In fact, by 1860, the game of eclecticism had become too complicated. For this reason it was overthrown, and vilified sixty years later because it had failed to signify those meanings architects found important. But it needn't have broken down if an adequate theory of eclecticism had been in operation.

Nonetheless, revivalist architects did at least justify their choice of a style in terms of appropriateness; and this gave a degree of coherence to their formal choice. One architect, J C Loudon, proposed a theory of 'associationism' based on the notion of 'association of ideas', and even went so far as to say that each house should convey in its manner the character and role of its owner.[14] If the inhabitant 83 were a country parson, the house should be dressed in castellated Gothic or related clothing. Thus the environment would become more and more legible as society became more differentiated.

To a certain extent, this doctrine was followed in the nineteenth century, and we find that the introduction of a new style is assimilated into the appropriate semantic field. The Neo-Egyptian Style, popular in 1830 because of the Rosetta Stone and 84 Napoleon's previous campaigns, was used sensibly on banks, tombs, prisons and medical colleges. The argument for its use might be based either on *conventional* or *natural* meanings. In the first cases, Neo-Egyptian was appropriate because the Pharaohs buried their treasure in temples of this style; or famous Egyptian doctors, healers and practitioners of medicine were sometimes also architects. Hence by the association of ideas, you could properly use the Egyptian style on banks and chemists' shops. Secondly, this style had natural meanings of heaviness, impenetrability and massiveness. The walls are battered and the openings small – use it on prisons, it 'naturally' signifies high security.

By the same line of reasoning, the Neo-Baroque, or Second Empire Style of 1860 had a series of natural overtones. It was massive, overarticulated, splendiferous, muscular, angst-ridden, tempestuous, bombastic, playful, exuberant, pretentious, and very expensive to build. Where should it be used? On the opera house of course. Garnier's Parisian confection of the 1870s was most suitably clothed; and 85

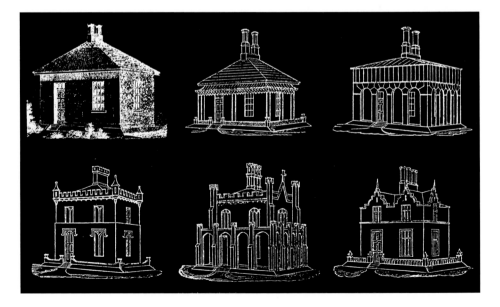

it was no accident that when he conquered France, Hitler danced a jig on its steps. His choice of this style for the Third Reich (an Empire meant to last longer than the French attempts) was both appropriate and inadvertently ironic. It symbolised strength, but as with so many governments which have chosen this style, the strength didn't survive its leader. Today, for this historic reason, Neo-Baroque conventionally symbolises 'vanished power' or 'ineffectual dictatorship', and is used in innumerable movies and television dramas to signify this ambivalent pathos. The short-lived nature of the architectural code, and its distortion by historical events thus brings out once again the domination of conventional meaning over natural signification.

We can clarify this issue by looking at the Classical language of architecture, the way the Three Orders constituted a semantic system, and how this system changed under the pressures of eclecticism. Vitruvius characterised the Doric Order as bold, severe, simple, blunt, true, honest, straightforward, and in sexual terms, masculine. In part, this characterisation stemmed from the natural metaphors inherent in the form, but it also had origins in historical accident (at least, according to Vitruvius' account of the Doric Order's birth).

The Corinthian Order was, by contrast, delicate, dainty, slender, ornamental and, sexually speaking, a young virgin. As one would guess, the middle Order, the Ionic, was a kind of architectural hermaphrodite, a neuter — in fact for Vitruvius, a matronly Order, because it was slightly more feminine than masculine (with elegant volutes). But these characterisations really only begin to make sense, as E H Gombrich has pointed out, when the Orders are put in *opposition to each other*.

The rigid orders of ancient architecture would seem to be a fairly recalcitrant matrix for the expression of psychological and physiognomic categories; still it makes sense when Vitruvius recommends Doric temples for Minerva, Mars, and Hercules, Corinthian ones for Venus, Flora, and Prosperina, while Juno, Diana, and other divinities who stand in between the two extremes, are given Ionic temples. Within the medium at the architects' disposal, Doric is clearly more virile than Corinthian. We say that Doric expresses the god's severity; it does, but only because it is on the more severe end of the scale and not because there is necessarily much in common between the god of war and the Doric order.[15]

Clearly there is nothing in common between warfare and the Doric except with respect to comparable things or elements: they each occupy equivalent semantic zones. In other words, if we map the Three Orders in a semantic space, it is the relationships (r1, r2, r3) which really matter, and not the 'natural' meanings of the forms, nor the particular semantic axes we choose whether Vitruvius' or our own.

As long as we can distinguish clear differences between elements, it doesn't matter too much what these differences are, because custom and usage will first set them in one semantic space and then transform them to another. This can be seen in the nineteenth century with the rapid shift of stylistic meanings. For instance, in very crude terms, the concept of state power was indicated successively by the Roman revival, the Greek Neo-Classical, the Gothic (at least in the Houses of Parliament), the Italian High Renaissance, the *Rundbogenstil*, the High

84 THOMAS USTICK WALTER, *Moyamensing Prison*, Philadelphia, 1835. The Egyptian style, with its battered walls, heavy columns and small openings, naturally signified a structure from which it was hard to escape. (HABS, Library of Congress, photo Jack E Boucher)

85 CHARLES GARNIER, *Paris Opera House*, 1861-74. The giant, heroic order is played double height against a smaller one. Surfaces are covered with sculpture and polychromy. Everywhere statues take up operatic poses, flexing their muscles — even the women look intimidating. The interior grand staircase displays people as if they were to make an entrance on stage. The internal corner, with its re-entrant angles, medallions and general grandiloquence, is the most muscle-bound corner of the time. The Second Empire style *naturally* signified power: it took a lot of money to build.

86

Victorian Gothic, and finally in the 1870s, the Second Empire Style. There was a general trend in this evolution towards more and more bombast and articulation, understood metaphors of power; but all of a sudden the semantic system could be overturned. Simplicity could become a correlate of potency, as it was with the Neo-Classical and the International Style. There is nothing to keep an age from inverting the semantic space of its predecessors. The relation of form to meaning is mostly conventional.

We can see this transformation of meanings in the jump from the Classical language of architecture to Eclecticism, and in the work of one man. Nikolaus Pevsner has summarised the way John Nash used a different 'style for the job'.

> [Nash] had a nice sense of associational propriety; as shown in his choice of the Neo-Classical for his town house and of the Gothic for his country mansion (complete with Gothic conservatory). Moreover, he built Cronkhill in Shropshire (1802), as an Italianate villa with a round-arched loggia on slender columns and with the widely projecting eaves of the Southern farmhouse (Roscoe's *Lorenzo Medici* had come out in 1796); he built Blaise Castle, near Bristol (1809) in a rustic Old-English cottage style with barge-boarded gables and thatched roofs (one is reminded of *The Vicar of Wakefield*, Marie Antoinette's dairy in the Park of Versailles, and Gainsborough's and Greuze's sweet peasant children); and he continued the Brighton Pavilion in a 'Hindu' fashion, just introduced after 1800 at Sezincote in the Cotswolds where the owner, out of personal nostalgia, insisted on the style 'Indian Gothic'[16]

87

In effect, Nash has substituted a revival style for each of the Three Orders. Roughly speaking, Hindu has been substituted for Corinthian, Gothic for Ionic and Classical for Doric (the Old English and Italian styles occupy new niches).

88

More significantly, a single form has taken on its opposite meaning in the system. The Corinthian (or Nash's Classical Order) has become masculine, simple and straightforward, because now it is set against other formal elements. This inversion is a good illustration of the semiotic rule that it is relationships between elements which count more than their inherent meanings. We could find countless other examples throughout architectural history: the Picturesque aesthetic being 'functional' in 1840 and 'anti-functional' in 1920; simple, Platonic forms symbolising truth and honesty in 1540 and deceit and artifice in 1870, and so on. Although our intuition and perception of form may feel straightforward and 'natural', it is based on an elaborate set of changing conventions. It is the differences between juxtaposed elements which constitute one of the bases for their meaning – not the natural overtones inherent in the elements themselves.

Even though aesthetic and technical issues dominate architects today, they still pay some measure of attention to semantics. An architect will use a curtain wall for an office building, because glass and steel feel cold, impersonal, precise and ordered – the overtones of methodical business, rational planning and commercial transactions. One could argue that the architect should deflect these meanings, that business might be made to look more adventurous and domestic than it is; yet the basic classification is suitable.

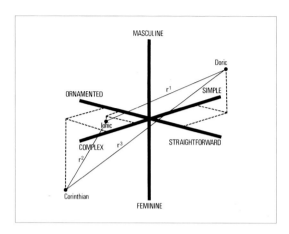

86 The THREE ORDERS. I have used these particular axes of Vitruvius for the sake of simplicity and comparison with the subsequent diagrams. But more interesting oppositions could be chosen, as long as they are semantically distinct enough to give different information from each other. For instance, 'nature' might be opposed to 'culture', 'power' to 'impotence', etc. Semantic meaning consists partly in *oppositions within a system*.

87 JOHN NASH, *Royal Pavilion*. Brighton, 1815-18. Nash threw into his soufflé a bit of Gothic, a bit of Chinese, a bit of cast-iron (palm tree columns) and his own version of a bulbous Hindu style. Ersatz, the first exuberant Kitsch building in England. Bad taste has been a positive creative force since then, reaching one high with the Victorian country house. All this obscures, however, the appropriateness of choosing the Indian style for an escape palace next to the sea. If you are designing a 'pleasure dome' for the Prince who wants to get away from London sobriety, what better than the style of Kubla Khan (published 1816)?

Wood is intrinsically warm, pliable, soft, organic, and full of natural marks such as knots and grain, so it is used domestically or where people come into close contact with the building. Brick is associated by use with housing, and is inherently flexible in detail, so it is also used domestically. In spite of the fact that there are much more economic building systems available, the wood-and-brick hybrid still accounts for seventy-five per cent of speculative and council housing in Britain – a clear indication that semantic issues take precedence, in the public's mind, over technical ones.

What about new materials such as nylon, which make up pneumatic buildings? The inflatable system is naturally pudgy, squashy, cuddly, sexual, volumetric and pleasant to touch, so it has naturally found a secure niche in the semantic field and is used appropriately on swimming pools, blow-up furniture, entertainment areas 89 and other unmentionable places. Its occasional use as a church or office building brings out different, less dominant semantic overtones.

These comparative aspects of building systems can be graphed in a semantic space similar to that already used, although axes other than the ones I have taken 90 over from Vitruvius would be more relevant. The **relations** between brick, pneumatics, concrete and steel set up the semantic field which will differ slightly for each individual and particular usage employed. Several architects have made hesitant steps to contrast materials for semantic reasons; one building emerging from this process – a multi-use structure in Rome – has been heavily criticised for being made up of clichés, and for being schizophrenic. This building, completed in 91 1965 by the Passarelli brothers, uses the conventional forms for office: smooth black steel and glass, and below conventional signs for dwelling – hanging vines, broken silhouette, picturesque massing and balconies. A third building system below ground, in monolithic, Brutalist concrete, is the parking garage. The standard joke was that each of the brothers designed a different part of the building and never talked to each other. Part of the criticism directed against this building was for its obvious use of styles already better developed by Harrison and Abromovitz, Paul Rudolph and Le Corbusier; and one can see the point of this censure.

But also, and perhaps a more deep-rooted reason for the pique was the use of various structures and materials. Architects and critics brought up with the International Style were ingrained with the Purist notion that one aesthetic and structural system should be used on a building. Attendant ideas supporting this were the notions of harmony, the classical ideal that a part cannot be added or subtracted without disturbing the integrated whole, and that each building had, Platonically speaking, one and only one best solution.

There were even further assumptions which this building called into question: the self-conscious use of opposite styles as *styles*. Le Corbusier had said, 'the "styles" are a lie'. Frank Lloyd Wright and Walter Gropius believed that a single style, expressing the character and integrity of the architect, must animate all his work – otherwise he was guilty of insincerity, pandering to the whims of a client and ultimately to a corrupt ruling taste. Eclecticism meant slick facility and lack of conviction.

There are two obvious problems with this single-style approach (still the reigning

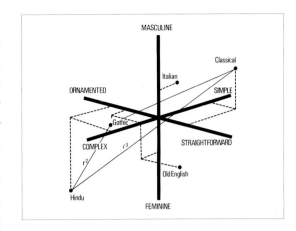

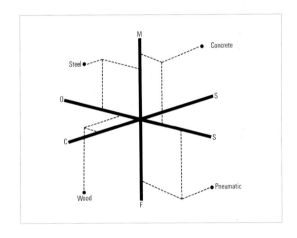

88 JOHN NASH'S *Five Styles* compared in the same semantic space as the Three Orders (86). The comparison brings out the fact that it is the *relationship* between styles, or Orders, which matters most in determining semantic meaning. The Corinthian, or Classical Order, has thus taken on its exact opposite meaning in Nash's system, because now it is more masculine, simple and straightforward than the Hindu style

89 BARBARELLA, 1968, is always shown surrounded with viscous, shiny plastic and soft, hairy fur. (ALA Fotocine)

90 FOUR BUILDING SYSTEMS. Particular uses of each building system have to be established before these relationships can be plotted: eg the particular use of concrete may in fact be more complex and feminine than the use of steel. Then the functional aspects have to be mapped in the same semantic space, and the two mappings compared.

one, even if it is less explicit than at previous times). First, as the Passarelli building shows; mixed styles are an aid to communication, and an architect must master at least three or four to articulate any complex building today, especially if he is to design the interior.

Secondly, the connection of any particular style with sincerity, whether it is the International Style or the *ad hoc* aesthetic of Handmade Houses, is a matter of history and convention, not something eternally true. By that typical process of historical inversion, we have actually arrived at a position where consistency and Purism do not equate with integrity, but quite the reverse. How has this happened?

Precisely because the International Style has been accepted on a massive scale by those who build cities. It is now the conventional style of the ruling class and its bureaucracy (at least for its large-scale offices and civic buildings), so its use hardly ensures that same sincerity which preoccupied the pioneers of the style. Furthermore the 'Masters of Modern Architecture' (I take the phrase from a series of books) have become like the consumer products Coca-Cola, Xerox and Ford, each with their own house style and corporate brand image. They did not intend this of course, but since they couldn't advertise and since they had to work within a consumer society, the main way of selling their reputation was to develop a single recognisable style which could be purveyed through magazines, books and TV. In short, their authenticity, and their sincerity itself, became a marketable commodity, just as that of Picasso and Ché Guevara did in other fields.

The followers of the 'masters' are led in the same direction, with the result that we can now recognise the Safdie style, the brand marks of Kurokawa and Tange, the Stirling manner, and so forth. How does a client or committee know which one to pick? They choose from books or articles which show his style distinguished from those of competitors. Originality and distinctiveness are saleable items.

The result of this hidden process, of the marketing of reputations, has been to produce a recognisable style of the élite, middle-class architects: it tends towards univalence because of the pressures toward consistency. It is made up from repetitive geometrics, divorced from most metaphors except that of the machine, and purged of vulgarity and the signs common to semiotic groups other than that of architects. The environment which is created by such a situation is one where every building is a monument to the architect's consistency, rather than appropriate to the job or the urban setting.

The issues involved are obviously complex. An architect must, to a certain extent, develop his own way of doing things, his own details and mannerisms; but these no longer guarantee or signify authenticity as they tended to do before the avant-garde was incorporated into consumer society. And if this practice now produces essentially boring, idiosyncratic sculpture, oversimplified in a single language, then today the architect's sincerity can be measured by his or her ability to design in a plurality of styles. Consistency equals unconscious hypocrisy (or, occasionally, conscious élitism).

91 PASSARELLI BROTHERS, *Multi-use structure*, Rome, 1965. The concrete and hanging vines classify the flats, the black steel curtain wall indicates office, and below ground, exposed concrete articulates parking. Termed 'Schizo' by *Architectural Review* and attacked by Modernists for its impurity, the building none the less makes basic distinctions which are obscured in Purist design.

PART THREE
Post-Modern Architecture

Historicism, the Beginnings of PM

The question of what period of architecture might be plausibly revived was fiercely and rather uncharitably debated by the English and Italians in the late fifties. Reyner Banham and his teacher Nikolaus Pevsner launched quite different kinds of attacks on Italian Neo-Liberty and what they took to be a return to Historicism (not to be confused with Karl Popper's use of this term in politics). Professor Banham, calling the class to order, attacked 'The Italian retreat from Modern Architecture' as 'infantile regression', because it went back to a pre-machine age style. Pevsner listed the other retreats from the faith and found shades of deviant 'neo-Art Nouveau and neo-De Stijl', neo-this and neo-that sprouting everywhere like poisonous weeds. Their articles and attacks, lasting from 1959 to 1962, were meant to wipe out these heresies with a little critical weed-killer, but in the event the Italians fought back at this Puritanism, the refrigerator school of criticism.[17]

The kind of buildings which were provoking this debate all had vague or repressed historical allusions: Franco Albini's museums and Rinascente, 1957-62, were reminiscent of traditional Roman building; the Torre Velasca, Milan, 1957, looked somewhat like a medieval tower; Luigi Moretti used an actual rusticated base in the Casa del Girasole, Rome, 1952, while Lubetkin, in England, used, ironically, a caryatid *porte-cochère* as early as 1939. One of the most convincing historicist buildings of the fifties was Paolo Portoghesi's Casa Baldi, 1959-61, an essay in free-form curves definitely reminiscent of the Borromini he was studying, yet also unmistakeably influenced by Le Corbusier. Here is the schizophrenic cross between two codes that is characteristic of Post-Modernism: the enveloping, sweeping curves of the Baroque, the overlap of space, the various foci of space interfering with each other and the Brutalist treatment, the expression of concrete block, rugged joinery and the guitar-shapes of Modernism. I give the dates of this Italian historicism to set it against the slightly later emergence of the same thing in Japan, Spain and America (where critics sometimes claim it happened first). Although Saarinen built his 'orange-peel dome', the Kresge Auditorium and chapel, in 1955, and these were reminiscent of Renaissance and medieval prototypes, it wasn't really until his Stiles and Morse colleges at Yale, 1958-62, in 'peanut-brittle Gothic', that overt historicism arrives. Here we have a conscious medieval layout, picturesque massing, an attention to the local Yale context – in sum the beginnings of a sensitive urban place-making. The detail and massing may be diagrammatic, and slightly cheapskate, but this is the Modernist inheritance.

Semi-historicism starts in America, in a big way, about 1960 with the major

92 LUBETKIN and TECTON, *Highpoint II*, Highgate, 1938. Because of local hostility to Modernism, the architects, half-ironically, incorporated casts of the caryatid removed from the Erechtheum. The Classical reference was perhaps fitting to their ordered, Classical geometries, but at this stage in time it is the presence of the human figure and the representational boldness, where it is appropriate – at the door – which are noteworthy.

93 PAOLO PORTOGHESI and VITTORIO GIGLIOTTI, *Casa Baldi I*, Rome, 1959-61. Half Baroque, half Modern in its curves and materials. The wall planes curve to acknowledge windows or doors, or create overlapping foci of space. Unlike later buildings by the same architects, the forms aren't entirely sculptural but keep semantic memories (eg cornice, building block, closed bedroom). (Oscar Savio)

works of Philip Johnson and the more kitsch variants of Yamasaki, Ed Stone and Wallace Harrison. Yamasaki and Stone produce their sparkling version of Islamic 'grilles and frills' in 1958 and then 'almost-real-Gothic' in 1962 – at least this is the date of Yamasaki's infamous instant arches (awaiting their cathedral, in Seattle). The historicism is attenuated, embarrassed, half-baked – neither convincing appliqué nor rigorous structuralism – a problem for many of the architects who left Mies setting out for decoration (and never quite arrived).

Philip Johnson is easily the most accomplished and intelligent of this group; indeed he probably thought about the problem of historicism far sooner and longer than other architects. His first, tentative break with Mies was the Synagogue in Port Chester, 1956, on the outside a startling simplification recalling those of   95 Ledoux, on the inside reminiscent of the Soane Museum. These historical quotes are located within a black picture-frame of Miesian steel, and the absence of ornament and content mark it as Modernist, so Johnson really – like so many others – is looking two ways. His writing and sensibility probably outdistance his architecture in contributing to Post-Modernism.

In 1955 the essay attacking 'The Seven Crutches of Modern Architecture' exposed some of the formulae behind which Modern architects hid, or tried to escape responsibility for formal choice: for instance, the pretence to utility and structural efficiency were two such 'crutches'.[18] Johnson later, in 'The Processional Element in Architecture', 1965, also debunked the spatial rationalisations of the Modern Movement. Combined with his play with historicist shapes (the redundant segmental arch appears in his Amon Carter Museum, 1961 and Folie 1962) these arguments no doubt pushed the door of history open further: 'Mies is such a genius! But I grew old! And bored! My direction is clear; eclectic tradition. This is not academic revivalism. There are no Classic orders or Gothic finials. I try to pick up what I like throughout history. We cannot not know history.'[19] So, by 1961, we have at least a camp, laconic statement in favour of eclecticism. What keeps Johnson from developing this is not only his jocular tone, his preference for surface

94 EERO SAARINEN and ASSOCIATES, *Stiles and Morse Colleges*, New Haven, 1958-62. Wandering medieval spaces and the heavy crude masonry of San Gimignano were partly sought because of the neo-Gothic campus of Yale. In retrospect the historicism seems diagrammatic, as homogeneous and scaleless as the Modernism it was criticising.

95 PHILIP JOHNSON, *Kneses Tifereth Israel Synagogue*, Port Chester, 1956. A thin plaster canopy is stretched tent-like across the nave to break it up into vaulted bays. This use of a traditional compression form in tension, and back-lit, clearly recalls, as Johnson intended, Soane's amazing distortion of Classical grammar. (Ezra Stoller)

96 *EVOLUTIONARY TREE*, showing the genealogy of the Post-Modern movement, 1960-80.

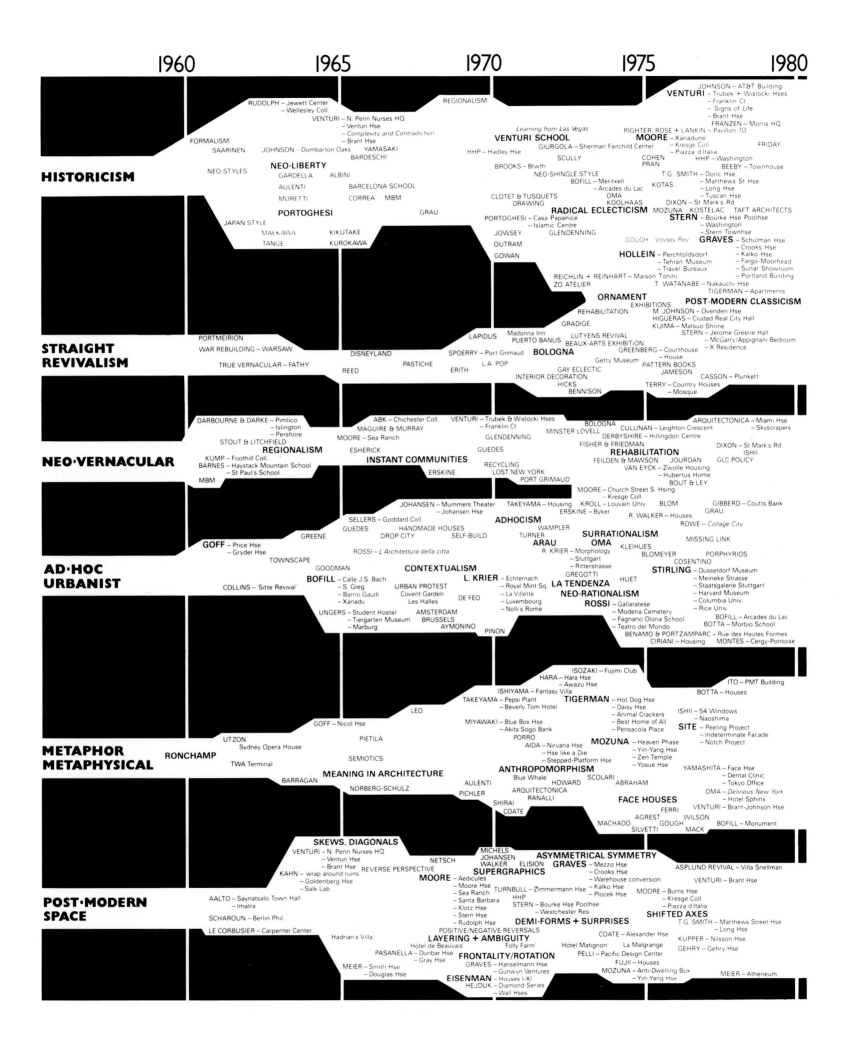

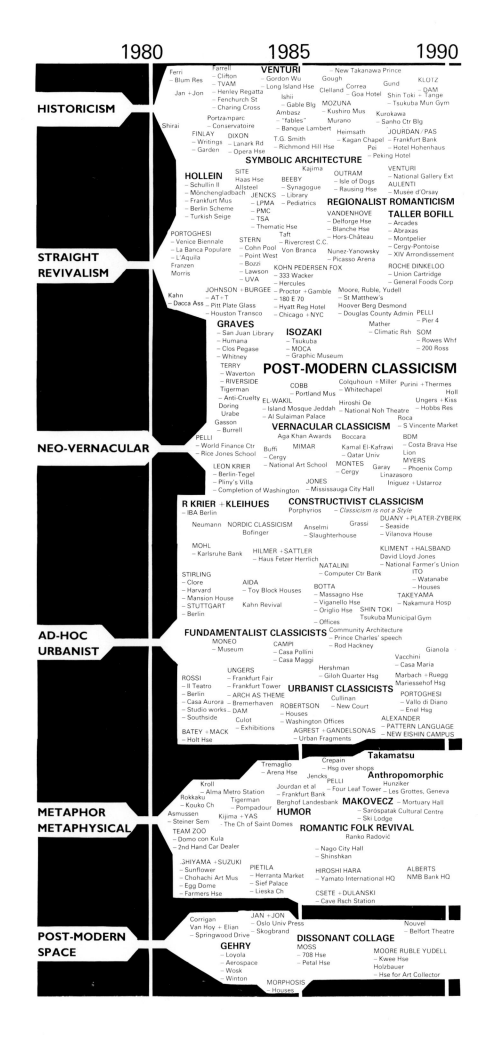

97 EVOLUTIONARY TREE, 1980-90.

wit over deeper investigation, but also his very Modernist commitment to 'pure form – ugly or beautiful – but pure form'.[20] The historicism of Johnson remains on the level of spotting the source, on esoteric codes rather than on more accessible and conventional ones. He thus never really develops an argument for ornament, regional suitability, or contextual appropriateness – three potential aids to his eclecticism that might have strengthened it.

96, 97 If Johnson and Saarinen can be classified as semi-Historicist, or one-half Post-Modern then so too can the 'Japan Style', and the 'Barcelona School' which developed at the same time, but toward a regionalist expression. The 'new Japan Style', a phrase used by Robin Boyd, is best exemplified in the sixties work of Kunio 98 Maekawa, Kenzo Tange, Kiyonori Kikutake and Kisho Kurokawa.[21] It incorporates nationalist and traditionalist elements within a basically Corbusian syntax. So projecting beam ends, brackets, torii gates, gentle curves, bevelled masts, constructional expression – all the hallmarks of Japanese architecture in wood – are translated into reinforced concrete and juxtaposed according to the method of 'compaction composition'. Le Corbusier developed this method of Cubist collage, and the Japanese, with their traditional Zen aesthetics of asymmetrical balance, frequently push it toward the refined and exquisite. While they use Brutalist materials and smash them through each other, they still end up with something as elegant as a Tea Ceremony Room (albeit in stained concrete). As with Johnson and Saarinen they remain hesitant about tradition, and wary of a full-blown eclecticism: 'So-called regionalism,' remarked Tange in 1958, 'is always nothing more than the decorative use of traditional elements. This kind of regionalism is always looking backwards . . . the same should be said of tradition.'[22] What, it might be asked, is really wrong with the decorative use of traditional elements – indeed straightforward ornament and the Trad styles? No one was prepared in the sixties to pose these questions in a radical way, and so the vague Modernist suspicion of ornament and convention remained.

I suppose the first *Modern* architect to use the decorative moulding and traditional symbol (such as the doorway arch) in an aggressive way was Robert Venturi.
99-101 His Headquarters Building for Nurses and Dentists, 1960, has decorative mouldings placed as exaggerated eyebrows over lower windows, and a paper-thin arch bisected by diagonal struts which shouts out 'public entrance'. All sorts of ideas which were to have later influence are present in this building, so it could be called quite appropriately the first anti-monument of Post-Modernism. Robert Stern was to develop the ornamental ideas and many architects, such as Charles Moore, were to learn from its funny corners, inflected walls, ugly ironies and 'Post-Modern space' (but more of that later). Suffice it to say here that we have, finally, a building that was wilfully traditional in some respects; like Baroque buildings, it was designed in terms of the urban context, the street line and flowing spatial requirements; like a Mannerist conceit it played tricks with scale, bloating certain windows and doors, while diminishing others. Certainly its calculated ugliness and awkwardness were Mannerist: the roof is an insult to the strength of the weather, the boxiness carved up is an insult to the International Style (as it was meant to be).

Robert Venturi's polemics against Modernism mostly concentrated at first on

98 KIYONORI KIKUTAKE, *Tokoen Hotel*, Kaike Spa, Yonago, 1963-64. The 'Japan Style' is evident in the constructional elements and the roof restaurant with its gentle curves. In addition the building is highly readable and broken into different semantic areas: boardrooms and conference rooms at the base, an open deck, two levels of hotel rooms (on the inside proportioned by tatami mats) and the vertical stairway.

99, 100 ROBERT VENTURI and SHORT, *Headquarters Building*, North Penn Visiting Nurses Association, 1960. The arch, a sign of door, is contrasted with rectangular and diagonal elements, to (over-) articulate the public entrance. Traditional decorative mouldings are also distorted on the windows. This bizarre, even 'ugly' usage was nevertheless one of the first buildings to incorporate historical ornament in a recognisable and symbolic way.

101 VENTURI and SHORT, *Headquarters Building*, plan, is a distorted box which, on the outside forms an embracing court, and on the inside directs movement with its diagonals. The odd angles and skewed space of Post-Modernism developed from such plans.

102, 103 VENTURI and RAUCH, *Allen Art Museum*, Oberlin College, 1973-77. This addition to an Italian Renaissance revival building of 1917 tries to harmonise and contrast with the previous building through its proportions and pink and red stone. Semantically, however, this 'elegantly decorated shed' is more a gymnasium than a museum, and awkwardly, not gracefully, integrated with its neighbour.

the question of taste, and then later on symbolism. In his first book, *Complexity and Contradiction in Architecture,* 1966, he set up a series of visual preferences in opposition to Modernism: complexity and contradiction vs simplification; ambiguity and tension rather than straightforwardness; 'both-and' rather than 'either-or', doubly-functioning elements rather than singly working ones, hybrid rather than pure elements, and messy vitality (or 'the difficult whole') rather than obvious unity. In addition to these stylistic codes, Venturi provided two more important contributions to the growing argument: first was his interest in pillaging from disregarded historical work, such as that of the Mannerists and Lutyens (who now with Gaudi becomes a paragon for nearly all the PMs), and second was his plunge into Pop Art, then Main Street, Las Vegas, and finally Levittown. Along with his wife, Denise Scott Brown, and his design team, Venturi looked at these hitherto snubbed manifestations of popular taste for their 'Lessons in Symbolism'. The results were collected in what could be appropriately called the first anti-exhibition of PM architecture, 'Signs of Life: Symbols in the American City' ('anti' because it went against the conventional museum codes of displaying artifacts).

The Venturi argument, taken as a whole, insisted on revaluing commercial schlock and nineteenth-century eclecticism for how they communicated on a mass level. There were certain problems of focus, however: no developed theory of symbolism was put forward, so the examples multiplied every-which-way; no standards for selecting and judging schlock were presented and the argument was conducted on the level of personal taste – not semiotic theory – so that the Venturi 'bill-ding-boards' triumphed somewhat arbitrarily over their 'ducks' (to use two of their fairly primitive categories). In fact, the Venturi Team's wholesale commitment to argument by taste and to inverting the taste of the previous generation was exclusivist and Modernist at its core.[23] By contrast, Post-Modernism, which has developed from semiotic research, looks at the abstract notion of taste and its coding and then takes up a situational position: ie, no code is inherently better than any other, and therefore the subculture being designed for must be

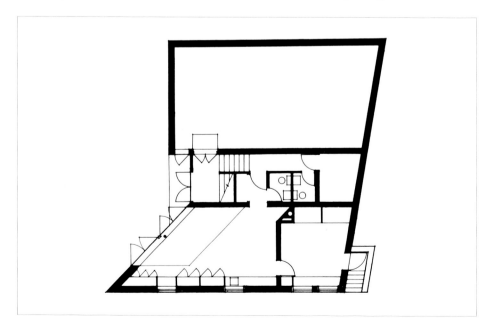

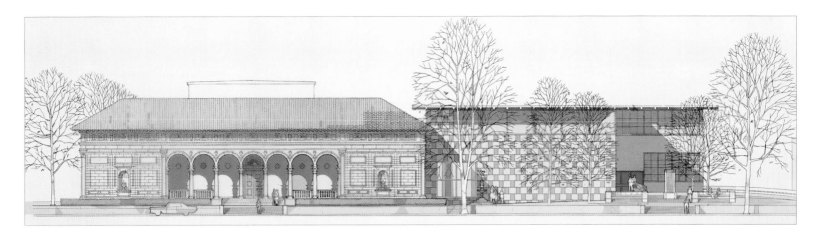

identified before one code can be chosen rather than another.

The Venturi Team would exclude a whole repertoire of codes, not only 'ducks', but also 'Heroic and Original' architecture, the grand gesture, the revival of the *palazzo pubblico*, and all the work they conceive in opposition to their decorated sheds.[24] Why? Because they still keep a Modernist notion of the *Zeitgeist*, and their particular spirit of the age 'is not the environment for heroic communication through pure architecture. Each medium has its day'. Our day, you might have heard from McLuhan, is one of symbolism via the electronic media – the 'electrographic architecture' of Tom Wolfe. It's amusing to note the symmetrically opposite positions of Team Venturi and Philip Johnson. They both take *a priori* stands on 'pure' form – one anti, one pro – as if such one-sided views of communication were adequate. Since Post-Modernism is radically inclusivist (like Renaissance architecture), it must fault the oversimplification of both polemicists and attack its causes. After all, Modernism is in an important sense nothing but the pretence of one *Zeitgeist* after another, each one claiming to occupy the centre stage, each one swinging the pendulum too far its way, each one adopting the war tactics of shock, slogan and exclusion. A difficulty of Post-Modernism is in adopting plural coding without degenerating into compromise and unintended pastiche, and a way of doing this, as we will see later, is through participatory design. This gives the designer a respect for codes and tastes which are not necessarily his own.

The Venturi Team have definitely responded to several codes which have heretofore remained unserviced by architects: those coming from the lower middle class and the commerce of Route 66. Their actual buildings, however, have usually been for a different taste culture – for professors or colleges, or 'tasteful clients' – thus creating a kind of hiccup between theory and practice.[25]

Their practice varies in its commitment to 'ordinary and ugly' architecture. The
102 Oberlin College Addition, 1973-77, is a decorated shed of pink granite and red
103 sandstone – 'a high school gym of the 1940s' as they call it – slammed onto a quietly harmonious Neo-Renaissance building. The juncture, the texture, the roof and pattern are all discordant and calculatedly ham-fisted. One wonders if the justification – 'the artists don't want architectural heroics' – is enough. There is an obvious jump in logic, caused by their prior commitment to ugliness. For why should the coding of a 1940s high school gym be used?

The Brant House, 1971, *does* make the argument for its coding by way of
104 association: since the owners have one of the great collections of Art Deco objects, there are various signs of this in the detailing. On the outside, two shades of green-glazed brick slide on the diagonal, and flat streamlines in shiny metal edge the surface. On the inside, taking cues from Lutyens, black and white marble stairs vibrate in opposition and the entrance sequence is punctuated by a series of shifts in axis and scale.

But arbitrary coding again enters at the back-side, which is '1930s Post-Office and Walter Gropius' – as if those two sources were adequate to Art Deco. Clearly the Venturis are slumming and enjoying the 'dumb' side of things. One more quote brings out the esoteric nature of the codes involved: they say the southern front 'resembles a plain Georgian country house (except there is no central motif)'.[26]

104 VENTURI and RAUCH, *Brant House*, Greenwich, 1971, southern exterior. The green glazed brick in two shades and the metal strips are in tune with the Art Deco collection of the owners, but the intended references to country houses are so oblique and under-coded as to go unnoticed.

105 VENTURI and RAUCH, *Franklin Court*, Philadelphia, 1972-76. An open frame of stainless steel approximates Franklin's old mansion, the 'surprise garden' houses his memorabilia, while the surrounding buildings have been restored – a convincing if modest knitting together of old and new.

Once this comparison is made, however, as with so many other Modernist buildings trying to have historical overtones, it is the *non*-historical parallels which dominate. The bow front has expanded to the point that no Georgian would recognise it, as has the gigantic side porch. The windows, colouring and details are all anti-Georgian in their Mannerised proportions. One can enjoy the building for its marvellous idiosyncrasy, for its careful distortion of codes, and its delightful wit – a nice green trellis jumps up the west side – but still wonder why the Venturis have to try so hard at being original in this esoteric way? It's as if their sensibility were still Modernist, while their theory were Post.

Two buildings which are more straightforward in their historical allusions and enjoy an easy-going but interesting commerce with the past, are the Trubeck and Wislocki houses, 1970, which use the Cape Cod vernacular in a conventional yet fascinating way, and the Franklin Court design, 1972-76, a Bicentennial homage to Benjamin Franklin. Here a very appropriate ghost image in stainless steel marks the profile of the old, non-existent mansion. Below are the archaeological remains, which can be spied through various bunker-like slits thoughtfully provided above ground. A neo-colonial garden, laid out roughly on Franklin's description, is peppered with various of his morally uplifting slogans. Thus the Venturi Team has produced here not a building, but a very amusing garden which combines meanings from the past and present in a way that isn't excessively idiosyncratic. It's fitting to the urban context, it's within both popular and elitist codes, it's ugly *and* beautiful and thus could be called their first pro-monument of Post-Modernism.

Perhaps because Robert Venturi and Denise Scott Brown have had to fight Modernism to establish their style and positions, they haven't yet been able to relax with traditional codes, the way their followers have. Clearly, Robert Stern, who will be discussed later, has a kind of exuberant facility with the 'Venturi Style', and the Barcelona School can turn it to its local purpose.[27] One group of Barcelona designers, Mora-Pinon-Viaplana, has taken cues not only from Venturi's formal ideas, but also from semiotics in general, to produce ironic juxtapositions of entrance space and circulation, column and wall; while another Team, Clotet and Tusquets, produce a heightened sarcasm by juxtaposing new and old. They place a paper-thin trellis above an heroic order of piers; within the piers and on the roof of the house is the place to park the car surrounded by a balustrade; finally, the piers, which come down to the ground, act as a screen behind which are rustic shutters and windows – out of phase with the piers. The syncopation of verticals is masterful, the layering of space a surprise, the contrast of meanings a delight. It's rather as if one composed a Classical building according to International Style aesthetics (or vice versa), a typical conceit of Post-Modernism.

With such a building then, finished in 1972, the Modern architect *almost* makes his peace with historicism and allows himself to quote tradition directly where it has a purpose (the building is on a Classical estate). I emphasise the word 'almost' because these designers really can't go very far down this traditional road yet, and are fearful of meeting interior decorators and Reactionaries coming back the other way. For this is what has partly stopped their full use of the past – the nostalgia boom, the continuation of reproduction architecture with its Reproduction

105

106

106 LLUIS CLOTET, OSCAR TUSQUETS and PER, *Giorgina Belvedere*, Gerona, 1971-72. This belvedere-bedroom is meant to relate to and contrast with the classical estate. You drive in – on the roof – between the temple's colonnade. Double-height space is set off against small-scale trellis and balustrade, and rustic wood shutters against white stucco, a grand irony of Post-Modernism.

Furniture, the Traditionalesque Style that never died and often became kitsch. The ex-Modernists still do not want to be tainted with establishment values, the eclecticism that has been the style of wealth and opportunism for the last two hundred years. So when they make hesitant steps towards this eclecticism it is always distorted enough to be recognisably still 'Modern' – structurally, at least, the opposite of kitsch.[28]

Thus, Post-Modern architects must distinguish themselves from the next group, those revivalists who never were Modern in the first place. The only reason they are included in this book is because of their influence on Post-Modernists, and the fact that they further opened the field to more options.

Straight Revivalism

One is often surprised to read how Gothic architecture survived in England through the sixteenth, seventeenth and eighteenth centuries right into the Gothic Revival. It never entirely died because people liked this 'national style', and there were always a few crumbly cathedrals in need of repair. In like manner, the old way of doing things never really stopped. Rather historians stopped looking – except H R Hitchcock, who called one small chapter of his contemporary history 'Architecture called Traditional in the Twentieth Century'. Even Hitchcock stops his account in the 1930s and no one, to my knowledge, tries to bring the story up to date in a comprehensive way. The reason for this is partly due to the fact that revivalist styles become kitsch, traditional becomes traditionalesque, and the whole thing a form of ersatz – that is, a clear substitute for the period being revived, neither a very creative extension to tradition nor a scholarly copy.[29] Thus Pittsburg's 'Cathedral of Learning', a forty-storey Gothic cathedral given over to study, or Moscow's seven
107 skyscrapers designed in Stalinist Baroque (or what Intourist guides call euphemistically 'The Fifties Style'). Many such confections were built, and some like the Karl Marx Allee in East Berlin, or the Laboral University in Gijon, are being revalued by Aldo Rossi and others for their urban implications.[30] Rossi and the other Rationalists such as the Krier brothers have stated that, despite accusations, their work is not Fascist; indeed that there is no such thing as an ideological architecture. Their confusions on this score are grandiloquent inasmuch as they also proffer a Communist architecture from time to time.

> [The defamatory critics] are stupid because a 'Fascist Architecture' does not exist. There is, however, an architecture of the Fascist era, Italian or Nazi, just as there is also of the Stalinist era.
>
> I do have a profound admiration for the architecture of the Stalinist period and I consider today works such as the University of Moscow and the Karl Marx Allee in Berlin, to be among the monuments of modern architecture.[31]

Why? Because they were 'enormous, collective feats' popular with the 'simple people', and they have lessons today for the idea of the street and the monument.

On the positive side, Rossi has contributed to the growing concern for the role of monuments in perpetuating, even defining, historical memory and the image of the city – key ideas for Post-Modernism in coming to terms with the collective, or public realm in architecture. Without a clear insistence on public symbolism – and

107 *Moscow State University*, Moscow, 1947-53? Classical realism, the architectural form of Socialist Realism, here borrows the repressive forms of czarism, the stepped pyramids, and the signs of bourgeois power. This coercive and boring symbolism – the architecture of monotony – is tied to an appropriate megalomania: the building houses 18,000 students in a kind of battery-hatch palace. That several western Marxists such as Aldo Rossi admire these buildings as socialist dreams is their luxury; but that they should be offered as urban prototypes is laughable. The insensitivity to context and historical meaning is droll. (Novosti Press Agency)

this means monumental, permanent gestures that self-consciously articulate certain
108 values – the image of a city becomes inchoate, the architecture evasive. But
negatively, Rossi fails to understand how symbolism works, why critics and ordinary
people have a perfect right to go on calling his architecture Fascist even when he
sees and intends it as recalling Lombardy farmhouses and memories from his
childhood. That is to say, once again, the architect has no general theory of codes,
how they are built up through usage and feedback and how they differ according to
class and background. Like the Modern architect, he naively perceives only the
meanings he sees and assumes they, and not other ones, are simply *in* the building.
As opposed to this Naive Realism, Post-Modernism acknowledges the all-
important contingent nature of meanings (for instance, whether Fascism has just
used stripped, Classical forms or not). The Post-Modernist then designs with these
transitory signs in mind. Of course there is no inherently 'Fascist architecture', but
equally obvious is the fact that recent usage has connected totalitarianism with
Neo-Classicism. The Rationalists are trying to resemanticise this form instantane-
ously, as the Fascists did: but it will take another twenty years of new usage before
the old is obliterated and they can use it more neutrally.

If time and usage are the crucial variables in architectural meaning, the case of
the Straight Revivalists becomes more problematic, for they, like the Modernists,
are often insensitive to nuances of time and context. Raymond Erith and Quinlan
Terry in England have produced very adequate, scholarly exercises in the Classical
109 style – a country house in Kingswalden Bury, Hertfordshire, that is Adamesque and
Palladian, even Georgian in parts. But it was finished in 1971 and there is no
indication of this fact other than a kind of wooden propriety in expression.
Although the Modern Movement may have over-simplified and encouraged all
sorts of disasters like Pruitt-Igoe, one can't pretend, as these designs do, that
Modernism never existed. The climate of opinion has to be acknowledged
precisely because it is not the *Zeitgeist* that Modernists claimed, but rather a
custom like the manners and speech of a nation.[32] It is adopted or honoured out of
respect, not necessity.

The indifference of the Revivalists on this level is paralleled, it is sometimes
claimed, by their lack of creative force, the absence of 'the life of forms' (to use
Focillon's expression) in their art. Henry-Russell Hitchcock has pointed out the
problem: '. . . whatever life twentieth-century traditional architecture retained as
late as the second and even the third decade of the century had departed by the
fourth. Post-mortems on traditional architecture have been many – and often
premature. The causes of death are still disputable, but the fact of dissolution is by
now [1958] generally accepted'.[33] Well, Post-Modernism would dispute anything
so final as death, and Quinlan Terry has argued the case that the Classical tradition,
like any other, is potentially alive. 'It is like a three dimensional game of chess – the
more you play the game the more fascinating it becomes. When I design I am
playing this game; I am not making a pastiche. The designs develop as if they have a
life of their own. I find it quite fascinating.'[34] The chess game of working out moves
not yet taken in a tradition is one source of inspiration and life; but contrary to
110 Terry, this may include pastiche – a rather misunderstood game of the moment.

108 ALDO ROSSI, *Modena Cemetery*, project 1971, realisation
1980+. The 'House of the Dead' is made more haunting
because it is given a flat top (no roof) and voided windows – as
if it had burned. Behind this, an empty street will lead towards
the towering 'common grave', which is unfortunately coded as
a crematorium funnel. This partly inadvertent coding, striking
but questionable, has heightened experience of the design.
Whether a cemetery should be so remorselessly deadly is
open to doubt, but beyond question is the monumental
presence, the image of architecture as public memory and
symbolism.

109 RAYMOND ERITH and QUINLAN TERRY, *Kingswalden
Bury*, 1971. Symmetrical temple front is placed in a recessed,
diminished entrance. Very slight visual rhythms can just be
detected in window bays, but the Palladian exercise lacks any
strong underlying idea, or any extension of the Classical
tradition.

110 *8834 Dorrington*, Los Angeles, c1972? Bungalows re-styled
in various neo-neo-modes by interior designers. The basic
eighteen-foot box is extended in front by a fence, a hedge, and
then a stuccoed or veneered facade with various exaggerated
signs of status and entrance. But the Neo- styles are mocked
with a certain creative wit: note the pediment monsters –
lobsters – the disjunction in scale, and the violent contrasts in
material. These scenographic tricks are highly readable, like all
good caricature.

The respectable design world, the academics and serious architects, are a little too quick to dismiss this sort of design, but happily there are now several talented semi-designers who are at work in the field. These vary from the Gay Eclectic designers of Los Angeles – the interior decorators who go exterior on their 'Bungaloids' (converted bungalows whose sex is changed from 1930s Spanish to 1970s Rococola and other modes) – to the Japanese architects, such as Mozuna Monta, who consciously travesty the Modern Movement and the Renaissance, making an enigmatic art form out of parody. Toyokaze Watanabe, for instance, bifurcates Le Corbusier's Villa Savoye and Aalto's Town Hall into one building, or builds a colisseum inside an Ottoman castle. Monta, who is the supreme ironist, a 111 man who sees and feels all the cultural confusion of a Japanese living in Western dress – simultaneously in the twentieth and fifteenth centuries – has crossed various Renaissance prototypes: for instance Michelangelo's Palazzo Farnese with Brunelleschi's Pazzi Chapel. The results of such hybridisation have a certain formal integrity and interest; the game of chess had these undiscovered forms of checkmate inherent in its rules. For a culture, like LA or Japan, which is always copying or essentialising trends a little bit too late, there is an exquisite sweetness to be enjoyed by making this time-lag into a conscious art.

This caricature, or parody of serious culture, of course undermines its pretensions, as the unconscious travesty devalues it. But the subversion is only momentary, a short space of time before the latent humour asserts itself and establishes the travesty as a new level of culture. Monta, Watanabe, Shirai, and to a certain extent Isozaki and Takeyama, are using travesty as a kind of mirror-image genre of cultural confusion, and if it's practised long enough, it may have the unintended consequence of uniting a fragmented society.[35] One of the virtues of parody, besides its wit, is its mastery of cliché and convention, aspects of communication which are essential to Post-Modernism.

Are there moments when Straight Revivalism is appropriate, without any ironies? Conrad Jameson would argue 'yes' when it comes to housing, particularly mass housing, where pattern books are called for.[36] The argument here might be that Georgian or Edwardian terraces work better than Modern estates, because a tradition – whichever one it is, as long as it is unbroken – contains more values, and well-balanced ones, than a Modern architect can invent or design. People enjoy these terraces more than new inventions, they are often cheaper to build than the system-built alternative, and they fit into the urban context, in language and scale. Thus one selects a pattern language suitable to the area and only modifies it 112 piecemeal, if there is need for a garage door here, or a refrigerator there. 114 Otherwise tradition always gets the benefit of the doubt: architecture is a social craft, not a creative art.

While Jameson's arguments are welcome, for mass housing, it seems to me they are not as exclusivist as he intends: 'Radical Traditionalism' is just one approach among many, and there is no reason an architect can't use it also to signal non-social, aesthetic and metaphysical meanings addressed to the few. Thus Jameson's traditionalism may well be adopted as a leading strand of Post-Modernism, but it will be used as a language which occasionally includes eclectic elements and speaks

111 MOZUNA MONTA, *Okawa House*, project, 1974. 'The renaissance of the Renaissance', with the outside of the Palazzo Farnese crossed with the inside of the Pazzi Chapel. Since the Japanese, like the Angelenos, re-broadcast culture and get it slightly wrong, artists such as Monta have taken this parody as their starting point and created serious works based on caricature. The result is sometimes an extension of traditional language.

112 *Warsaw Old Centre*, rebuilt 1945-53 in replica form based on old photographs, measured drawings and personal accounts of the people who lived there. The market place was rebuilt after the Nazi destruction as a symbol of Poland's rebirth. The interiors were, of course, remodelled in a new way, piecemeal, to suit modern requirements and plumbing. (Embassy of the Polish People's Republic)

of personal, élitist ideas, as well as the social meanings he demands.

Already there is one strand of commercial revivalism which is a major industry: the popular house and speculator's development. There are also the well-known pastiches of Portmeirion, Disneyland and their world-wide variants. This tradition is developing most quickly in the Far East, Los Angeles and Houston where ersatz new towns, or at least vast housing estates, spring up as fast as a plastic polymer gone berserk. Some communities are so artificial that when you walk in the door for the first time the Van Gogh *Sunflowers* are already hanging on the wall and the concrete logs are crackling out the heat from concealed gas jets. This 'total service' obviously aids a family that has to move every two years and hasn't the time to choose real paintings, and cut the wood. In Europe, various ersatz towns are being created, especially by the seashore, such as Port Grimaud, La Galiote, Puerto Banus. When compared with Modernist new towns, or even modern seaside resorts, these fabrications are clearly more humane, appropriate and enjoyable – hence their commercial success. Maurice Culot, a *soi-disant* Stalinist, even sees them as the answer for the communist future, a nice irony of hypertensive capitalism being the midwife of history.[37] Whatever 'historic compromises' actually occur over ersatz new towns, it is time architects followed speculators into this field and took advantage of such commercial and social pressures for architectural ends. Both society and architecture would gain from this arranged marriage.

An American example of revivalism, which has elicited all sorts of response from architects and critics, is John Paul Getty's Museum in Malibu, California, a scholarly recreation of Herculaneum's Villa of the Papyri – plus other Pompeiian delights. Architects have damned the building as 'disgusting', 'downright outrageous', 'too learned', 'frequently lacking in basic architectural design judgement', 'fraudulent', 'recreated by inappropriate technologies' and, of course, too expensive ($10 million – or was it $17 – a mere hors-d'oeuvre for Getty). These predictable outcries have been rebutted by David Gebhardt, the incisive historian from Southern California, who, pointing out its obvious functional appropriateness and its popularity, thinks it one of the most important buildings of the last ten years:

113

115

113 FRANCOIS SPOERRY, *Port Grimaud*, 1965-69. Drive your sailing boat right up to the manicured lawn of a Provençal fishing village in reinforced concrete. No two houses are the same, and the variety of spatial experience is well above the Modernist counterpart, making this village the major model for resort centres in the Mediterranean. Several Far Eastern versions are planned . . .

114 HASSAN FATHY, *Gourna New Town*, Egypt, 1945-47. A rediscovery of the vernacular. This mud-brick village, with its tight protected streets and traditional forms, is an instant re-creation of villages that have existed for 2000 years. An example of self-build, the town is not only far cheaper than any Modern counterpart could be, but also more varied and delightful. Jameson contends that the architect's role is to rediscover such past building traditions and keep them operative by piecemeal modification. Gourna proves it can be done – but where is the western barefoot architect? (Dalu Jones)

115 DR NORMAN NEUERBURG *et al*, *Getty Museum*, Malibu, 1970-75, inner peristyle garden. False windows, replica statues and wall paintings imitating first-century imitations of marble – a very amusing and colourful re-creation whose wit is perhaps not intended. (The Trustees of the J Paul Getty Museum)

116 *Getty Museum*. The Villa dei Papyri was never quite like this since it lacked a parking garage and chlorinated water, but several parts of this seaside palace have been replicated. Its transplantation to Southern California and a magnificent view overlooking the Pacific is appropriate especially as a museum for antiquities. Because it has the greatest budget, and therefore upkeep, of any museum there is a slightly miraculous polish about the ambience which the Romans would have envied. Note, below, the *trompe l'oeil* columns, garland and false marble. Several Pompeiian styles made a virtue of deceit which here is ironically more deceitful – for instance the contradictory painted shadows. (The Trustees of the J Paul Getty Museum)

As a functioning object, the Getty Museum appears to work as well as – or even better than – most recently built museums . . . [the designers] have evinced a far more sympathetic response to the needs of a popular audience than that expressed in any of the recently completed 'modern' image buildings which have been constructed in the U.S.[38]

Reyner Banham, known for his sometime celebration of such Pop recreations, condemns the whole thing for its lifeless air, the 'bureaucratic precision' in detailing: 'The erudition and workmanship are as impeccable, and absolutely deathly, as this kind of pluperfect reconstruction must always be . . . no blood was spilled here, nor sperm, nor wine, nor other vital juice.' Basically, then, it isn't really Roman *enough* in its feeling and creation, the old charge of Modernists that traditionalists tend, in our century, to give birth to the corpse. Charles Moore, otherwise sympathetic to this sort of thing, has also faulted it for lack of spatial invention.

My own impressions of this over-praised/over-condemned villa are somewhat different. It's exciting in its setting, certainly delightful to experience as a good replica (like Sir Arthur Evans' reconstructions at Knossos), very sympathetic to the antiquities displayed and even a challenge culturally, for it is saying that our time can indulge, like no other, in accurate historical simulation. Through our reproduction techniques (xerox, film, synthetic materials) and our specialised archaeologies (in this case archaeological and landscape specialists), with our high technologies of air-conditioning and temperature control and our structural capabilities (of putting the whole thing over a parking garage), we can do what nineteenth-century revivalists couldn't do. We can reproduce fragmented experiences of different cultures and, since all the media have been doing this for fifteen years, our sensibility has been modified. Thanks to colour magazines, travel and Kodak, Everyman has a well-stocked *musée imaginaire* and is a potential eclectic. At least he is exposed to a plurality of other cultures and he can make choices and discriminations from this wide corpus, whereas previous cultures were stuck with what they'd inherited.

Thus I would argue that the Getty Museum is a passable, if unintended, example of Post-Modern building, commendable for its pluralism and opening of choice, but neither brilliant nor especially moribund. Perhaps the reason it has aroused a disproportionate amount of praise and blame is that it raised, at the right time, the question of what architecture should be in the seventies, but it didn't give the answers (so all sides were agitated).

Another similar event, Arthur Drexler's exhibition at the Museum of Modern Art entitled 'The Architecture of the Ecole des Beaux-Arts' (October 1975-January 1976) also posed the same question without giving a clear answer. Here was MOMA, the mother of the International Style in 1932, seeming to propose a return to nineteenth-century values: ornament instead of pseudo-functionalism (as Drexler would have it), urbanism and public buildings instead of mass housing, an attention to historical detail instead of an abstract, timeless statement. While the exhibition implied such alternatives, it was nevertheless indecisive about advocating a direct return to borrowing from Beaux-Arts building. One obvious problem was that this architecture had many of the faults of Modernism: it was often as impersonal, heavy, and academic as the worst excesses of the International Style.

116

More importantly, at the MOMA exhibition there was no theoretical context given for the use of the past, and without a coherent theory the show could only appeal to the sensibility, the new taste for the past – for 'roots' shall we say?

In the same context, many important books were published on Victorian and Edwardian architecture in the early seventies, which implied an historicism without advocating it. Among those in English which contributed to the developing argument were Walter Kidney's *The Architecture of Choice: Eclecticism in America 1830-1930* (1974), *Edwardian Architecture and Its Origins*, edited by Alastair Service (1975), *Bay Area Houses*, edited by Sally Woodbridge (1976), *The Architecture of Victorian London*, by John Summerson (1976). These historians, especially younger ones such as John Beach, Gavin Stamp and Mark Girouard, are on the edge of influencing present practice, but their commitment has been mostly to the past as being over and done with. Still, if we are concerned with the growth of a Post-Modern tradition, their historical research is needed because they show the virtues of an eclectic architecture just before it was overpowered by Modernism. The examples of a rich vocabulary, that of 'Queen Anne Revival', that of Lutyens, were brought into the limelight to be studied by the current eclectics.

Neo-Vernacular

Another response to the obvious failure of Modern redevelopment and comprehensive renewal was a return to a 'kind of' vernacular. The inverted commas are necessary here (ersatz is the age of quotation marks) because the vernacular wasn't straight revivalist nor accurate reproduction, but 'quasi' or 'in the manner of' – a hybrid between Modern and nineteenth-century brick building. The style, however, is highly recognisable and has the following attributes: nearly always pitched-roofs, chunky detailing, picturesque massing and brick, brick, brick. 'Brick is humanist', so the slogan goes (or gets caricatured), so humanist that you even find the ex-Brutalist Maekawa using it on skyscrapers in downtown Tokyo. One understands why many Still-Modernists like James Stirling poke fun at 'The return of people's detailing in Noddy land'.[39] There is a kind of cosmetic thinness about much of this work, a folksy face disguising a grim, Modern housing estate.

At any rate, ever since Jane Jacobs launched her attack on Modern planning, there has been increasing demand for mixed renewal. This was in 1961, about the time Darbourne and Darke won the Pimlico competition, in London against groups such as Archigram who favoured comprehensive rebuilding. The Darbourne and Darke solution nicely illustrates several of Jane Jacobs' points: it incorporates old buildings such as the dark brick nineteenth-century church; it mixes various activities, such as corner pubs, library, old age home and housing; it has a rich variety of spaces full of trees; and gives a definite sense of what every sixties architect was about – 'place'. Finally, it used a 'Victorianesque' aesthetic of chunky brick and thus established, if not invented, the neo-vernacular style.

This style became, in the seventies, for an impoverished and ideologically uncertain Britain, *the* style to fall back on when there were no other clear directions. It was or is acceptable to the majority of English people because it doesn't depart too far from the traditional family house (although Darbourne and

117

118

117 SIR EDWIN LUTYENS, *'Heathcote'*, Ilkley, Yorkshire, 1906. Lutyens' 'High Game' style uses the full repertoire of Doric elements – bases, columns, friezes, cornices – plus French refinements, to produce a magnificent pile befitting a royal residence or Town Hall. The articulations and re-entrant angles make it an enjoyable game, as do the face metaphors of both wings. Lutyens is being reassessed today not only for his eclecticism, but also for his mastery of spatial contrast, and humour.

118 DARBOURNE and DARKE, *Pimlico Housing*, 1961-68, 1967-70. The chunky brick aesthetic and volumes treated as giant decoration. This scheme mixed various uses in relatively low-rise high-density, and also mixed new and old building, landscapes and masonry. The D&D projects always show a sensitivity to contrast which stems from the Picturesque tradition. G E Street's Church of St James-the-Less has been preserved to become the focal point of the design. Brick was chosen partly for economic reasons, partly for associations which the inhabitants wanted: substantiality rather than 'flimsy-like panel construction'. (Brecht-Einzig Ltd)

Darke have added such 'un-English', Modern elements as streets in the air, quasi-Mansarding and staccato, rather than individual house-by-house, massing).

In an exhibition of work, from May-July 1977, Colin Amery and Lance Wright from the *Architectural Review* marked what they took to be the typical if understated mainstream of English architecture running from Pugin through Shaw, and Howard to the Letchworth Garden Suburb.

[It] restates particularly English virtues of domestic architecture. At the same time as many local authorities were indulging in an orgy of inhuman system building, Darbourne and Darke quietly proved that some of the essentials of domestic life like privacy, small gardens and good landscaping could be provided at high densities in cities within a framework of vernacular materials. ... Then there is the side so developed at Pershore — which is concerned with bringing back traditional (and therefore genial) materials and forms — a brick arch over the front door, windows that are more vertical in proportion ...[40]

A more radical traditionalist like Jameson would, of course, show how many quirky neologisms Darbourne and Darke have introduced. Most seriously they have abolished the traditional street and created instead a large 'housing estate' — however fragmented in appearance. Thus this Neo-Vernacular was yet another half-way house, as the hyphenated appellation suggests, and not intended to be either Modern or traditional, but a bit of both.

Other English architects who worked in the method and style, again being acutely sensitive to scale and picturesque massing, were McGuire and Murray, Ahrends Burton and Koralek, Edward Cullinan, on occasion the GLC, and interior designer/architects such as Max Clendinning. So strong did the approach become that, by 1975, it could almost be proclaimed as official British policy (although policies such as these are never official, and certainly not proclaimed, in Britain). An indication is the Hillingdon Civic Centre, 1975-77, in its higgledy-piggledy Victorianesque of-course-brick, designed very much for and within the Welfare State by Andrew Derbyshire. He was explicit in justifying its intentions at the RIBA Conference: '... we set out in this project to design ... a building that spoke a language of form intelligible to its users (its occupants as well as the citizens of the borough) and used it to say something that they wanted to hear'.[41] There follow the grandiose claims that the building will break down administrative barriers and get everyone talking cordially with their elected representatives, as if the friendliness of the forms would suddenly induce a corresponding outbreak of hospitality in the neighbourhood. These claims, that architecture can radically change behaviour, are Modernist ones, although the attention to 'user-reactions' and actual social research are Post-Modern. Indeed the great emphasis on the *language* of architecture and the codes of the various groups who might use the building is precisely the Post-Modernism being advocated here. But the arguments are being applied with a kind of naive populism and literalism: 'Pitched roofs cover the steps of the wall section almost to ground level so that more roof — the protective, welcoming element — is seen than wall — the defensive, hostile element.'[42] One form equals one straightforward meaning is the implication. The whole notion of multiple readings, and readings which change over time, is reduced

119 ANDREW DERBYSHIRE of ROBERT MATTHEW, JOHNSON, MARSHALL and PARTNERS, *Hillingdon Civic Centre*, 1974-77. Decorative brickwork around the windows, a large bureaucracy fragmented into a village scale, a collision of several pitched roofs with Frank Lloyd Wright and 'human values'. The building is also curiously reminiscent of the large nineteenth-century resort hotels in America. The architects consciously attempted to design within the users' language. (Sam Lambert, *Architects' Journal*)

120 FEILDEN and MAWSON, *Friars Quay Housing*, Norwich, 1972-75. Picturesque layout and the north European merchant's house adapted to this historical site near the Cathedral Close. The steep pitched roofs, variety of colour, and semi-private space add to feelings of historical continuity. Bernard Feilden has been involved with major restorations at St Paul's and York Cathedral.

for the grand, popular meaning – pitched roofs = 'the protective, welcoming element'.

While it is impossible not to commend the new interest in actual, popular codes, the impression cannot be avoided that these are subtly being distorted and limited to good taste, middle-class versions of these codes. Indeed, the work in the Neo-Vernacular sometimes suffers from a pervasive smugness, a kind of piety about being homespun that seeks to proclaim itself. This piety may be preferable to the deserts of mass-housing, with which this architecture is always contrasted, but it is somewhat less than a close reflection of existing architectural taste codes. Already the work of Venturi and Scott Brown had shown these to be richer than this 'Architect's Architecture' in brick.

The Neo-Vernacular made obvious and fitting connections with the trend towards rehabilitation and re-use that also became public policy by 1975 – this time it was proclaimed as European Architectural Heritage Year and a major approach of the GLC. A firm such as Feilden and Mawson could divide its time between restoration of historic monuments, straight Modernism, and vernacular revival – such as their brick housing in Norwich designed on the model of the tall North European merchant's house. These designs not only went back to old prototypes, but also adopted ancient city patterns, existing street lines, and the wealth of accumulated accident – or rather the specific historic facts that made a street bend here, a row of houses twist and angle there. These quirky picturesque odd-spots, a delightful hallmark of the medieval city, finally became design formulae in the recent work of Aldo van Eyck and Théo Bosch.

Their scheme in Zwolle, built between 1975-77, renovates many buildings in the old historic centre and adds to these a mixed development: twenty-one businesses and seventy-five new houses. These, narrow and high like the traditional Dutch prototype, also conform to the existing bending street pattern. Thus a series of spaces which are diverse: short alleys, small streets with arcades, streets with external staircases leading to residences on higher levels, semi-public space with gardens. The dwelling form truncates the gable roof – a typical Modernist decapitation showing the building is of Our Time – but otherwise extends traditional form in a marvellous way: for instance, the interior spaces open through a veiled loggia, where one may look over the semi-public gardens, or up into sun-filled, distorted attic space. This rich ambiguity is characteristic of Post-Modern space, as we will argue later.

Van Eyck was called in on this project in 1970 in a typical protest of the time against inhumane city redevelopment. His arguments for renewal and infill housing can be taken as the toughest, unequivocal statement of a Modern architect just as he is becoming Post:

> What the snow image suggests in terms of the city is a careful adjustment, adaptation, modification and addition. Cities are chaotic and necessarily so. They are also kaleidoscopic. This should be accepted as a positive credo before it is too late . . . Add to this the notion that no abstract norm imposed from above, or any other motive, sanitary or speculative, can further justify the wanton destruction of existing buildings or street patterns . . . Ultimately,

121 ALDO VAN EYCK and THEO BOSCH, *Zwolle Housing*, 1975-77. Diverse functions and renovation combined with a new scheme based on the narrow Dutch facade – only the gable has been lopped off. The curving blocks are knitted into the traditional urban patterns to keep the street lines and neighbourhood identity. Sixteen types of residences were incorporated, many with semi-private gardens looking out on the public space.

122 VAN DEN BOUT and DE LEY, *Bickerseiland Housing*, Amsterdam, 1972-76. Narrow, deep houses with oriel windows, 'lightyards' in the centre, truncated gables (compare with the seventeenth-century example) and semi-Brutalist detailing. Again a half-way house, or *neo*-Vernacular job, this cheap housing saved the area from being developed by outside commercial interests, much to the gratitude of the remaining community. An example, like Zwolle, of urban protest resulting in positive action.

123 JOSEPH ESHERICK, *Cannery*, San Francisco, 1970. Nearly every historic city now has a converted area that has been somewhat pedestrianised to the great joy of shoppers. This middle classification of Victoriana (above all) robs it of guts, but supplies it with cash flow, a worthwhile mephistophelian deal. Twee but alive, clean but rugged, phoney but authentic history, are the contradictory signs.

124 MARTORELL, BOHIGAS and MACKAY, *Santa Agueda*, Benicassim, Spain, 1966-67. A serious version of popular vernacular housing done in a picturesque way with pantiles and window blinds (that extend the living room space). MBM, exemplary eclectics, modify their style to suit the job; this is in one of their five current modes which also include the Industrial Style, Barcelona School Style, Pop Manner and Eclectic Mode. (Xavier Miserachs)

the world today can no longer afford such waste, nor can it afford to overlook the right of people to maintain both the built form as the social fabric of their domicile if that is their choice. Anything else is sociocide – local genocide with only the people left alive.[43]

Another project which came out of the urban activism of the late sixties was the Bickerseiland renewal in Amsterdam, where architects Van den Bout and De Ley 122 also worked with the local community to provide infill, vernacular houses. Again, these were tall, narrow and deep with a Dutch head flattened off just above the eyebrows, raising the question – if a Modernist could go this far backward, why couldn't he go the next step and get the remainder right?

It is interesting, in this context, to compare the Neo-Vernacular of different countries, let us say Joseph Esherick's Cannery in San Francisco and MBM's Santa 123 Agueda in Benicassim, Spain – both worked on in the mid-sixties. The former is a transformed nineteenth-century warehouse with Modern graphics, where elevators shoot through and enliven a tarted-up brick vernacular. Curves and arches are accentuated, the old fabric is heightened by reducing the window mullions to a minimum and using strong, contrasting colours. The result is very popular with the middle-class shopper, which is why such rehabilitations have been swiftly repeated from Australia to Canada. What they lose in terms of authenticity they gain in terms of jollity and it is probably this quality that is both their economic saving and psychic curse.

The same is partly true of Martorell, Bohigas and MacKay's traditionalesque 124 housing with its picturesque pantiles and inevitable brick. Like tourist resorts and Port Grimaud, the aesthetic formula is really a class (and therefore an economic) formula, because such comfortable and cosy images appeal to the middle class. In fact, they cut across many social lines and appeal to the rich and poor in different countries. It would be false to term this a universal taste, or more popular than its opposite, Neo-Classical terrace housing, but it clearly articulates codes of meaning that go deep: friendliness conveyed through warm mixtures of wood and brick, individuality and ambiguity conveyed through broken massing, familiarity with respect conveyed by the choice of well-known elements. If it never quite lifts you off the ground with its brilliance or originality, then it can be termed a success, because it was meant to be modest – not heroic. In summarising this emergent strand of Post-Modernism at the RIBA Conference in 1976, I put together the following hodge-podge of a conclusion which tried to define what all the participants would agree is an unexceptional, common position.

[Housing] should be small in scale, incorporate mixed uses and mixed ages of buildings, be rehabilitated where possible and put more on a craft than high art basis. It might be architect-designed, or based on pattern books modified to the particular situation. Wherever possible, it would be dweller controlled and sometimes it would be even self-built out of garbage and built in a pseudo-vernacular, depending on the taste of the culture for which it was built. Housing signifies a way of life . . .[44]

No other architect came closer to this goal (without reaching it) than Ralph Erskine.

Adhocism + Urbanist = Contextual

Erskine has designed in several styles, including the Neo-Vernacular which he used with consummate wit at Clare College, Cambridge, 1966. Here the small scale and domestic verge on the cloying and cutie-pie, but the whole thing is saved from mawkish charm by typical Erskinisms such as the cheapskate corrugated detailing and outrageous jokes – twelve feet of cantilevered doorway, cantilevered in brick, three inches from a support! Erskine has turned the expedient and ad hoc into a kind of art form, where his own happy-go-lucky style is clearly recognisable. At Byker, outside Newcastle, he has built a community of housing which will probably rank with the Weissenhof Settlement, Stuttgart, 1927, in establishing the paradigm to follow.

First among its principles and most important for the Byker community is a degree of self-government, a certain local power to balance that of the central city. To support this, the architect set up his office on the building site and allowed the people being rehoused (9,500) to choose their location, friends and apartment plan (within a restricted budget). This participation in the planning process helped form and continue the community, as much as did the preservation of the existing social ties. Since eighty per cent of the people remained within the area during the building, most of the old associations remained too.

Indeed, several important buildings were preserved – churches, a gymnasium and local buildings, so that the resultant patch-work has a depth of historical association much greater than the typical Modernist new town. Classical elements, discarded building parts, ornament from previous buildings were incorporated either as decoration or use – such as seats and tables transformed *ad hoc* from column capitals.

In the Byker renewal, Erskine allowed the multi-use of activities and corresponding multi-expression of function, although it must be admitted this articulation is more in his own *ad hoc* style than in the local codes of Byker. Every house, and seventy per cent are on ground level, has a private domain and is surrounded by semi-private space such as gardens and small walkways. Even the exterior apartment corridors in the Byker 'wall' are broken up and given local planting, so that this large block has the identity and safety so lacking in the old paradigm, Pruitt-Igoe and other famous monsters of Modernism.

Erskine shows that, in the words of John Turner, architecture really is a verb, an *action* – not just a set of correct theories or prescriptions. His office became immersed in the Byker community by setting up shop in a disused funeral parlour, selling plants and flowers (an obvious popular activity in England), acting as the local 'lost and found', that is, doing countless non-architectural things as he got to know the people, and they his team. Then the slow process of design and construction took place, endless discussions and rather small decisions, so that landscape, 'doorway', colour, history, idiosyncrasy and other non-commensurables could find a place. The success of the result, both as an amusing and humane environment make this a key Post-Modern project in theory, if not in precise coding (there might have been more, traditional houses and renewal). But the success depends in large part on Erskine's inimitable free-wheeling openness which could, without intimida-

125 RALPH ERSKINE, *Clare College*, Cambridge, 1972, entrance showing brick cantilevered almost to a support, but then saved in time – all doors should have *something* odd about them.

126 RALPH ERSKINE, *Byker Architects' Office*, Newcastle, 1972-74, in a converted funeral parlour. The red, white and blue graphics rise as optimistically as the balloon on this office in the heart of the renewal. The designers were accessible to the inhabitants who had a say in their future location, neighbours, and type of apartment.

tion, gain the confidence of the people and allow the process to happen – the verb to conjugate. How one generalises or teaches this art, apart from example, remains a mystery.

It does seem, however, that the pluralist language of Byker results partly from the participatory process. 'Participation in design' became in Britain, during the seventies, a respectable if loaded term which usually meant a one-sided consultation with those being designed for: they could see the plans beforehand, but didn't have the expertise or power to propose viable alternatives.[45] At Louvain University, Lucien Kroll and his team took the process further and really involved a community (or part of it) in design decisions.

The students, who were divided into flexible teams, participated in designing the buildings along with Kroll, who acted rather like an orchestra leader. They shifted 128 small bits of plastic foam around in working out the overall model. When disputes arose, or one group became too dogmatic and fixed, Kroll reorganised the teams so that each one became familiar with each other's problems, until a possible solution was in sight. Not until then did he draw up the plans and sections which made it workable. The resultant buildings show a complexity and richness of 129 meaning, a delicate pluralism, that usually takes years to achieve and is the result of many inhabitants making small adjustments over time.

The variety of codes and uses in the buildings clearly reflect the fact that opposite values are being realised, but even here there are biases in the result. The aesthetic is everywhere picturesque, as if normality and the silent majority have been rigorously snubbed.

By following only one mode of interaction in design, Kroll has actually precluded everyday, impersonal architecture, and thus one longs here for a judicious bit of the International Style. Post-Modernism accepts Modernism not only for factories and hospitals, but also for semiotic balance, for its place within a system of meaning. As soon as the system swings too far towards the idiosyncratic and *ad hoc*, it invites the return of the Neo-Classical, even 'Fascist Style', not for the 'rational' justifications which its adherents may proffer, but for reasons of signification and richness.[46] Meaning consists in oppositions within a system, a dialectic in space or over time.

The politically motivated group in Brussels, ARAU, have used these oppositions for their own ends: stopping large-scale redevelopment in the capital of the Common Market. Basically they use pastiche, Port Grimaud and true Brussels vernacular in opposition to the Modernism proposed by ITT and other multinationals. When the multinational comes with its scheme for a disruptive highrise, ARAU (*Atelier de Recherche et d'Action Urbaine*) meet it with a counter-proposal. This action group organises neighbourhood support, calls a press conference, agitates through the newspapers and uses its *counter-design* to stop or redirect the original proposal. ARAU has successfully fought a dozen or more such battles, using attractive pastiche as an urban weapon, and it's interesting to note that this style, or 130 several modes, come about through the participatory activity. Maurice Culot, one of its members, has said:

For ARAU members the city is a place where democracy could live – they

127 RALPH ERSKINE, *Byker Wall*, Newcastle, 1974. A mixture of materials used in a semantic way: brick in the lower two floors, corrugated metal and asbestos in the upper ones; semi-private deck in green stained wood, circulation in blue, and untamed nature at the base. These articulations break down a potentially massive wall, and give it a human scale.

128 LUCIEN KROLL and ATELIER, *Medical Faculty Buildings*, University of Louvain, near Brussels, 1969-74. An artificial hill town of various activities, articulated with different building systems. The large glazed area is communal, also the restaurant space; the other materials – wood, brick, plastic, aluminium and concrete – are also used semantically. Traditional signs are incorporated: greenhouses, pitched roof and chimneys signify the more private areas. The variety and detail simulate the piecemeal decisions which take place over time and give identity to any old city.

reject any proposal that banishes inhabitants from the city . . . My mission is not to create new forms but only to explain the options and programmes being debated by ARAU. We do not force our own architectural tastes on people, but follow the advice of the people involved.[47]

The next step could be a form of architectural larceny: ARAU might appropriate the commission from the original designers and actually build their counter-design; then neighbourhood participation would begin to mean something.

While it's unlikely that such illegalities would be supported by Shell, Ford and the World Trade Center, it's also wrong to assume that this activism is entirely barren. Aside from changing the climate of opinion (and multinationals are now themselves adopting a form of local pastiche), such protests have stopped destruction in many large cities – for instance, in the Covent Garden area in London and the Nieumarket in Amsterdam. Advocacy planning in America was also effective in stopping urban disruption, although it too couldn't initiate development. At Zwolle, as we have seen, the community finally acted positively after it was threatened by redevelopment, and the same is true at Byker in a somewhat different context. Maurice Culot's relative success is suggestive, I think, not only for its use of various styles and counter-schemes, but also because it stems from an institutional base. ARAU is formalised, it has links with lawyers and other professionals, and can work with the hundred or so already existing action committees in Brussels. If these neighbourhood groups can become stronger, as strong as their suburbanite counterparts, then the long history of indiscriminate city destruction may be reversed.

The Modern Movement has played a role in the deterioration of cities by supporting new towns, disurbanisation and comprehensive redevelopment – all anti-city trends – but apologists would claim that really the villain at large is consumer society, the motor car and the pull of suburbia. Whoever is finally convicted of the crime, it's clear that the Modern Movement did nothing much to solve it. They had no great political and social theory of how a city thrives and how civic virtues are cultivated and nurtured.

The Post-Modernists, Culot, the Krier brothers, Conrad Jameson for instance, take a different view of city life and stress the active, valuative aspect. The planner, architect or market researcher *intervenes* to bring about those values he supports, but he does this within a democratic, political context where his values can be made explicit and debated. The proper place for much that now happens as architecture or planning, Jameson contends, is the political forum – the neighbourhood meeting or the meeting of political representatives. While no adequate city forum exists to express or guarantee this process, Post-Modernists insist on its desirability.

Basically, this is a return to an old and never perfect institution, the public realm – the agora, the assembly area, mosque or gymnasium that acted as a space for people to debate their varying views of the good life or assert their communality.[48] While it would be premature to claim a unanimity of views on this, the public realm comes back as the major focus of design in the schemes of the Rationalists, Charles Moore, Ricardo Bofill, Antoine Grumbach and the Krier brothers. Only Robert

131

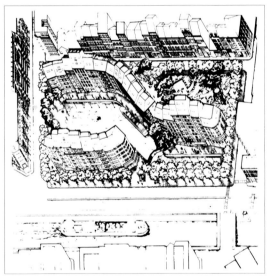

129 *Medical Faculty Buildings*, University of Louvain. View across the main Piazza showing builders' contribution to design. The rocks grow up from the ground into brick and then tile. Participation and individualism have produced a witty environment, which only lacks normality. One longs for a bit of straight Modernism here, or even Aldo Rossi.

130 ARAU, *Brussels*, 1975. This group uses various counter-designs to stop massive redevelopment, leaving it up to the community to choose which alternative, or combination, they want. Using pastiche, Port Grimaud, or here, Honfleur and Van Eyck as alternatives to Modernist redevelopment, they seek to confirm the underlying city patterns.

Venturi, among the Post-Modernists, takes a stand against the agora and *palazzo pubblico*, and he does this, as we have seen, for communicational and not political reasons.

Rob and Leon Krier, in particular, have celebrated the public realm in many of their design schemes and competition entries. They have also mounted well-observed attacks on the devastation of city fabric. They criticise all the forces, whether economic, ideological or Modernistic, which have destroyed the texture of cities, and then propose elegant alternatives to patch it up, or to create new wholes.

Basically, the Krier brothers follow Camillo Sitte's notion of articulating continuous urban space as a negative volume that flows and pulsates and reaches a crescendo around public buildings – a cathedral or school may serve as the pretext for the agora. This patching of urban, public space is the antithesis of Modernistic practice – the free standing, functionalist monument.

In the Echternach project, Leon Krier inserts a traditional arcade and circus, using   132
the existing morphology of the eighteenth century to create an identifiable spine to the town and a culmination of the entrance route at the existing abbey. Height, scale, silhouette, building materials are all compatible with the existing fabric, although accentuated to give a new emphasis to the public realm. Leon Krier uses the traditional aerial perspective of tourist maps to stitch these forms together, and a master-planning concept whose grand sweep is reminiscent of Bath. Such historicist methods are combined with a Corbusian language of form resulting in that characteristic schizophrenia of expression about which the reader must now be tired of hearing.

In his entry for the La Villette Competition, Krier has proposed a return to the intimate scale of historic cities by creating a unit urban block based on a collectivity   133
of twelve or so families. These closely-grained blocks are then used as a background fabric against which the more public buildings stand out along a centre spine. The idea is a return to the historic city of Paris, and to an architectural language based on socially recognisable types.

These large buildings crystallise Types of buildings like The Theatre, The Library, The Hotel, into specific architectural models. They are not to be   134
understood as unique signs – as words in an esoteric language – but rather as   135
an attempt to create a system of social and formal references which would make up the landmarks of a contemporary city, replacing the traditional religious and institutional landmarks with building Types of a new social content.[49]

The 'new social content', inevitably Marxist for Krier, is as Modernist as his Rationalist language of Types, and the latter is not bound to communicate socially, as intended, because of its abstract, atemporal character. Nonetheless the intentions of establishing a language, a public symbolism, and knitting this within the fabric of Paris are exemplary. Furthermore, Krier sees this city building as gaining its meaning from various dialectics – that between the private and public realm, the present and the past and the morphology of solid and void. This semiotic intention and city of dialectical meaning takes us to the writings of Colin Rowe and the practice known as Contextualism.

131 NIEUMARKET *protest in Amsterdam*, 1975, to protest constant demolition of the old quarters for a new metro. Continual battles have helped save some buildings and areas, but the slaughter can be read as 'handwriting on the wall' (inside the ghost image of the destroyed buildings): 'loss of apartments through war 366, 10 years of renewal 335, from the metro 115; new buildings 1946-74 6 apartments'. The Amsterdamers never tire of finding new ways of announcing their plight.

132 LEON KRIER, *Echternach project*, 1970. The tourist map view of this Luxembourgeois city stitches together medieval, Baroque and Modern elements. Circuses, grand avenues, and endless bay repetition are reminiscent of Bath or Haussmann. Every city, Krier seems to be saying, should have its urbanist-eye-view kept in order so that the public parts – squares, streets, monuments – articulate its memory.

133 LEON KRIER, *La Villette Competition*, Paris, 2nd prize, 1976. Made up of small, community units of almost a dozen or so families which, Krier contends, would have local control, this scheme nevertheless has a grand, centralised imagery (all the housing looks the same). A grand public boulevard runs north/south (right/left) containing the Place Centrale, Place de la Mairie, and Square des Congrès. Rolling English parks create the other axis which focuses on historic Paris. The biplanes are also reminiscent of Le Corbusier.

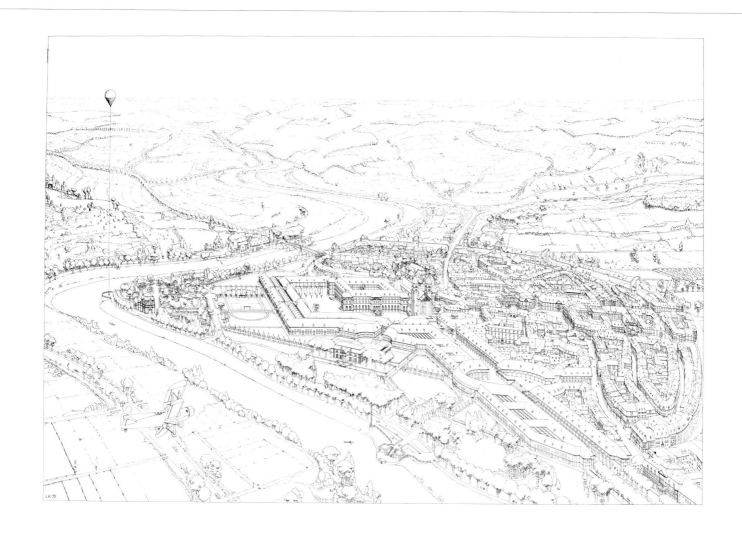

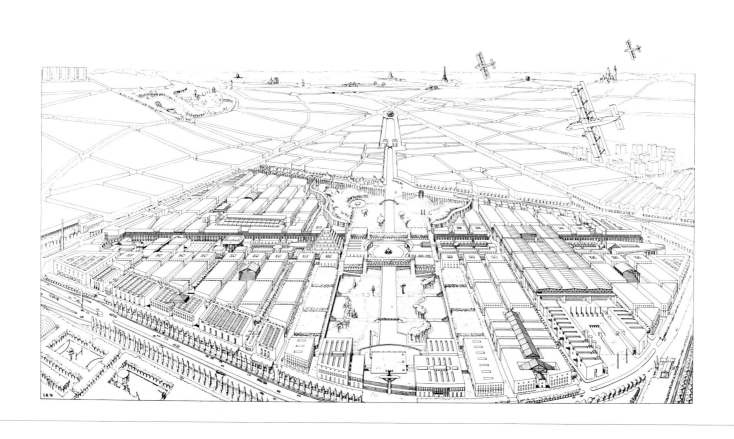

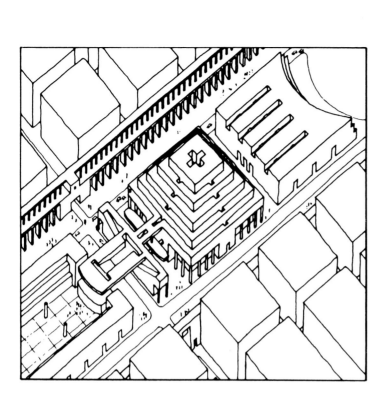

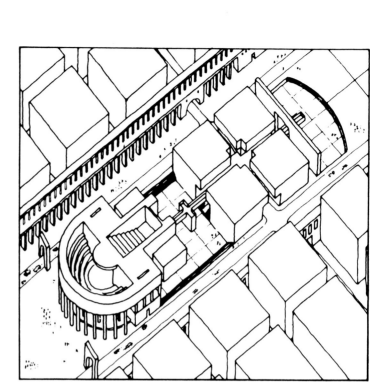

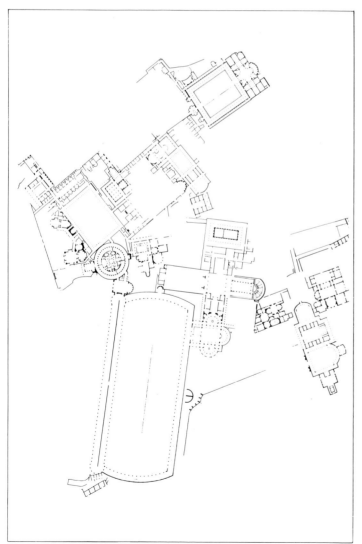

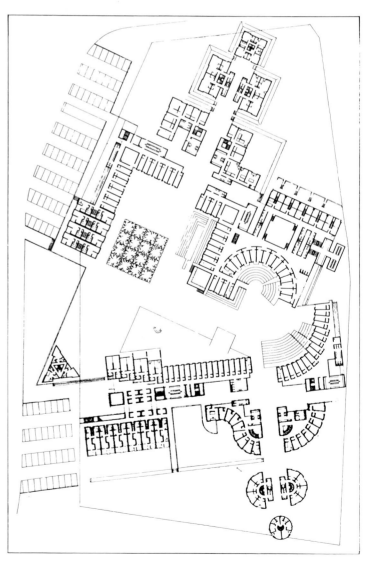

As a philosophy and movement, Contextualism started in the early sixties at Cornell University with studies into the way cities formed various binary patterns of legibility. Alvin Boyarsky looked at Camillo Sitte's work for its implications, just as George Collins was doing at the time, and the most important binary pair emerged from Sitte's drawings: the opposition between solid and void, or figure and ground. As Grahame Shane describes the language of Contextualism, with its inevitable abstract dualities (as if the theorists had all been trained by Heinrich Wollflin, with two slide projectors) there are urban patterns of *regular* vs *irregular*, *formal* vs *informal*, *types* vs *variants*, *figures* vs *fields* (if effectively combined known as *set-pieces*), *centre* vs *infill*, *tissue* vs *boundary edge* and ho vs hum.

Such a glossary could begin with the term *context*. By definition the design must fit with, respond to, mediate its surroundings, perhaps completing a pattern implicit in the street layout or introducing a new one. Crucial to this appreciation of urban patterns is the Gestalt double image of the *figure-ground*. This pattern, which can be read either way – solid or void, black or white – is the key to the contextualist approach to urban space.[50]

According to this argument, the failure of Modern architecture and planning, very briefly, was its lack of understanding the urban context, its over-emphasis on objects rather than the tissue between them, design from the inside-out rather than the exterior space to the inside. By pondering hard on the large chunks of blackened areas in Sitte's drawings, and studying Nolli's seventeenth-century map
138 of Rome, the Contextualists found, as did Robert Venturi, a new respect for *'poché'* or left-over tissue building, the 'ground' for any city's attractive 'figures'.

To Colin Rowe and his Gibbonian prose fell the job of weaving all these dualities into a spellbinding dialectic of binary pairs, which recommended itself perhaps more as suggestive analogy than as precise prescription. His 'Collage City' set up arguments between the mechanism of Enlightenment thinkers and the organicism of the Hegelians, the Olde Worlde fantasies of the Americans without roots at Disneyland, and the Brave New World of Superstudio with too much past in Florence. He contrasted the fixed, Platonic utopias of the Renaissance with the 'utopia as extrusion' of the Futurists, the single, big ideas of the 'hedgehogs' and the many, little goals of 'foxes': 'Palladio is a hedgehog, Giulio Romano, a fox; Hawksmoor, Soane, Philip Webb are probably hedgehogs, Wren, Nash, Norman Shaw almost certainly foxes . . .'[51] Such games and analogical thinking work most effectively when Rowe uses one side of his equation to criticise the other and comes up with a compound which includes both antinomies. Thus his 'Collage City', based on the *bricolage* of many different utopias (or the 'vest pocket utopias' – Swiss Canton, New England village, Dome of the Rock, Place Vendome, etc) has everything both ways with a beneficent vengeance: 'the enjoyment of utopian poetics without our being obliged to suffer the embarrassment of utopian politics'.

The buildings of Hadrian, his pluralist Pantheon, his Rome, especially his villa at
136 Tivoli are *ad hoc* compilations and dialectical utopias. In fact, during the sixties, Hadrian's Villa becomes *the* exemplar, a model and point of reference for such
137 various architects and critics as Louis Kahn and Sigfried Giedion, Mathias Ungers and Vincent Scully – in short Modernists and Post-Modernists. For some, it is the

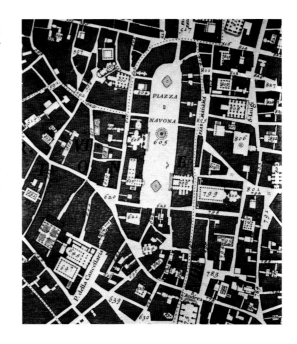

134,135 LEON KRIER, *La Villette typology*, of the Hotel and Cultural Centre. The ziggurat is lifted from its historical context, and Ledoux's design for a barn is turned into a town hall cut into four parts. Krier's hope for a universal language that could be understood founders on the same misunderstandings that plagued Ledoux and Le Corbusier. The meaning of form is social and temporal, and cannot be established by fiat, especially when based on abstractions. It is curious that Krier, who attacks Le Corbusier for his urban insensitivity, should have such similar notions, but the theory of how architecture communicates is not widely understood.

136 HADRIAN'S VILLA, Tivoli, AD 118-134. A series of axially oriented set-pieces brought from all parts of the Roman world in this early eclectic complex: temples and canals were copied from Egypt, caryatids from Greece, and there was even a place for 'Hades' here. The most exquisite part of this villa retreat (it is really a small town) is the Teatro Marittime (middle left) with its circular canals and overlap of exedra, convex and concave. Hadrian retired to this 'library' to read, eat, and bathe. Colin Rowe has said 'The Villa Adriana presents the demands of the ideal and recognises at the same time the needs of the *ad hoc.*'

137 OM UNGERS *et al*, *Student Hostel Competition*, 1963. Like Hadrian's Villa, a series of set-pieces are repeated and organised on their own axes which cross and collide. Multiple geometries, dissonant angles, and a subtle public order.

138 GIAMBATTISTA NOLLI, *Map of Rome*, 1748. Private building in grey cross-hatching is hollowed out by public space in white, which may be street, piazza, courtyard or church interior. The map gives an idea of semi-public space and how it mediates between the major antinomy, public and private.

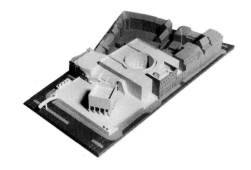

139 JAMES STIRLING, *Düsseldorf Museum Project*, 1975. A sensitive example of contextual infill, where the height, scale and masonry of the area are respected, but the symbolic elements are still allowed expression. The entrance cube inflects from the grid and is also a major focus for site lines which relate to other monuments. The nineteenth-century facade to the left is wrapped around part of the new museum. Glass sheeting, the only Modernist remnant, is appropriately used as public circulation and congregation area. (John Donat)

140 MAISON DES CARIATIDES, *28 rue Chaudronnerie*, Dijon, c1610. Something like thirty-seven heads decorate this house, perhaps too many even for a Mannerist. The mixing of architectural and human members is quite extraordinary in its ingenuity: note for instance the careful asymmetries set against the ordered use of pilaster-people. Windows, doors, chimneys and other places of transition or focus were celebrated with complex metaphors, quite appropriate for the erogenous zones of architecture.

richness of overlapping spatial foci which is the lesson of the Villa, for others, the eclecticism of sources (Egypt and Greece), the palimpsest of meaning or the Mannerism of sharp juxtaposition. For Rowe, it is the supreme instance of fox-like dialectic:

> For if Versailles may be a sketch for total design in a context of total politics, the Villa Adriana attempts to dissimulate all reference to any single controlling idea . . . Hadrian, who proposes the reverse of any 'totality', seems only to need accumulation of the most various fragments . . . The Villa Adriana is a miniature Rome. It plausibly reproduces all the collisions of set pieces and all the random empirical happenings which the city so lavishly exhibited . . . It is almost certain that the uninhibited aesthetic preference of today is for the structural discontinuities and the multiple syncopated excitements which the Villa Adriana presents . . . the bias of this [anti-hedgehog] argument should be clear: it is better to think of an aggregation of small, and even contradictory set pieces (almost like the products of different regimes) than to entertain fantasies about total and 'faultless' solutions which the condition of politics can only abort.[52]

This argument for Collision City was, like that of *Adhocism*, based on the method of *bricolage* and the importance of memory in forming a base for prophecy and city design.[53] It mustered the examples of several semi-historicists mentioned here at the outset – Lubetkin and Luigi Moretti who juxtaposed past with present to gain a richer meaning. I mention these common points of interest not to prove any priority of influence, but rather to show an emergent consensus in some quarters, a consensus which is perhaps best represented by the Düsseldorf scheme of James Stirling. Because here, by 1975, we have a leading Modern architect using *bricolage* as a technique to knit and sometimes jam the past and the present together, and mediate between that basic antinomy: the solid urban tissues and the void of public realm. Stirling uses a wraparound nineteenth-century facade on one side to fit into the context, and crumbles it away on the other side in a knowing pastiche. He pulls a pedestrian route from the more dense urban fabric into a circular court and then inverts this, dialectically, into a square object (the ground has become figure, the circle squared). This pronounced object is then inflected on its podium to acknowledge a major city axis and act as a focusing monument – becoming thereby one more in a neighbourhood group. Except for esoteric references to Schinkel and Albert Speer, and the reticence in historical detailing (blank pediment, no pilasters) this project represents a new stage in Post-Modern urbanism, because it shows a Modern architect acting with the kind of sensitivity towards the historical context one would expect of a traditionalist, with the freshness and invention of a Renaissance architect.

Metaphor and Metaphysics

Another motive causing architects to leave the tenets of Modernism was its obvious inability to deal with or pose general questions of architectural meaning: what was architecture 'to be about', especially now that the Modernist beliefs in progressivist technology and the Machine Aesthetic were seen to be so naive (or boring)? Architecture must have a signifying reference – the Renaissance had its Platonic metaphysics, the Romans their belief in Imperial organisation – what is ours to reflect, beyond a polite agnosticism?

One of the particularly defining characteristics of Post-Modernism is its pursuit of odd metaphysics, 'after strange gods' as it were, instead of the familiar and tired gods of process and pragmatism.[54] But even with the machine metaphor dead, our age is not much closer to credible metaphors or a developed metaphysics. Science, in its agnosticism, can hardly provide the answers although it can refute them. Furthermore, any metaphysics is thrown into question today for two quite different reasons: it is often too idiosyncratic to capture the imagination of society at large, and it doesn't build up a foundation in habit and ritual, since industrial society tends to erode or commercialise this traditional base.

Nonetheless, the spiritual function of architecture remains, in fact, it will not go away – even if a religion and metaphysics are lacking. Thus the Post-Modern architect, like the Surrealist painter, crystallises his own spiritual realm around the possible metaphors at hand. The metaphysics are then expressed as either an implicit or explicit metaphor which is signified in the form. Perhaps my earlier argument should be summarised. The most renowned metaphorical buildings – Ronchamp, the Sydney Opera House, TWA – vary in their coding from implicit to explicit, from mixed metaphor to congruent simile. On the one hand, architectural 'simile' is, as in writing or speech, the formal and explicit statement of a metaphor – the hot dog stand that has so many other cues, such as mustard and bun, that one can say it is explicitly intended.

On the other hand, most architectural metaphors are implicit and mixed. The overriding metaphor which recent architects have just started to express grows out of the organic tradition of Modernism and relates very closely to body images and man's continuity with the natural and animal kingdoms. We can see a metaphysics in its primitive stage now making use of very direct similes. The human body, the face, the symmetry of animal forms are becoming the foundation for a metaphysics that man finds immediate and relevant. Beyond this, he responds willingly and unconsciously to body images, the haptic metaphors of inside and out, up and down, projections of his own internal body orientation. Even his description of architecture is coloured by this imagery. Buildings 'lie on the horizon', or 'rise up from it', have 'a front' which is more acceptable than 'a back' (just like living beings) and are 'dressed up' or 'plain'.

Charles Moore and Kent Bloomer who have analysed these body images in relation to architecture, claim they form a basic model for the experience of the environment, and one not limited to the priority of sight.

By combining the values and feelings that we assign to internal landmarks with the moral qualities that we impart to psycho-physical co-ordinates, [right/left etc] we can imagine a model of exceptionally rich and sensitive body meanings. It is a comprehensible model (because we 'possess' it), although it is much more humanely complex than a mathematical matrix.[55]

For such reasons the city is considered empty without its anthropomorphic dimensions, its central 'heart' or equivalent to the main piazza, the symbolic focus.

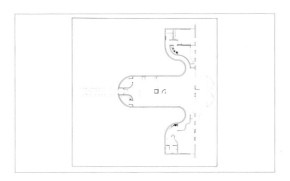

141 MINORU TAKEYAMA, *Hotel Beverly Tom*, Hokkaido, 1973-74. Eighty rooms are syncopated in three quarters of the cylinder; a restaurant and roof garden are indicated by other syntactic changes. The phallic form is not absolutely legible – this symbolism is coded with other, functional meanings.

142,143 STANLEY TIGERMAN, *Daisy House*, Indiana, 1976-77. The plan and parts of the elevation mapped with varying degrees of subtlety to well-known parts of the male and female anatomy. These shapes, partly due to the client's wishes, are again finished off with a series of oppositions – the flat, stucco wall versus textured cedar curves, rectilinear window grid versus curvilinear viewing panes. One blank side is for public entrance and kitchen, the other flat side for viewing the lake. This elevation is a transformation of the plan which visually implies that the phallus continues forward on to the deck and the windows go on into the ground. The symbolic arched entrance presently lacks its Spanish Mission bell.

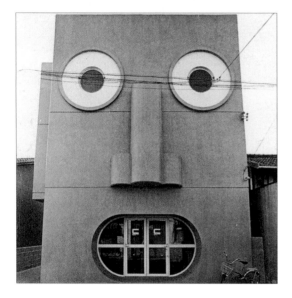

144 *Gable watching in Amsterdam* is an enjoyable pastime; the faces of these buildings are as different and engaging as those in typical portraits of Dutch burghers. Animals as well as the face and body are also literally present in the decoration.

145 FEDERICO ZUCCARO, *Palazzo façade Via Gregoriana*, Rome, c1592. The metaphor of windows as eyes of a building is here dislocated to the mouth. The doorway grimaces, the windows smile. Note how pediments, keystones and cornucopia intersect the face. Is this the conventional entrance to Hades?

146 KAZUMASA YAMASHITA, *Face House*, Kyoto, 1974. You are swallowed by a scowl, the eyes bulge, the nose needs plastic surgery. Such literalism suggests a question – 'Ah, but where are the ears?' Either less or more explicit coding should have been attempted. (Ryuji Miyamoto)

The house has so many such anthropomorphic foci that it may be considered a living proof of the validity of the 'pathetic fallacy'. We project not only a heart (hearth) but, as Carl Jung has pointed out the whole anatomy of the face and body.[56] In his example, an eighteenth-century Hebrew text, the turrets of the house are the ears, the furnace is the stomach and the windows, as usual, are the eyes. The house, as I have already mentioned, is often perceived as a face, and found to be decapitated when given a flat roof.

During the Renaissance, such body images were conventionalised and incorporated into architectural dimensions. The human body was inscribed both into the plan and elevation of churches, and the metaphor was taken so seriously that Bernini was even criticised because his piazza for St Peter's resulted in a contorted figure with mangled arms.[57] Any doubt that man is obsessed by an architecture in his own image, or at least his own image projected onto architectural facades, can be dispelled by counting the caryatids, herms, terms and so forth that are peppered throughout any large European city, a veritable menagerie of funny faces and strange races. 140

Recently, Post-Modern architects have taken up the anthropomorphic metaphor and metaphysics in a direct and sometimes vulgar way, turning the image into an explicit simile. Thus Minoru Takeyama's Beverly Tom Hotel, 1974, is in the shape of the Shinto 'tenri' symbol, that is to say a phallus – a symbol repeated throughout the hotel in the details, down to the ashtrays! What metaphysics justifies such metaphor? It is clear that the vertical shape may have led to the symbol, and hotels are, in a banal sense, corridors of power, but neither rationalisation can sufficiently explain the phallus, which seems to be the abstract statement of primitive power in the industrial landscape. But then again why *this* hotel as a phallus? It's not the equivalent of a dolmen, Place Vendome, obelisk, or Christian spire – the building task can't carry here such strong content. 141

Stanley Tigerman also uses explicit metaphors to generate architecture: the 'Animal Cracker House', Hot Dog House, Zipper apartments and again a phallus-shaped building called euphemistically the 'Daisy House'. Here the justification came from the client, who had seen the Hot Dog House and wanted something visually edible too. Various lubricious reasons led to the final form, perhaps the most printable being that Tigerman wanted to make his client laugh. At any rate, the significance for us is not so much whether Tigerman's or Takeyama's similes are ultimately justifiable and profound, but rather that, unlike Modern architects, they have felt a need to use the metaphorical plane of expression. The results may be raw and occasionally ludicrous, but the architect has *intended* to use this mode of speech, formerly confined to the commercial sector with its giant donuts and hot dogs, and his buildings, thus, are not the misfired metaphors of Malapropistic Modernism, but the overfired metaphors of Post-Modernism in its first stage. 142 143

Possibly because metaphor and symbolism were suppressed by the Modern Movement, their re-emergence now at a time of unsettled metaphysics is bound to be overemphatic; but Post-Modernists are nonetheless committed to exploring this level of meaning.

One of the most pervasive, implied metaphors in house building has been the suggested image of the face. Children often draw their home as a face, and we project, empathetically, our feelings and dimensions onto buildings. Other anthropomorphic parts have been represented in traditional architecture – a balance of supports suggesting legs, a bodily symmetry, a proportion suggesting human ratios of arm to torso – which have given it a familiarity and welcome disposition. The row houses of Amsterdam with their high, pitched gables,

144 symmetrical visage and face-like orifices, stare out at you like so many prosperous and individualistic burghers in a guild portrait by Rembrandt. This metaphor, a commonplace for centuries, is coded in such a way that the contradiction between competition and civic pride is directly portrayed: each is given equal weight in these 'cheek by jowl' facades. Furthermore, the coding is mixed and ambiguous, unlike,

145 say, the face buildings of the Italian Renaissance – the Zuccaro Palace in Rome, and the faces at Bomarzo. These latter so overcode the forms that the face no longer welcomes but alienates, or mystifies.

The Japanese architect Kazumasu Yamashita has taken this strand of tradition to its logically absurd conclusion in Kyoto. Here his Face House, with its round eyes

146 and gun-barrel nose, scowls and yells and ultimately swallows the inhabitant. By mapping the forms so literally the metaphor becomes reductive – 'this is nothing but an inscrutable face'. This reductivism, always a danger of simile, should be contrasted with the Amsterdam examples or the popular bungalows in America with their multi-projecting foreheads, or the anthropomorphic creations of Bernard Maybeck.

I have attempted a similar mixed coding in a studio building. The profile is the

147 normal Cape Cod pitched roof, the mouth, teeth and eyebrows are more purely architectural in their suggestion and even the explicit eyes and nose are here familiar enough architectural elements to seem merely arches and plane. The face is then perhaps not immediately recognisable; at least it was intended to be subliminal and work as an extension to the architectural meanings, providing them with a penumbra of vague feeling.

Michael Graves has concentrated his attention on suggesting anthropomorphic

148 metaphors without naming them. His elaboration of windows, doorways, and profiles, the erogenous zones of architecture, is conceived not just to call attention to their syntactical role, but also to dramatise the everyday human experience of familiar actions: standing beside a window ledge, holding it and gazing; noticing the visual juncture between the roof and the sky. The bodily metaphors are here much more general and implied. Indeed, they may not even be perceived as such. But the constant attention to tight space, to touchable, close-grained details adds up to a consistent bodily experience and is an extensive field for metaphorical play. We naturally anthropomorphise the world in speech, and while this may be unacceptable science or the pathetic fallacy, it is still fitting to give this ubiquitous activity a response in architecture. It, of course, does not yet constitute a full metaphysics and that realm remains a primary question mark for Post-Modernism. What indeed, beyond the human and animal realms, is architecture to be about?

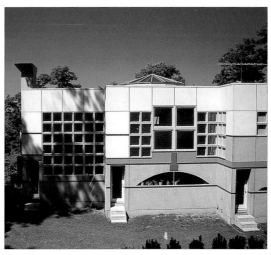

147 CHARLES JENCKS, *Garagia Rotunda*, Wellfleet, 1977. Symmetrical ends of pitched buildings often produce a physiognomic expression quite by chance. Here the face is partly in purdah, with the teeth basement hidden by shrubbery. The eyes and nose are painted blue on the inside face to give a reflected light and contrast with the sky. The metaphor is somewhat veiled as a geometric pattern of arches and verticals.

148 MICHAEL GRAVES, *Plocek House*, Warren, New Jersey, 1978-82. The windows form an implicit image of the face.

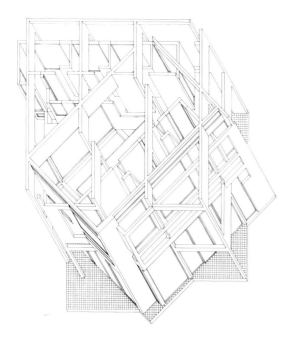

149, 150 PETER EISENMAN, *House III* for Robert Miller, Lakeville, 1971. A careful collision at 45 degrees of structure, volume, function, space, wardrobes, and what-have-you. Following through these collisions rigorously makes you look for and expect the presence, or absence, of a diagonal. This is an architecture of implication, where once you know what is implied you can follow the game. (Martin Tornallyay)

Post-Modern Space

Modern Architecture has often taken as its main subject matter the articulation of space, that is, abstract space as the content of the form. The origins of this go to the nineteenth century and Germany when space, *Raum*, void etc had a kind of metaphysical priority: not only was space the essence of architecture, its ultimate stuff, but also each culture expressed its will and existence through this medium. Sigfried Giedion's 'space-concepts' are the culmination of this tradition, just as are the Bauhaus, the Barcelona Pavilion and the Villa Savoye – which illustrated Giedion's ideas of transparency and 'space-time' perception. Another tradition of Modern space, perhaps stronger, comes through the 'rational' Chicago frame and its development by Le Corbusier in the domino block. Here space is seen as isotropic, homogeneous in every direction, although layered in grids at right angles to the frontal plane and floor lines. The ultimate development of this 'warehouse' space is with the vast, enclosed halls of Mies and his followers. Besides being isotropic, it can be characterised as abstract limited by boundaries or edges, and rational or logically inferable from part to whole, or whole to part.

As opposed to this, Post-Modern space is historically specific, rooted in conventions, unlimited or ambiguous in zoning and 'irrational' or transformational in its relation of parts to whole. The boundaries are often left unclear, the space extended infinitely without apparent edge. Like the other aspects of Post-Modernism, it is however evolutionary, not revolutionary, and thus it contains Modernist qualities – particularly the 'layering' and 'compaction composition' developed by Le Corbusier.[58] His La Roche house, 1923, develops several of the key Post-Modern themes: back-lighting, punched-out screen space, and the implication of infinite extension created by overlapping planes. To these formal motifs Venturi added the skew or distorted space, created by sharp angles which exaggerate perspective. Both he and Eisenman increased the complexity of Le Corbusier's compaction composition. Where there were a few, bold elements juxtaposed there became a major traffic accident of collisions; where a few cardboard cutouts had existed the walls were carved up like paper-dolls, and layered on top of each other like a patch-work quilt. If Le Corbusier's space is the equivalent of a Cubist collage, then Post-Modern space is as dense and rich as a Schwitters' *Merz*. Indeed, one could say it developed partly, if indirectly, from Kurt Schwitters' great *Merzbau*, the column of memories that he constructed inside his house, which was a literal accretion of every aspect of his life (unfortunately the assemblage was destroyed by the Nazis).

Yet in spite of this free-form precedent, and the Expressionist spaces of Hans Scharoun, Post-Modern space is more an elaboration of the Cartesian grid than an organic ordering. Thus Eisenman's or Graves' houses always keep a mental co-ordinate system no matter how free-form and baroque they become. The reference plane is always an implied frontality, and the route through the building or the curvilinear elements then relate to this conceptual cage.

Eisenman's House VI is, of course, supremely Modernist in its rigid exclusion of every contextual fact: there are no indications of the regional style, the strong colonial clapboard tradition, the woodland setting, the Frank family that inhabit it, or even their books, paintings and memorabilia (rather hard for a photographer and his wife, an art historian). The building could be upside-down or tilted on its side and it wouldn't make much difference (especially since columns hang in tension six inches from the ground and a stairway runs downside-up in mirror image). But the space and certain humorous touches are definitely Post-Modern: not only the Escher-like tricks I have mentioned, but also the play on the transformations of syntactic elements, particularly the column.

Columns are painted shades of grey and off-white – anything but a colour – to sometimes indicate their load-bearing role, or their mechanical function, or their
153 decorative use, or for no reason. Walking through the house one becomes sensitised to these variations, and the game of architectural chess commences. The column may be in one of the four states mentioned above, or as its path is implied
151 throughout the mental grid-system, it may be present or absent, or – and this is most extraordinary – it may be continued as a rectangular cut in the surface. This *absent* column cuts through roof, wall and even floor, wreaking its ultimate havoc on domesticity (such is Eisenman's sardonic hatred of function). It divides the
152 marital bed in two. A false step or leap and you'd land in the living room, or would have until the Franks glazed over the hole made by their absent column. Because of their unexpected baby (unexpected by the designer, that is), who occupies the living room, several open areas have now been acoustically shielded by plexiglass; other spatially flowing tricks remain, however.

Again the column has its revenge, and again in the master bedroom, by transforming itself into a door. Ever seen a door as a column which rotates? And in three shades of grey and white? It's easy to calculate the snag. When the column is 'closed' there is still about two feet of left-over open space letting in all that kitchen smoke, guest gossip and baby talk. But if I've made this sound totally undesirable it's unintentional, because this pivoting column which is 'not a door/door' is startling and beautiful as a volumetric object and very amusing in its context. As a single conceit it may be questionable, but as the transformation of a theme well prepared for in advance, it's delightful and even sensual. One of the unlikely things about this

151 PETER EISENMAN, *Two steps of transformation*, drawing for House VI. One can see the stairs, real and virtual, existing in counterpoint; the two reference planes, real and virtual; and the underlying presence or absence of the column grid. The general grid layering is kept throughout, thus continuing the movement in frontal and 90 degree turns, but there is a slight shift of reference planes on the diagonal, 45 degrees.

152 The absent column marching through ceiling, roof and floor divides the marital bed. Originally the gap opened right up into the living room below.

153 PETER EISENMAN, *House VI* for the Franks, Washington, Connecticut, 1975. The back side of the house continues the theme of a large flat plane placed frontally to the approach, and various lesser, vertical motifs placed at right angles to the direction of movement. Note the column lines marked on the outside either as extended pilaster, or wedge of space between two volumes. The front door is around to the left, the main bedroom is on the first floor to the right, above the living room. Find the hanging column in the middle if you can. (Norman McGrath)

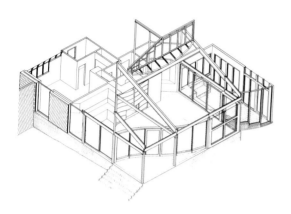

154, 155 ROBERT STERN and JOHN HAGMANN, *Pool House*, Greenwich, Connecticut, 1973-74. Relating to the parent house in some details and the Shingle Style in others, this little folly celebrates the sun and water, through orientation and rippling rhythms. A double-height porch rotates to the view; the entrance to the left curves in under a colonnade (of three columns) which have odd, very odd, capitals. The column, beam and roof systems have undergone, like Eisenman's, several complicated transformations which are fun to mentally unravel. (Ed Stoecklein)

156, 157 ROBERT STERN and JOHN HAGMANN, *Westchester Residence*, Armonk, NY, 1974-76. Pool front with fragmented signs relating to Classical architecture, Frank Lloyd Wright and Tuscany (the light ochre paint is stopped by a thin, virtual cornice of two red bands). An odd scale and tension are set up with the woods and rusticated base: the stuccoed wall seems too small and thin for the base – as if it would be blown away into the woods. This fragility and delicacy is presented in such great contrast that it may be termed Mannerist, frustrating.

building, at least it surprised me, is that the internal coding, the consistency of interrelated meanings created *ex nihilo*, made up for the lack of any external, historical coding, the conventional signs which architecture usually depends on for meaning. While the Purist language of Eisenman may be Modernist, his witty semantic use of this language is Post-Modern; while his exclusive concern for syntax and contempt for function are Modern, the ambiguity and sensuality of his spatial invention are Post-Modern.

Robert Stern, a *soi-disant* Post-Modernist, is by contrast actually quite Modern, or at least Moderne. All of his work has the linear, cardboard quality of the International Style behind it; all of it makes use of vast planes of pure white wall separated by primary colours and good taste graphic abstractions. They may defer towards the vulgar and Art Deco, because Stern believes in the importance of Route 66 and 'inclusivism' (he was taught by Venturi at Yale), but he can't get over his inherent fastidiousness.[59] Basically, Stern has the sensibility of a New York cosmopolite crossed with an enlightened dilettante from Lord Burlington's circle, and his natural inclinations would drive him towards the Country House Set – not Main Street; but his theory steers him sideways in more pluralist directions. (It seems at first surprising that Eisenman, a 'White' and Stern, a 'Grey', should be smoothing over their non-colour ideologies to co-edit the writings of Philip Johnson, until one understands they are all, first, New Yorkers, and second, of related sensibility.)

The Pool House Stern has built, near its slightly colonial mother house, shows an appreciation for the local context and has historical allusions, two aspects he singles out to define Post-Modernism. It does not indulge in much applied ornament, his third definition, and actually concentrates on spatial and syntactic transformation *à la* Eisenman to become a very Modernist building indeed. And yet the Shingle Style, the complexities of roofscape and skylighting, the masterful use of the indirect, back-lit bow shape are not found in rational architecture. One cannot infer the detached column from the regular column grid, nor the distortions in entry and stairs – these are circumstantial articulations that, by varying from the norm, call attention to themselves. In other words, it is heterogeneous not repeated space, modified to communicate a message of entry way or passage, gutter or calculated nonsense. 154, 155

Stern's residence in Westchester County also continues the wit and absurdity of Post-Modernism, but combines these with a corpus of Modern motifs: careful asymmetries slide across an off-white (light ochre) plane; there's an absence of sills and of decorative articulation except for the two bands of red at the top (a diminutive cornice, or misplaced stringcourse?). There's a Wrightian podium of flat-chested, fieldstone terraces, again without the copings and horizontal ornaments one would expect in a more traditional building. The interior, with its bold splashes of colour used to accentuate volume, could an Art Deco version of a Le Corbusier, so pure, light and undecorated is it. Thus the Post-Modern architect by name is, as my litany insists, indelibly schizophrenic, tainted with a sensibility of Modernism which he will throw off, yet picking up eclectic fragments where he wants. 156 157

The notion of 'fragments' is as important to Stern as it is to Graves, and it

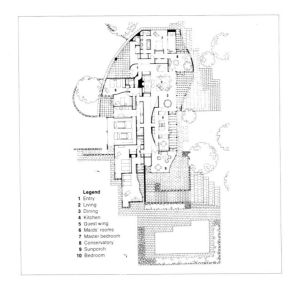

158 *Westchester interior space* is stretched along a major axis that connects the master bedroom (7) to the sun-porch (9). Parallel with this axis are five minor planes of space, also layered frontally to the entrance (1). The way space is brought in and out across these axes is delightful, if hard to read: the curving wall disappears into a colonnade and screen to emerge again as a curving wall.

159 *Chinese garden space* is, like Post-Modern space, ambiguous and eternally changing. Here one of many walls is punctured by a 'moon gate' whose sign, the circle, also symbolises money and perfection. These meanings are further reinforced by the greyness of the wall so that, at dusk, the hole glows as the 'moon who washes her soul' in the pool. Other representational elements include the rockery and bushes (landscape painting) and writing above the door ('night time'). Because the signs are traditional they have a wider base than the fast-changing ones of Post-Modernism. (Maggie Keswick)

becomes a kind of compositional method in both of their hands. The south facade is partially unified by broken S-curves and by broken stringcourses and planes in shear, that is to say, fragmented motifs lifted from the Baroque and Edwin Lutyens. The plan contains semi-circles, semi-ovals, semi-rectangles and a semi-spine of circulation, that is to say, 'semi-forms' rather than completed ones, forms that, as in 158 Zen aesthetics, demand a completion in the imagination.

The handling of space is equally suggestive and diffuse – none of the obvious unities of Modern Architecture, but everywhere complex implications which always lead on to a climax that is never present. There is an undeniable frustration to this, both mental and psychological, used as we are to a strong 'sense of an ending' and graspable whole. In part, the parallel must be with the decentralised space of Mannerism, with its self-conscious ambiguity and contradictory spatial cues. In fact, C Ray Smith has termed recent American architecture 'Supermannerist' because of the plethora of spatial tricks – the omnipresent diagonals, violent scale changes, supergraphics and whimsical punctuation.[60] The comparison of Post-Modern with Mannerist space is helpful in many ways, but I think there is another analogous model, one of a quasi-religious nature.

Post-Modern, like Chinese garden space, suspends the clear, final ordering of events for a labyrinthine, rambling 'way' that never reaches an absolute goal. The Chinese garden crystallises a 'liminal' or in-between space that mediates between 159 pairs of antinomies, the Land of the Immortals and the world of society being the most obvious mediation.[61] It suspends normal categories of time and space, social and rational categories which are built up in everyday architecture and behaviour, to become 'irrational' or quite literally impossible to figure out. In the same manner, Post-Modernists complicate and fragment their planes with screens, non-recurrent motifs, ambiguities and jokes to suspend our normal sense of duration and extent. The difference, and it is a profound one, is that the Chinese garden had an actual religious and philosophical metaphysics behind it, and a built-up conventional system of metaphor, whereas our complicated architecture has no such accepted basis of signification. Our metaphysics often remains private, as in the Surrational creations of John Hejduk. Thus, although Post-Modern space may be in every way as rich and ambiguous as Chinese garden space, it cannot articulate the depth of meaning with the same precision. Its metaphorical and metaphysical bases are just being laid, and it is questionable how far they can grow in an industrial society.

Charles Moore is, in his own way, trying to develop an architecture of public metaphor and his work, which pulls together practically all the themes of Post-Modernism, shows the possibilities and present limits of this approach. Moore has written about Hadrian's Villa and the importance of images and historical allusion in creating a sense of place, so he is well qualified to design for the public realm.[62] His Kresge College dormitories combine many historical memories that are only vaguely presented – alluded to rather than precisely quoted. The overall plan 160 meanders and shifts violently, a cross between the serpentine walk through a Chinese garden and a tight Italian hill town.

The image of the Mediterranean village is inescapable and reinforced by several cues: large white planes, a public, two-storey arcade, angular junctions between volumes. But whereas the southern European village gives stability and a sense of permanence, because it is built of an encompassing stone, Kresge is made from a cardboard-like wood, that 'cheapskate' material that has always plagued Modernism. Thus a feeling of insubstantiality is created at the very point that the metaphor of enclosure is about to be consummated, and the image of the Italian hill town criticises, rather than reinforces the meanings intended.

In like manner, the references to the Spanish Steps, the *Arc de Triomphe*, the cascades and waterways of the Alhambra – all memories Moore has collected on his many travels – call into question their present use. Is this a kind of *haute vulgarisation*, or the pastiche and travesty we have noted before? Perhaps the first. Moore has spoken, not pejoratively, about whimsy and nostalgia in architecture and this work has some of the virtues and vices of both these genres. On the negative side, we can see how the insubstantial feel of the place combines with its bright supergraphics and flimsy construction to lead to the student epithet, 'Clown Town'. There is always the danger with Moore's work that its relative cheapness will combine with the whimsy to produce a kind of tawdry pathos, like a run-down summer resort; but by and large these meanings are overtaken by the more powerful metaphors of place, which he has intended.

Thus Kresge mixes the very personal scale of a village with the calculated surprise of a walk through a garden, whether English or Chinese. The two-storey arcade screens have varying syncopated rhythms, combined with syncopated colours behind them, to increase the feelings of suspense and discovery. Since, in plan, the buildings pinch in perspective they can heighten the sense of movement and depth; since various 'anti-monuments' punctuate the route – post office, laundromat, telephone altar, etc – there is some content, however banal, to anticipate. Moore has justified this low-keyed approach as fitting for the modest, egalitarian role of the student dormitory:

> . . . All the inhabitants are students, there for four or five years together. So it seemed important to us to establish not a set of institutional monuments along the street to help give a sense of place to the whole, and a sense of where one was in one's passage up the street, but rather to make a set of trivial monuments, of things like drainage ditches made into fountains, of the laundromat facade a speaker's rostrum with garbage collection under . . . [63]

This bricolage, an ironic debunking of the public realm, has the double meaning intended – to punctuate and define experience and to deflate pomposity – but one longs, by contrast, for a modicum of public decorum, the straight gesture of communal well-being. Moore has studied the scenic planning of Disneyland and its stage-set quality has been successfully incorporated here, but at the cost of overwhelming normality.

Still, if we contrast this dormitory village with others built in the last forty years its virtues become very much apparent. As opposed to the Modern university – Mies' IIT for instance – it is carefully set in its context rather than dropped unceremoniously, like an urban bomb. Thus the backs of the buildings, in wood painted ochre, are sympathetic to the forest, and the plan slides this way and that to avoid existing redwoods. Opposed to the predictable spaces of rational

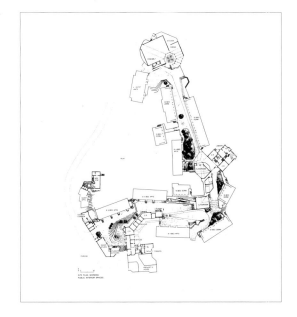

160 CHARLES MOORE and WILLIAM TURNBULL, *Kresge College*, University of California at Santa Cruz, 1972-74. A meandering route threaded through a redwood forest has each plaza with a separate monument to define the 'place'. Many buildings set up their own axial and rhythmic systems rather like Hadrian's Villa, but here on a linear L-route. The sense of place was further underlined by creating opposite activities at two ends of the scheme – Post Office and entrance arena at bottom and assembly and dining areas at the top. Hence the street is well used and keeps students going from one side to the other. A complex water works and orange trees reinforce the Spanish image: 'a laundromat stands for the village well' unfortunately not having quite the same importance, and telephone kiosks are turned into major archways. (Morley Baer)

161 *Kresge College* two storey arcade and entrance stairs, traditional elements which are slightly exaggerated here in scale as are the conventional number plaques. Complicated rhythms are set up which run through the whole scheme like a Mannerist palazzo: here ABCBCDBAC. The porches which serve for sunning and street watching are painted underneath in strong primary reds and yellows. (Morley Baer)

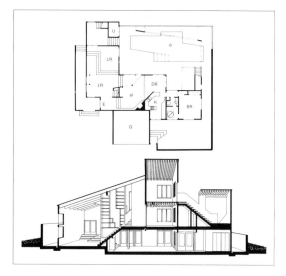

162 CHARLES MOORE and ASSOCIATES, *Burns House*, Santa Monica Canyon, LA, 1974. The organ up the stairs gives this view a religious overtone, but in the whole space it is set off against elements such as the Mexican balcony. Light spills from various points, and back-lighting suggests a greater depth than exists; the opposition of layered, skewed space and monumental object is quite delightful. Moore uses traditional elements for their contrasts, in an easy-going, relaxed way.

163 *Burns House*, section and plan. Space flows and zigzags to the private study at the top. Several walls are punched out and skewed off the right angle.

164 *Burns House*, exterior, in seventeen shades of earth colours, which create interesting recessions in depth. Moore develops the stucco-box tradition of Southern California for its economic and figurative potential.

165 *Kresge College*. The backs of the buildings, in wood painted ochre, relate to the redwoods, while the light coloured arcades form a background to the street life.

architecture, there is always a twist and surprise around every corner and nook.

The depth of the metaphor involved here becomes greater on examination: 'place' results not just from strong images, but also from the careful distribution of activities. Since the post office and assembly areas are located at opposite ends of the L-shape, there is a natural to and fro of movement that keeps the streets occupied, and since functions are fragmented and interspersed, there are the chance encounters, and the richness, of the historic village. Thus the metaphors of place and community are created through use as well as image.

Moore has extended his type of public (sometimes whimsical) imagery in a more representational direction, incorporating in one scheme for New Orleans precise iconography such as the boot of Italy, and a play on the real, historic orders (turning some metopes into fountains called 'wetopes'), but his most convincing Post-Modern building, to my mind, is the Burns House, for a professor at UCLA. Here the cut-out stage sets, something of a Moore brandmark, have a perplexing mystery which is delightfully confusing but not frustrating. The walk through the house is peppered with surprises and other forms of architectural spice.

Each image that appears en route – a Mexican balcony, an altar-like organ, 162 inglenook, etc – is at first the focus of visual attention and then, because of back lighting, merely the pretext for further discovery. The layering of cut-out walls has the same effect as that in Eisenman's work, providing the suggestion of infinity, except here many are set at a skew angle, so that scale and orientation are dislocated. As you move up the stairway towards the attic-study, two extraordi- 163 nary mysteries unfold: the view back reveals a perspective distortion of such complexity that the relative scale and position of object are impossible to determine, while the route forward splits and then widens in reverse perspective. (by 1971 a conventional motif).

This is the left-over, idiosyncratic stairway we might expect near the sanctum, the professor's lair, but then the lower route suddenly turns into an Art Deco dressing room. From Mexico through a church with its organ to an attic stair that reveals a Hollywood, back-stage dressing table the images and moods are quite unexpected, but not inappropriate. One looks in the first mirror, a natural stop on the walk, to admire one's finery, then the next – which turns out not to be a mirror at all, but a hole, cut and placed like the previous mirror. It opens over a drop of fifteen feet. This joke and use of human vanity is just another characteristic surprise of Moore's Post-Modern space. Everywhere there are details of colour and form that remain to be discovered – eye-traps which can spring shut.

The outside, with its seventeen shades of reds and oranges and earth colours, is 164 equally amusing and profound. Several shades are contrasted to give the effect of shadows where they don't exist, thus turning the corner on a volume where it doesn't. Other shades mark out a progression from dark to light, from the dull, underplayed tower to the more important, bright functions. But all these tonalities are so subtly related that they actually integrate and create a whole feeling of pleasant domesticity, appropriate for Southern California. Without specifically invoking the Spanish Mission Style and the other local associations, Moore has managed to design something equivalent in feeling yet superior in wit.

Radical Eclecticism

If Post-Modern space continues to develop in this direction towards the mysterious, ambiguous and sensual, it will start to conventionalise certain metaphors of a quasi-religious nature. There's not much chance these will ever be supported by a socially shared metaphysics, and so they will signify a general spirituality when not an obvious idiosyncrasy. What I would guess, but it's no better than other prophecies, is that the present developments towards complication and eclecticism would continue and that we might see an architecture emerge that is quite similar to the Neo-Queen Anne and Edwardian of eighty years ago. Every 166 indication points towards increasing complication in formal and theoretical concerns: the work of Graves, Eisenman, Moore *et al* is an elaboration of a 1920s syntax to the point of Mannerism; on a completely different level the theories of Jane Jacobs and Herbert Gans point towards a corresponding heterogeneity of urban villagers and taste cultures. No doubt a case can be made for simplification and large-scale decisions concerning utilitarian structures such as roadways, but by and large the natural development of a city towards increasing complexity – a patchwork quilt of contradictions and mixed intentions – is positive, because it reflects the mixed desires and goals that any large metropolis must fulfil.

If one looks for a historical parallel, when many styles and ideologies were competing, the period 1870-1910 becomes even more pertinent. At that time, at least fifteen styles were in opposition (no doubt too many) and complication and eclecticism were rife. The general trend of all styles towards heterogeneity was reaching a peak – High Gothic couldn't get any more articulated or the Second Empire Style any more bombastic. If complexity was a natural metaphor for power, then there was no place more complicated to go than the Paris Opera except to a thorough-going eclecticism, like the 'Queen Anne Style' as seen in Texas, Los Angeles and San Francisco. In fact, all styles were hybrid and becoming syncretic if not eclectic – one has only to think of the borrowings between Art Nouveau and the Second Empire Style. Today precisely such borrowings are occurring, perhaps because all designers now belong to the world small-town of architectural magazines, and an idea in any backyard on the map soon spreads elsewhere – thanks to cheap half-tone reproduction. Hence the fragmentation in design, not only the conscious 'fragments' of a Graves or Stern or Kroll, but also the natural one that comes from a compound set of sources. Furthermore, the return to the past has become something of a backwards race that might reach Renaissance proportions: we only have to recapitulate the historicism of Venturi, the straight revivalisms of Disneyworlds, the Neo-Vernacular, Neo-Ornament and Contextualism; all point in the same direction – over the shoulder.

Finally, if our pattern books today include four hundred building systems, if 'local' materials now mean everything down at the hardware shop, then our natural vernacular is eclectic if not polyglot. Even the present attempt at a simple Neo-Vernacular is bound to be infected by these mixed sources. In semiotic terms, the *langue* (total set of communicational sources) is so heterogeneous and diverse that any singular *parole* (individual selection) will reflect this, even if only in excluding the diversity. Such are the facts of architectural production.

166 J CATHER NEWSOM, *1330 Carroll Street*, Los Angeles, c1888. A twelve-room house with 'Californian' ornament, lacy spindle and lattice in the 'Moorish manner'. The elaborate shingle patterns, stained glass, circular contrasts and eave recessions add a depth and grandeur to entry. Such virtuosity in wood was helped by the great carpenter-builder tradition which already existed. The results, like Charles Moore's, were not as expensive as they look, and equally wide in reference.

A corresponding argument can be made concerning consumption. Any middle-class urbanite in any large city from Teheran to Tokyo is bound to have a well-stocked, indeed over-stocked 'image-bank' that is continually refilled by travel and magazines. His *musée imaginaire* may mirror the pot-pourri of the producers, but it is nonetheless natural to his way of life. Barring some kind of totalitarian reduction in the heterogeneity of production and consumption, it seems to me desirable that architects learn to use this inevitable heterogeneity of languages. Besides, it is quite enjoyable. Why, if one can afford to live in different ages and cultures, restrict oneself to the present, the locale? Eclecticism is the natural evolution of a culture with choice.

There are, however, objections. It is constantly pointed out that eclectic systems, both in philosophy and architecture, didn't produce much originality, nor confront key issues with any kind of tenacity. The charge is that eclecticism is a kind of weak compromise, a mish-mash where second-rate thinkers can take refuge in a welter of confusing antinomies. They combine contradictory material in the hope of avoiding a difficult choice, or seeing through a problem to a creative conclusion.

Thus eclectics have been trimmers or dilettanti, and the architecture often botched. Furthermore, eclecticism in the nineteenth century was often motivated more by opportunism than conviction, and architects mixed their modes as much out of laxness as desire. We are all familiar with the vague pastiche, 'in the manner of' Something, without being much of Anything'. The motivation was essentially one of mood and comfort and while these are perfectly honourable goals, they certainly are not sufficient for architecture as a whole. The lack of semantic and social argument made nineteenth-century eclecticism weak. Indeed, there was hardly any theory of eclecticism beyond choosing the right style for the job.

In contrast to this weak eclecticism, it seems to me that Post-Modernism has at least the potential to develop a stronger more radical variety. The various formal, theoretical and social threads are there, waiting to be drawn and woven together. Indeed, the seven aspects of Post-Modernism I have outlined do constitute such an amalgam, even if it isn't yet an interrelated whole. As I have constantly reiterated, there is room in this amalgam for Modernism, precisely because the theory of semiotics postulates meaning through opposition, and the possibility of rich meaning using a restricted language.[64]

By way of summary, the common ground of the seven approaches can be stressed and an emergent Radical Eclecticism can be projected as a possibility, an alternative to the weak eclecticism of the past.

A Radical Eclecticism would include areas of extreme simplicity and reduction, not only for their contrast in space, but also because of a dialectic in meaning over time. As opposed to the theory of Modernism, however, this reduction would never be more than momentary, or situational, depending on the particular context. It would be motivated by the original Greek meaning of eclectic – 'I select' – and follow the basically sensible course of selecting from all possible sources those elements which were most useful or pertinent *ad hoc*.

In a studio building on Cape Cod for instance, I selected elements from the existing vernacular, from traditional shingle construction and a basic catalogue of

167 CAMPBELL, ZOGOLOVITCH, WILKINSON and GOUGH, *Phillips West 2*, Residences and Offices, London, 1976. Art Deco mixed with London vernacular and pantiles create a *mélange* which is suitable to this mixture of functions.

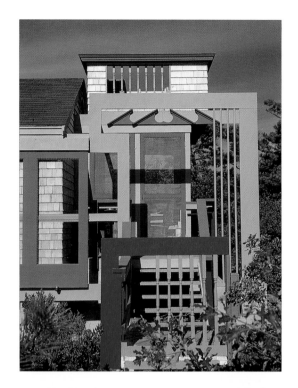

168 CHARLES JENCKS, *Garagia Rotunda*, Wellfleet, 1977. Architecture as prefabrication plus cosmetics. The prefabricated garage, doors, ornament, pediments etc, were all chosen out of a catalogue, the same Cape Cod catalogue and the initial studio was constructed without supervision. Because the techniques and materials were all traditional, the shell cost a minimal $5,500, and the rest of the available money could be spent on cosmetics, on rectifying mistakes, on articulating the basic garage. Level changes, 'widow's walk', bay window, porch, entry gate and interior harmonics were added to the basic shell. The view shows the entry head with its seven doors and twice-broken split pediment, which articulates the actual door of entry.

169 *Garagia Rotunda* interior with part of the harmonies visible. The 4 x 4 inch studs are painted differing shades of blue on their sides to bring out the 3/9/5 rhythm. The underlying symmetry and axes are brought out by blue tile lines, while corner angles are painted in *trompe l'oeil* to imitate a mirror image.

prefabricated building parts. The selection was a mixture of new and old, traditional balusters and modern pivot windows – all of which were local to the area and easy to build. The basic shell was a prefabricated garage (although finally hand built) and the garage door was the cheapest way to get a large, framed opening (and the effect of a *baldacchino*). Since all the basic choices were absolutely minimal, inexpensive and based on builder's vernacular, the majority of the money could be spent on articulation, on changing levels, and painting harmonic colour combinations. I wouldn't claim this studio as a model of Radical Eclecticism – the programme was too limited for one thing – but it does have the mixture of languages and can be read by the local inhabitants (for instance, those who built it while I wasn't there). 168 169

There are, I think, no completely convincing examples of Radical Eclecticism in existence besides the venerable buildings of Antonio Gaudi; just hints of what it might be adumbrated by designers such as Bruno Reichlin in Switzerland, or Thomas Gordon Smith in California. In general, however, some of its aspects have now clarified. 170 171

Unlike Modernism, it makes use of the full spectrum of communicational means – metaphorical and symbolic as well as spatial and formal. Like traditional eclecticism it selects the right style, or subsystem, where it is appropriate – but a Radical Eclecticism mixes these elements within one building. Thus the semantic overtones to each style are mapped to their closest functional equivalents – for instance in Thomas G Smith's work the entrance and porch are given Classical formality whereas the sides are in the vernacular of the region.

The examples cited are just individual houses and therefore too restricted in their coding and breadth of expression. At the present time a larger model is needed, greater in scope and urban – for instance, an apartment house in the inner city, which could take into account the existing local codes.

Theoretically, at least, several of the key issues are clear. One must start by defining a basic opposition in coding between the inhabitant and professional, perhaps taking as one departure point Basil Bernstein's fundamental distinction between 'restricted' and 'elaborated' codes.[65] The varying codes based on semiotic groups may not be determined by class alone, but are usually a complex mixture of ethnic background, age, history and locale. The designer should logically start with an investigation of the semiotic group and always keep in his mind the varying views of the good life as seen by the people involved, since architecture ultimately signifies a way of life – something not entirely understood by the Modern Movement. The training necessary for this needn't entail a degree in anthropology. Common sense, a willingness to understand the client's background, plus a certain appreciation of etiquette can suffice. Social research may help. Sympathy and constant consultation are minimum requirements. The difficulty is that since continuous traditions have been broken, and the profession has its own language and ideology, one cannot assume a commonality of values and architectural language, so an inevitably self-conscious theory must suffice to link this duality.

In any case, the designer should first study the area, the language of the tribe, and understand it fully before designing. The language may have an ethnic or cultural dimension based on the background of the inhabitants, and also a purely architectural dimension – the vernacular (which has usually been disrupted, but elements of which usually exist). The kinds of thing that can be said in this traditional language will conserve the values of the local group. Indeed, such a conservative approach is the *sine qua non* for any urban development, for the reasons that preservationists, the 'contextualists' and Conrad Jameson advance. But this traditional base does not exhaust the questions, as they sometimes argue.

In several studies concerning the way architecture is perceived, I've found an underlying schizophrenia in interpretations which, I believe, parallels the essentially dual nature of the architectural language.[66] Generally speaking there are two codes, a popular, traditional one which like spoken language is slow-changing, full of clichés and rooted in family life, and, secondly, a Modern one full of neologisms and responding to quick changes in technology, art and fashion as well as the avant-garde of architecture. One code is likely to be preferred by any individual, but quite likely both contradictory codes exist in the same person. Since there is an unbridgeable gap between the élite and popular codes, and since there is no way to abolish this gap without a drastic curtailment in possibilities, it seems desirable that architects recognise the schizophrenia and code their buildings on two levels. Partly this will parallel the 'high' and 'low' versions of Classical architecture, but it will not be, as that was, a homogeneous language. Rather the double coding will be eclectic and subject to the heterogeneity that makes up any large city. To some extent this is the 'inclusivism' that Venturi, Stern and Moore call for, but, in addition, it asks for more precise local or traditional coding than they have yet undertaken. Their work still gives priority to esoteric, fast-changing codes and treats traditional ones, often, just as an opportunity for historical allusion.

Radical Eclecticism by contrast starts design from the tastes and languages prevailing in any one place and overcodes architecture (with many redundant cues) so that it can be understood and enjoyed by different taste cultures – both the inhabitants and the élite. Although it starts from these codes, it doesn't necessarily use them to send the expected messages, or ones which simply confirm the existing values. In this sense it is both contextual and dialectical, attempting to set up a discourse between different and often opposed taste cultures.

Although it is generated in participation with those who will use the building, it transcends their goals and may even criticise them. For these contrasting reasons it can be read on at least two quite distinct levels telling parallel stories which may or may not be consistent, depending on the context and building involved.

Finally, Radical Eclecticism is multivalent, as against so much Modern Architecture: it pulls together different kinds of meaning, which appeal to opposite faculties of the mind and body, so that they interrelate and modify each other. The taste of the building, its smell and touch, engage the sensibility as much as does the sight and contemplation. In a perfectly successful work of architecture – that of Gaudi – the meanings add up and work together in the deepest combination. We aren't there yet, but a tradition is growing which dares make this demand for the future.

170 BRUNO REICHLIN and FABIO REINHARDT, *Maison Tonini*, Torricella, Switzerland, 1972-74. A well-proportioned villa in the Alberti/Palladian tradition, with grand arch framing view, symmetrical axes, and very simple mathematical harmonies (visible here is ABA'CA'BA and C = A + B). The finish and furnishings are unnecessarily prison-like, but one assumes this is a momentary Calvinism and will not last with these young designers.

171 THOMAS GORDON SMITH, *Paulownia House*, Oakland, California, 1977. A prefabricated Quonset hut, wood frame construction and a rusticated, Serlio arch which is mirrored to make it whole. The quoins, voussoirs and other traditional elements are made from stock pieces to suggest a more substantial construction than actually exists.

Towards Radical Eclecticism, Third Edition, 1981

Since I finished the second edition of this book in 1978 several important shifts in architecture have occurred which have led to this postscript. Major Modern architects such as Hans Hollein and James Stirling have now gone convincingly 'Post' in every way but name; major American practitioners in New York and Chicago have changed direction in a dramatic turnabout, leaving their previous faith in favour of the new creed; finally, important schemes have been built and, in one case, the Piazza d'Italia, the real 'major monument' to Post-Modernism is nearing completion. This book has had the (editorial) misfortune to be written just as Post-Modernism was becoming a world movement with developments occurring faster than new editions.

The situation is dynamic with sudden bursts of the new architecture arising in unexpected places such as Tokyo and Chicago, places where Modern and Late Modern Architecture have a strong following. Indeed, some architects like Helmut Jahn and Philip Johnson vary from one building to the next, from Late to Post and back to Modern – a confusing course to follow at least for the public, and one which has led me elsewhere to classify the three schools according to thirty variables.[67] There is no reason here to elaborate such a complex taxonomy. Just the basic distinction should be kept in mind: Late-Modern architecture is an exaggeration of several Modern concerns such as the technological image of a building, its circulation, logic and structure, whereas Post-Modern architecture, in an attempt to communicate, is double-coded, an eclectic mix of traditional or local codes with Modern ones.

The shift to Post-Modernism has occurred most strongly in the United States, a natural situation given the presence of the major protagonists as well as a relatively favourable building climate where experiments are welcomed. Now under way are at least three multi-million dollar commissions, those leviathans which gave Modernism such a bad name: Philip Johnson's AT & T building, Hardy, Holzman and Pfeiffer's Willard Hotel addition in Washington DC, and Ulrich Franzen's Philip Morris corporate headquarters in New York. In each case, the size and generality 172 of the building task have led to muted results only marginally more articulated than their predecessors. The mixture of Modern and Revivalist styles is smoothed over; sharp contrasts are avoided; imagery, ornament and historical allusion are present but subdued. The same can be said of the recent Chicago Post-Modernism of the large corporate practices: Peter Pran's skyscraper designed within the firm of Schmidt, Garden and Erickson and Helmut Jahn's work within C F Murphy Associates. The intermixture of codes is subtle and understated, a predictable fusion for large offices and conservative clients. More surprising is that this mixture has a refreshingly naive aspect. Crisply detailed and extremely archetypal in its use of historical form (*the* semi-circle, *the* cornice, etc) it seems at the start of a new tradition, not unlike Brunelleschi's first use of Classical details. Forms are not used expressively (beyond their representational role), they are not articulated or shaped with sculptural weight. Instead, they are treated as flat appliqué, or melted into the flat surface of a building, becoming thereby equated with constructional necessity.

172 ULRICH FRANZEN, *Philip Morris Corporate Headquarters*, New York City, 1979-82. Classical skyscraper design on Grand Central Station side, with base (echoing Station), vertical shaft and capital. The mouldings, echelon and cut-out loggia repeat the centralising symmetry of the base. To the side street the building presents a modern, horizontal facade; the meeting of this literal double-coding might have produced a more ironic corner joint.·(Ulrich Franzen Associates)

With the work of the Chicago Seven,[68] more particularly Thomas Beeby, we find an almost inevitable conjunction of Neo-Palladianism and Neo-Mies, elegant in its crisp detailing and refined structuring of space. Beeby's Townhouse, produced as one in a row of varying contextual buildings, mixes Modern structural grid with traditional aedicules and barrel vaults. The Classicism inherent in Mies is so close to Neo-Palladianism that when they are forced to meet in Beeby's work the conjunction seems natural; an inevitable consequence of Palladian rules being followed in reinforced concrete and steel. Beeby also mixes iconography in a thoroughgoing manner so that the grotesque face of Hades in the basement grotto seems at home with the polished chrome dragster on the ground floor. The strength of this work is its sure handling of structure and complex spatial rhythms which read horizontally and vertically in syncopation. Each 'internal facade' becomes a variation on the previous one and on the front *Serliana*. The ornament, such as it is, results directly from constructional elements – particularly the mullion, and in this way provides another bridge between Modern and traditional practice. It's as if Mies had gone Post-Modern, or at least back to his Schinkel period.

Perhaps the most important aspect of these town houses is that they return to the American street tradition by combining individual variation within an overall street morphology. This tradition (which exists notably in San Francisco, Chicago and New York) was one broken by Modernism. The Chicago town houses, variants of which are being built now, show an elegant handling of stripped Classical detail and ornament that re-establishes an urban grain and incident. In Europe, similar types of scheme have evolved with less individual expression of each house; in London, one version of this infill architecture has been completed. Jeremy Dixon has designed a scheme which fits into the nineteenth-century urban pattern both in plan and detail. Accepting the street lines and traditional layout, the bay windows of adjoining houses and their emphasis on the front door, the scheme manages to be both acceptably familiar and inventive. The inhabitants can recognise their traditional language and requirements; the stereotypes are used in a relatively straightforward way, as stock as the London brick with which it is built.

But then, on further inspection, there are esoteric meanings more directly accessible to the architect, or the inhabitant who cares to search for them: the physiognomic visage, the suggestion of a face, which is appropriately made by the front door (or rather two front doors combined over the traditional stoop). This 'face' is also another favourite image of Post-Modernists, an aedicule, a 'little house', the signifier of domesticity which has had such a long history in the West since its first conventionalisation in ancient Greece. Dixon masterfully repeats the aedicule form at different scales – in the windows, roof profiles and 'entrance gates' – to unite a complex array of formal quotes. These vary from the Neo-Vernacular brick to the Dutch gable with its crow-step articulation, from Art Deco ziggurats to Rationalist grids. Particularly ingenious is the way the aedicular gate-post becomes a cover for garbage cans on the house side.

In one respect, this scheme epitomises a search of Post-Modernists for a rich, flexible language which stems from the locale. The language is eclectic, as mixed as the Queen Anne of a century ago and as responsive to particular cultural

173

174

175

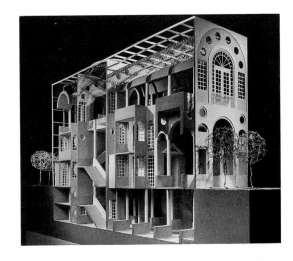

173 THOMAS BEEBY, *Townhouse Project*, Chicago, 1978. Based on Palladio's Villa Poiana, like Isozaki's Post-Modern work, with archetypal circles, rectangles and flat decorative detail, this town house also incorporates a Miesian structural logic on a five-foot module. A sequence of varying spatial character is defined with barrel vault, a dome over the stairs and subterranean grotto. (Thomas Beeby)

174 JEREMY DIXON, *St Marks Road*, London, 1976-79. Twenty-four houses and twenty flats placed on a tight site pick up the existing Edwardian street pattern and scale. By doubling the houses in a single, visual unit the appearance of a large house is kept; the angled plan, while an economic use of the site, produces odd internal conditions.

conditions. The attempt to derive such a language has been made by other architects in Amsterdam and Vienna, notably by the group called Missing Link. These young designers have undertaken empirical studies of pre-existing urban
177 signs – the towers, gates, doors, street corners and courtyards of Vienna. Elegant line drawings are made of these recurrent motifs – 'words' of the Viennese architectural language – and a new set of typologies is derived from them through a process of abstraction. Perhaps their design results do not yet completely forge the hoped-for 'missing link' with the past, but their analyses show one way of proceeding towards that goal.

The contextualists are also headed towards a regional historicism without, however, approaching too close to traditional syntax. Leon Krier's designs for Rome, and the other schemes produced for the show 'Roma Interrotta', summer
176 1978, are both contextual and disruptive, based on the Nolli plan of Rome and opposed to its grain. Krier has, in typical Rationalist manner, reinvented the 'primitive hut' of columns and triangular roof truss, but this time each column is the side of an eight-storey tower and the pyramidal roof encloses an awesome public realm – a cross between a train-shed and an open-air market. The drawings, when seen collaged into the Roman perspectives of Piranesi, actually stand up to these grand and disturbing images. The public buildings have the breadth of scale and heavy gestural quality typical of the Roman tradition. They are meant to support a local form of civic organisation, the *rione*, an alternative to the centralised bureaucracy and state. Each one would have restaurants, clubs, rooms for games and large top-floor studios for artists who would fabricate the syndicalist imagery.[69] The idea, as Krier describes it, is to revive the *res publica* and create new civic institutions which can support it, ones on a par with the seventeenth-century churches of Rome. This collage of new and old, utopian syndicalism and traditional city, is characteristic of the European Rationalists in Brussels, Barcelona, Paris and Italy generally.

So far, only imperfect fragments of the style and idea have been realised, one on the edge of Paris. Georgia Benamo and Christian de Portzamparc have completed a small urban scheme, the Rue des Hautes-Formes. This inevitably seeks to

175 JEREMY DIXON, *St. Marks Road*, London, 1976-79. Slight variations in stained glass and door colour give perceptible individuality to each house. The aedicular 'face' is repeated at different scales, in windows, gateway and roof pitch, providing variations on this domestic theme. The variety of texture and small scale elements also reinforce this theme.

176 LEON KRIER, *Rione project*, Rome, 1978, for the Via Condotti and Via Corso. An international centre and aeroport terminal are among the functions projected for this monument to a new public realm. Krier, as other Rationalists, both uses and distorts the existing language and morphology of the city, producing heroic images of a yet unborn society. The mixture of primitive construction and sophisticated technology is as striking as the contrasts with Piranesi. (Leon Krier)

177 MISSING LINK (Otto Kapfinger and Adolf Krischanitz), *Vienna Studies*, 1977. A series of elegant line drawings of typical Viennese buildings, here the Wohnhöfe (the public housing of the twenties), abstracts recurrent aspects of the local language – towers, gates, corners, courtyards, etc. From these studies a new eclectic whole is created which relates to the past. (Missing Link)

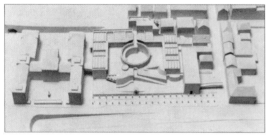

178 GEORGIA BENAMO and CHRISTIAN DE PORTZAMPARC, *Rue des Hautes-Formes*, Paris, 1975-79. Hanging arches, a 'thick wall' with various window types and a plan which acknowledges the street and central public realm; otherwise the scheme resembles Modernist slab blocks in many ways.

179 JAMES STIRLING, MICHAEL WILFORD & ASSOCIATES, *Staatsgalerie and Chamber Theatre*, Stuttgart, 1977, construction 1979-84. One moves under an entrance arch, a primitive hut, but then to left or right off axis. The U-shaped, symmetrical gallery is in front, but one has to approach it diagonally up a ramp. The circular open-air sculpture court can be reached on axis, but one moves through it on a perimeter, semi-circular ramp which finally connects up with a walkway into the more domestic urban fabric. In this circuitous way the public is brought informally right into the heart of the museum without actually gaining entry.

recreate 'the street, the square, the urban place' but at greater density than in a   178
traditional city. Tower and slab blocks of Modernism are combined and given a Post-Modern formal treatment of cut-out screens *à la* Moore, false hanging arches to signify entry *à la* Venturi and a variety of window treatment *à la mode*. The last is further justified as a method of breaking down the scale and reducing the feeling of being overlooked by a thousand eyes – something that would have resulted from an all-window version. If there are contextualist doubts about this scheme they concern the leaky space, the small size of the piazza and *res publica* and the neutralised relation of solid to void, urban poche to monument (the scheme lacks monuments).

A more convincing example of urban contextualism, now under construction, is the museum in Stuttgart by James Stirling. This scheme picks up formal cues from the surrounding context, in this case the height and grain of adjacent buildings and   179
the basic axial relationship to the main street. From this entrance axis it layers a sequence of space frontally and at right angles to movement; as in a Rationalist building the grid is felt conceptually throughout although one is forced to move around it in circles and diagonals. Thus a basic dualism is set up between rectilinear and rotational elements, a binary opposition which heightens the appreciation of other contrasts: in particular the De Stijl words collaged onto the Schinkel grammar.

The eclectic language incorporates Romanesque arches for the sculpture court and Egyptian cornices for the painting galleries; these references signify 'museum and art' in a stereotypical way while remaining quite subdued. Indeed, the Schinkelesque grammar has an overall rationale in this German context as it signifies 'culture' on a popular level. The virtue of this scheme is to use such obvious clichés with a dramatic inventiveness, one which plays up oppositions between past and present, circle and square. The focus of the museum epitomises this contrast; the circular court is a 'domeless dome', an inside-out space, the room towards which one moves to find oneself outside, cut off from urban noise and in touch with sculpture or the sky. The ideas behind this, the mandala, the 'dome of heaven – the sky', the 'heart of the city' and the circular *res publica* are, as we have seen, key ideas of many Post-Modernists. They are as much ideas of content as purely architectural ideas and seek to raise, if not answer, metaphysical questions which Modernists, in their pragmatic phase, overlooked.

One could speak of a Metaphysical School of Post-Modernism which loosely   180
unites architects from many different countries, particularly those in America and Japan. Monta Mozuna and Hiroshi Hara use themes of the mandala and 'centred space' which are similar to those of Charles Moore and James Stirling. Hara has written: 'Homogeneous space tends to atomise human relationships . . . if you agree that homogeneous space is negative and undesirable, then we must somehow regain control of the Post-Modern spatial order . . . a house . . . must possess a strong independent centre. This creates a regular order that is opposed to the surrounding homogeneous space outside.'[70] His work, like the others', makes use of strong enclosures, repetitive grids, axial symmetries, mirror images, Palladian motifs and a religious handling of objects. Interior volumes are arranged as

so many altars, hieratically fixed on an axis of light which runs down the spine of the building. They provide the body image and 'heart' which Charles Moore and others have called for in architecture.

More historicist in his metaphysical conceits is Kazuhiro Ishii, an architect who was trained under Moore at Yale. His '54 Windows', a house for a doctor, uses popular signs and colour codes which he argues are regional in nature; or his Naoshima School transforms the Renaissance colonnade into a Post-Modern, 181 syncopated paradox. In the latter building, he occasionally leaves out columns thus dealing with the Renaissance 'problem of the corner' in an ironic way. But he orchestrates these Mannerist jokes (hanging capitals of steel bars) with an obviousness that opens the reference out to non-architects.

Michael Graves, by contrast, is less explicit with his humour, as indeed his metaphysics. The work of Graves is coded with a depth and complexity that eludes quick understanding. His Schulman House addition makes use of historicist elements – the ziggurat, the Baroque stagger in plan, the column, entrance 'pediment' and so on – but it changes scale and colour to distort the perception of these elements sometimes beyond recognition. For instance, the decorative 182 moulding over the front door is just barely a pediment and keystone. Graves would argue that only a distortion of traditional syntax will foreground these elements and decontaminate their potentially kitsch quality, an argument that has some force. Yet at the same time, it raises corresponding problems: a certain archness of reference, a lack of focus and unity (which may be intended). Recently, Graves has 183 moved towards a more Post-Modern explicitness and one can actually identify certain traditional signs. Not only the elements mentioned, but the green of the earth, the blue of the sky and the conventional foci of the house, the hearth and front door. Then, as one examines the architecture further, more elaborate cues become apparent, such as an asymmetrical symmetry on the garden and entrance sides and the presence/absence of columns. This last is another Mannerist paradox. The column has jumped off the centre of the front and landed to one side, or conversely, the capital has jumped off the column-chimney and landed in the centre. Either way it's an amusing, if arcane architectural conceit.

The question of traditional, applied ornament has started to exercise Post-Modernists with increasing frequency. There have been exhibitions, conferences and magazines on the subject, not to mention countless projects and completed works.[70] It is safe to assume that ornament will flourish again soon, purged of its connection with 'crime' and other guilt-laden associations, to fulfil many of its traditional roles. These include not only the symbolic functions which Venturi and Stern have underlined but, more obviously, aesthetic ones: to give scale, depth and proportion to large, bureaucratic monoliths; to provide variation on themes stated elsewhere in the building and to highlight these; to 'hide faults in construction', something which Modernism in its more Calvinistic moments wanted to show; to give enjoyment, complication and visual games to a boring surface, and finally to accent the mood of a space rather the way spice and garlic accentuate taste. When Modernism cut ornament from the diet of architecture, a lot more than bad taste was purged, and it is one of the pleasures of Post-Modernism to bring back these

180 ARATA ISOZAKI, *Fujima Country Club*, 1975, in the primary shape of a black, silent barrel vault, which twists into the form of a metaphysical question-mark, ending with a version of Palladio's Villa Poiana. Why Palladio in a Japanese country-club, it asks? The primary form contrasts with the surrounding environment and the modifications of the Villa Poiana (round columns, thick arch, entrance pillars cut in half) have structural justifications, but the overall question-mark and its green 'period' show the arbitrariness of form, postulated by the Metaphysical School. (M Arai, *The Japan Architect)*

181 KAZUHIRO ISHII, *Naoshima School*, 1977. A colonnade and other traditional forms such as a pitched roof gate mediate a modern shed space behind. The complicated rhythm of the colonnade (A, B, A, C, A, B, 2A, C, A. C, A, B, 2A, C, A, B, A, C, 2A, C) plays on and syncopates Renaissance examples while other historicist comments include 'missing columns' (indicated by hanging capitals).

delicacies one by one.

Hans Hollein, already adept at the slick-tech look of Late-Modernism, has turned his attention towards the ornamental use of this aesthetic. In his renovation of the Perchtoldsdorf Town Hall, near Vienna, he has produced a grand, ornamental use of chrome and furniture elements to intensify the existing ornament. Here an undulating blue line edged in chrome divides the wall in parts above the traditional dado line, in order to accentuate the existing portraits of the previous mayors. The waves vary in breadth, as do the rippling panels below, to conform with the varying ovals of the paintings above. Over the side entrance doors, otherwise unarticulated except for handles, the waves invert to allow headroom and signal a change of function. This contextual use of ornament (reminiscent of Viennese Rococo) signifies a positive functional choice Hollein made when confronted with the difficult requirement of adding to the size of the council chamber. He decided that, rather than build a new chamber, he would crowd all the councillors into the old one and thereby preserve their historic link, with a room that has great emotional overtones (the commemorative portraits were painted soon after a Turkish deception that resulted in the massacre of the town's people). The crowded ornament, thus, not only half frames the elders, but also half frames the crowded councillors seated below, and thus acts as a metaphorical link between the two groups. The latter are squashed tight against each other in thin, Art Deco chairs which just fit into places allotted at the table. On the floor in the centre of the oval 184 is a stylised vine and bunch of grapes, a symbol both of the major source of revenue of this town and (because of the golden marble lumps) money itself.

In scale and concept, Hollein's designs are midway between architecture and furniture and thus lend themselves to ornamental treatment. His Austrian Travel Agency in Vienna consists of an ornamental series of giant furniture-pieces juxtaposed as a symbolic collage. On the exterior the neutral, grey urban fabric is preserved and yet the new function is subtly cued by the introduction of polished bronze which gleams out from the grey. On the inside, the various tourist fantasies and stereotypes become an excuse for an eclecticism I would once again term Radical because of its semantic appropriateness: ruined columns impaled by chrome shafts signify travel in Greece and Italy; desert travel is communicated by 185 bronze versions of the palm columns at the Brighton Pavilion; India by a bronze 186 solar topee, theatre tickets by a stage curtain, air travel by birds and, ironically, the place where one pays for it all, the cashier's desk, is signified by the outlines of a Rolls Royce radiator grille. All of this is sheltered under a light-filled coffered vault reminiscent of the local Post Office Savings Bank, the magnificent 'Modern' space Otto Wagner built in 1906. Thus local reference is set against stereotype, and existing urban fabric against infill. Because of the precision craftsmanship the stereotypes, like those of Dixon and Stirling, avoid becoming kitsch. Hollein thus speaks directly to a mass-culture and uses its clichés (something of a necessity in a travel bureau) — but with a wit and care not usually evident in the products of mass-culture.

The way architecture communicates with this industrial society has to be seen as a major challenge for Post-Modernism. Clearly Modernism failed to speak to this

182 MICHAEL GRAVES, *Schulman House*, Princeton, 1976-78. Asymmetrical symmetry is set up on the entrance and garden sides by emphasising both the centre and one side. The front forms diminish in plan to emphasise the door. (Norman McGrath)

183 MICHAEL GRAVES, *Plocek House*, Warren, New Jersey. 1977, built 1979-82. The column is stylised and placed as a pier to mark the two significant parts of the house — the hillside entrance and hearth. On the inside it becomes a stair-column. Colouring also is an abstraction of the ground and sky. (Proto Acme Photo)

184 HANS HOLLEIN, *Perchtoldsdorf Town Hall*, renovation, Austria, 1975-76. The wavy decorative lines in blue and chrome mediate between the ceiling, table and floor ornament while the stylised vine and grapes provide visual distraction during interminable debates. A sympathetic collage of old and new which has a semantic justification. (J Surwillo)

society in several of the ways outlined at the beginning of this book. Just as clearly Post-Modernists such as Robert Venturi have been equivocal about engaging this issue. Wrapped up in the problem are various questions which make a simple approach to it impossible – such as the balance between populist and élite codes, both of which architects have to serve, and their attendant threats of kitsch and mystification. Furthermore, there are the problems of a consumer society which celebrates private building and not public architecture. The architect, presuming he wishes to communicate positively with this society through his building, must steer a precarious course through these obstacles. To reiterate, he must appeal to different taste cultures using different codes, and this will make him an eclectic. Whether he produces weak or Radical Eclecticism depends on whether he finds compelling reasons for using a style. Simplifying somewhat, we can point to three basic justifications for choosing a style, or mixing styles, as the case may be: the context the building fits into, the character of the particular functions which must be enhanced by style and the taste-culture of the inhabitants. We can see these three aspects in Charles Moore's half-completed Piazza d'Italia in New Orleans.

As the aerial view of the urban context reveals, this piazza is set in a mixed area of New Orleans. To one side is a Modern skyscraper, whose black and white graphics have been taken up as a motif to generate a graduating series of rings. This circular form, at once a Modern 'bull's-eye' and Baroque urban form (Place des Victoires, Paris), permeates out into three streets giving a cue to the passer-by that something unusual occurs behind the existing buildings. This setting up of an 187 expectation, and the use of veiling devices that at once proclaim and hide – the archway, the pergola – dramatise the approach. We are pulled towards the centre of the bull's-eye and expect to find there a symmetrical, circular culmination. What actually occurs both satisfies and contradicts this supposition. There are indeed a centre and circular forms, but instead of confirming a Baroque centrality, they set up new expectancies. The circles are partial discs, screens of columns that spin asymmetrically on the diagonal of movement towards a new culmination point, the tallest point, an archway, in fact a Modern *Serliana*. This diagonal is reinforced by 188 the cascade of broken forms – the boot of Italy – which focuses on the highest plateau, the 'Italian Alps'. Thus we have a clear organisation of form and content. As Italy rises towards the Northern Alps, so too do the Five Orders of Italian columns, and they culminate in a new sixth order which frames the future restaurant. This invention for a German restaurant (they will hang sausages in the windows) Moore calls the 'Deli Order'. Neon necklaces around the neck of these columns further indicate that this is the twentieth century and that commercial bad taste is a part of it. Moore has a liking for architectural whimsy and puns (he calls the watering metopes 'wetopes') and it is a credit to his teamwork that these calculated lapses in taste don't get the upper hand. They are part of a rich mix of meanings, rather the way similar elements are absorbed into Shakespearean drama.

A point worth stressing is that the plurality of meanings in this scheme could not have been successfully incorporated by one designer (a point to be made generally about participation). Moore has teamed up with two local architects from the firm of Perez and Associates and these designers supplied much of the peculiar cultural

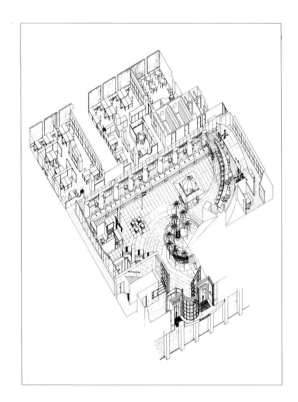

185 HANS HOLLEIN, *Austrian Travel Agency*, Vienna, 1976-78, axonometric, shows the symbolic centres collaged on to an abstract grid of space with circles, staggers and rise and fall of section articulating the zones between selling (above) and private work areas (top). Continuous open space is thus characterised and dramatised, as opposed to Late-Modern isotropic space.

186 HANS HOLLEIN, *Austrian Travel Agency*. Placed under the cool white light of a Secessionist barrel vault, which subtly mediates between different ceiling heights, are various signs of foreign travel: a bronze Lutyens dome for India, palm trees for exotic places, ruined columns for Greece and Italy.

knowledge. They were the ones to stress the importance of the annual St Joseph's festival, the pretext for the fountain and piazza. Once a year, the Italian community comes to the fore to celebrate its presence, by selling Italian specialities and local concoctions (muffalattas, salami, cheese, etc) on the day of their patron saint. Since the ostensible reason for the piazza was to give identity to the Italian community in a city where other ethnic groups dominate (the French, Spanish, the blacks and Anglos), there was a sufficient pretext for historicist rhetoric and explicit content. What was the content? 'Italianness' clearly, as symbolised by the echoes of the Trevi fountain, the Five rather than Three Orders, the strong earth colouring, the Latin inscription ('This fountain was given by the citizens of New Orleans as a gift to all the people') and most obviously the plan of Italy (with the Adriatic and Tyrrhenian seas represented by moving water). Since the community is made up mostly of Sicilians, this island occupies the centre of the bull's-eye, an emphasis which is increased by another focus, the black and white podium. This can function as a speaker's platform on St Joseph's day when the piazza works as a *res publica*. This particular function is the kind of detailed social content that emerges as a possibility only after patient exploration into a local culture, and it gives the rhetorical forms a credibility they would otherwise lack. But, it is a rhetoric that extends across many taste-cultures.

For historians there are references to the Marine Theatre of Hadrian and the triumphal gateways of Schinkel; for the Sicilians, echoes of archetypal piazzas and fountains; for the Modernists there is an acknowledgement of skyscrapers and the use of current technologies (the neon and concrete); for the lover of pure architectural form there are cutaway imposts finished in speckled marble and a most sensuous use of polished stainless steel. Column capitals glisten with this material as water shoots out of the acanthus leaves; or the stern, squat Tuscan columns are cut from this material leaving razor-sharp 'paramilitary' images, the silhouettes of Greek helmets.[72] The overall impression, finally, is a sensuous and rhetorical one, perhaps a bit too overemphasised at present because its background infill isn't finished. But conceptually it is a convincing example of Radical Eclecticism: it fits into and extends the urban context, it characterises the various functions, symbolic and practical, with various styles, and it takes its cues for content and form from the local taste-culture, the Italian community. Moreover it provides this community with a centre, a 'heart', to repeat the Post-Modern catchword. While engaging a mass-culture with recognised stereotypes, it manages to use them *both* straightforwardly and in an inventive, distorted way. Finally, and on a predictive note, it foreshadows an architecture like the Baroque, when different arts were combined together to produce a rhetorical whole. Clearly the success of this rhetoric depends on an area outside of architecture: the belief in a credible social or metaphysical content. The search for such content is the next challenge for Post-Modernists.

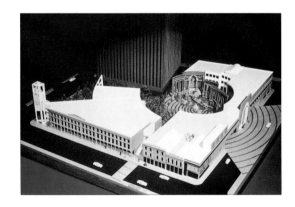

187 CHARLES MOORE (with Allen Eskew and Malcolm Heard Jr of Perez & Associates and Ron Filson), *Piazza d'Italia*, New Orleans, 1976-79. The aerial view shows the piazza (circle) set into the urban tissue (rectangle) like a mandala which announces its presence by various cues: a pergola, a campanile and archway or the rings of paving. This scheme, like many Rationalist ones, reinforces the historic urban fabric while at the same time changing its meaning. (UIC)

188 *Piazza d'Italia*. Columnar screens and flying arches lead up to one focus, the future German Restaurant with its 'Deli Order' of neon and the modern *Serliana* with raised keystone. Note the reflective glow of the neon. The dark, flat imposts look like an architect's rendering of a cross-section.

The Synthesis: Post-Modern Classicism, Fourth Edition, 1984

The last postscript to this book was written in 1979 when several buildings mentioned in the text, such as James Stirling's Stuttgart Museum, were under construction. The completion of these, and work in a new style, have led inevitably to this new conclusion. It completes the story told at the beginning of this book, first written in 1976. For what has occurred is the beginning of a new public language of architecture, a Post-Modern Classicism, which, if not elegant and perfected as a fully-developed mode of discourse, is at least clear in its broad outlines. Now architects are beginning to use the full repertoire again – metaphor, ornament, polychromy, convention – to try to communicate with the public. This attempt may not always be successful, and the results may suffer from the speed of current building practice, but the general approach has been established. It amounts to a consensus, like the International Style of the Twenties, but it is a consensus with a difference: Post-Modern Classicism is a free eclectic manner to be used where it is appropriate on public buildings. It's not a totalistic style, the claim Nikolaus Pevsner made for the International one, and it exists as a genre, with other styles. In short, it is the leading part of the pluralism which it supports as a necessary communicational device.[73]

In order to create architectural meaning, opposition must be used, and the Free-Style Classicism of the present gains its meaning as the public genre by contrast with more romantic and pragmatic modes.[74] It can be solemn and dignified as is 189 Aldo Rossi's work. It can be the commercial jazz of Charles Moore, the monumental fanfare of Ricardo Bofill or the sweet polyphony of Hans Hollein. The mode is various, but still identifiable. From Classicism it develops a universal grammar and syntax – the columns, arches, domes, methods of joinery and decoration – and from current social tasks and technology it gains a creative impetus.

The New Tuscanism – The Functional Mode

The synthesis of current trends was first apparent in the 1980 Biennale in Venice. 190 Organised by Paolo Portoghesi and a committee which included Robert Stern, Christian Norberg-Schulz, Vincent Scully and myself, the Biennale's real subject was Post-Modern architecture, although its actual title was 'The Presence of the Past'.[75] This title unfortunately distorted the meaning of Post-Modernism, bending it towards historical reference. But the great virtue of the show was to celebrate architecture and the new consensus. The public responded to this display, over 2,000 visitors came per day – a large number for an architectural exhibition. The show was demounted and reassembled in Paris and San Francisco. While certain critics such as Bruno Zevi attacked it, the majority of non-architectural writers supported the new approach.

If architecture is defined as the public art, then this exhibition vindicated the public part of the definition. It reached the broadest audience of Italians through television and newspaper coverage. For those hostile to the show it was mere publicity: a 'Potemkin's Village' of cardboard screens that would blow away with the next fashion. But, that it was more than this can be seen from the variety of

189 ALDO ROSSI, *Modena Cemetery*, 1984, view of ossuary. Balconies inside this roofless volume allow access to the burial cells within the thickness of the red walls, in what Rossi himself terms 'analogous architecture'.

190 *Strada Novissima*, Venice Biennale, 1980. The notions of the facade and street return, with most of the facades in a Free-Style Classical manner. From the left are the facades of Krier, Kleihues and Hollein. (Venice Biennale)

buildings completed in its language.

One of the contributors to the Biennale, Aldo Rossi, is a personal friend of Portoghesi. Perhaps this explains his primary place in the exhibition, designing the entry gate and the floating *Teatro del Mondo*. This combines Classical organisation 191 with vernacular construction, a hybrid that shares with Venturi's buildings an interest in the archetypal; the square-mullioned window, the flat, cheap, plainer facade. But as important as these fundamentalist images, was the presence, not of the past, but of Rossi himself. For this signalled a coming together of the Neo-Rationalists and the Eclectics, or in other terms the Urbanists and the Historicists, the opposing schools of Post-Modernism. Up to this date, Rossi's architecture was stern and repetitive, an image of death in life: after this show, his work is more buoyant and contextual. During this period, his all-important Modena Cemetery was being completed, the masterpiece of archetypal imagery and what he called 'analogous architecture'. But it wasn't just Rossi who was influenced by the climate of opinion. He had actually formed the school of Neo-Rationalism, *La Tendenza*, which influenced, in turn, the synthesis of Post-Modern Classicism. From Rossi, and others such as the Krier brothers and Mario Botta, it gained the aspects of controlled repetition and urban propriety: above all the restrained mood or style which can be called 'the New Tuscanism', or the 'New Abstraction'.[76]

This last term was coined by OM Ungers and myself to both contrast with the New Representation and refer to an emergent approach: a design concerned with abstract architectural themes. Rossi in his important book *L'Architettura della Città*, 1966, had emphasised the multivalent nature of architecture, how structures such as a Roman arena could be transformed in various cultures and re-used: as housing, for instance. Ungers in his book *Architettura come Tema*, 1982, generalised this notion to the point where architectural themes became so autonomous as to dominate over history and function. Culture may change but the abstract types of house and perimeter block go on *transforming* themselves forever:

191 ALDO ROSSI, *Il Teatro del Mondo*, The Floating Theatre, Venice Biennale, 1979-80. A Classical four-square geometry centering like the domed churches of Venice on a lantern and globe. The blue decorative elements relate to the context, while the wooden construction relates to the vernacular.

The New Abstraction in architecture deals with a rational geometry, with clear and regular forms in plan as well as in elevation . . . Emotion is controlled by rational thinking, and this is stimulated through intuition . . . [An architectural concept is something] which does not change at all, which is permanent, and which only proceeds through continual stages of transformation. The New Abstraction means exactly that – the transformation of ideas and concepts in the course of history.[77]

A transformational grammar based on universal archetypes or ideas has much to recommend it, especially as a means of creative thought.

192   Ungers, positively exploding onto the German scene with a sudden burst of work, has five or six large jobs in various stages of completion. His Perimeter Block in Berlin is an illustration of the transformation of an apartment type around an interior courtyard. One can literally read off the variations on the architectural theme: the window abstractions tell the educated viewer what type of apartment is within, even if they don't tell him whether it is inhabited by Germans or Italians. The New Abstraction is meant to be trans-cultural, inhabiting a kind of pure architectural heaven. Ungers' Frankfurt Fair Hall and Galleria is a culmination of other pure themes: the glazed arcade, the warehouse space and the stepped

193   platform. If the cypresses are ever planted on the roof, where the cars were meant to be parked, it will become a tough German version of that most sweet Italian garden, Isola Bella! This is another virtue of the New Abstraction: it forces one to combine opposite archetypes, think across functions, get away from the stereotypes of normal production. Ungers gets such creative pleasure from recombining and transforming his themes that he spends relatively little time in detailing or supervising their construction. Thus, like Rossi's buildings, they appear conceptual rather than built, schematic rather than personalised.

This aspect of the New Abstraction lends itself to mass production. It is obviously cheaper to grid everything and make every variation from the straight line into a simple curve or hemisphere. And here lies the Classicism of this approach. It is based on a fundamentalist, Platonic geometry. The circle, square, triangle, hexagon, octagon, or their fragments, exhaust the formal repertoire. One will not find a complex curve, or non-modular unit in this work. The parts are fitted together with a knowledge and precision which suits an industrial society. It is all basic and rationalised or, less generously, 'idiot-proof'.

If one is handling lots of work, and designing it, while constantly moving as Rossi and Ungers do, then this simple method pays dividends. Apart from this pragmatic value (which may entail cursory detailing), there is the aesthetic and moral virtue. The style is neutral, well-behaved and understandable. These qualities recommend it to those designers who are dismayed by pluralism and what they take to be the kitsch of Post-Modernism. The New Abstraction, with its emphasis on the autonomy of architecture, means one can more or less dispense with other people's taste and concentrate on aesthetic and organisational problems. And this means architecture can be controlled as an art.

No Neo-Rationalist has greater control of his craft than the Ticinese architect, Mario Botta. Studying under both Louis Kahn and the Atelier of Le Corbusier, he

192 OM UNGERS, *Perimeter Block*, Schillerstrasse, Berlin, 1978-82. The street line is kept and the basic Berlin apartment type is transformed around a courtyard to permit a variety of use and a lively, musical facade. (Waltraud Krase)

193 OM UNGERS, *Frankfurt Fair Hall and Galleria*, Frankfurt, 1979-82. A giant glazed arcade like those of the nineteenth century, connects one hall to another. Ungers' housing is like Rossi's, a repetition of a structural bay crossed with another type: the stepped platform, a kind of Isola Bella with cypresses and parked cars. (Von Hoessle-Frankfurt)

has gone the Classical Post-Modern route developing the late styles of these masters toward a primitive Classicism. Recognisable, in distorted form, are such Classical features as cornices, columns with capitals, rustication and the all-important pedimental skylight which can be seen as either an amplified fanlight or a diminished arcade. These last give an ordering, mythic element to all his buildings, 194 contrasting with the weight of the masonry, sign of the ground. The opposition between sky and ground, or more traditionally heaven and earth, roots the buildings in a very primitive way. Indeed the over-heavy concrete columns also take up this opposition, giving a fundamental permanence to our highly mobile society. It's as if Botta is re-inventing the Egyptian and Cretan house-columns which mark the centre of the social world and hold up the sky. Just as important is the geometrical ordering, not only of the plan but of the constructional elements, usually the concrete block. Botta invests these with an almost sacred quality, as if they were marble and not industrialised material. And he draws, and thereby controls, the placement of each one. Thus they take on a decorative, hieratic role rather like the Cistercian use of masonry. Kahn, Le Corbusier and Modernists such as Mies van der Rohe also treated industrial material this way; they also admired the primitive Romanesque where it turned construction into a transcendental art. What distinguishes Botta from his predecessors is the explicit Mannerism of his revival. Where these Modernists suppressed their Classicism behind a technological imperative, Botta lets his develop freely into a primitive symbolism. For instance, the constructional blocks in the Casa Rotonda fan apart to become a capital, or 195 stagger at forty-five degrees to become a dentil frieze.

The emphasis on Classical ordering is apparent in Botta's plans, which like Palladio's, are often divided conceptually into nine squares. Not surprisingly these

194 MARIO BOTTA, *House at Viganello*, Ticino, Switzerland. 1980-81. A monumental temple/bunker contrasts with the mountainside and greenery. Botta achieves further Mannerist effects by enlarging the fanlight, diminishing a dentil frieze, and cutting out voids in extreme chiaroscuro. Note the absolute symmetry, voided keystone and decorative use of concrete block. (Alo Zanetta)

are oriented to the four horizons and view, another way the buildings are rooted in place. What makes them excessively Mannerist, and non-Palladian, is the truncated roof, the diminished pediment, top, or dome. Here, as in the concrete block, we find the paradoxical expression of Botta's sensibility as a partial-Modernist. At the last moment, he won't have recourse to a proven formula or cliché but stops the building at its crowning statement, almost with a flat roof. These stops, like his strong use of chiaroscuro, the violent holes cut in the masonry wall, are a sign of disquiet and tension: the query of the new world to the old, the challenge of Modernism to traditional Western culture. In a very real sense the subject of Botta's Mannerism is concerned with this challenge, this collision of opposites. Like Stirling's work at Stuttgart, there is no attempt to smooth over the difference or opt for a facile reconciliation. In fact, both Botta and Stirling like to dramatise the conjunction of opposed systems and sensibilities.

Botta's work – like that of Aldo Rossi, OM Ungers and the other Neo-Rationalists – is in the New Tuscan Style partly because this is an inexpensive mode based on the simple repetition of walls and voids, and partly because the manner is both aristocratic and proletarian.[78] Like the Modernism Tom Wolfe satirised in *From Bauhaus to Our House*, this austere style is wonderfully ambiguous: it's both non-bourgeois and bourgeois.[79] Like designer blue jeans, it celebrates a sophisticated poverty. It's also the easiest mode to detail, or, as the case may be, leave without detail. Sebastiano Serlio recommended the plainest Classical style, the Tuscan, for use in prisons, fortifications and harbours: rough, heavy functions close to peasant life and the soil. It is these virtues, the nobility of the simple peasant, which recommend the manner to certain architects.

Another reason for its adoption is promoted by Demetri Porphyrios in his 'Classicism is not a Style'.[80] This polemic, published in 1982, makes the paradoxical assertion, contradicted by the examples illustrated, that the current spare Classicism of Rossi and Spanish designers is not a mode or genre. What I am terming the New Tuscanism Porphyrios wishes to see solely as a morality concerning construction, what he calls the 'mimetic elaboration of the constructional logic of vernacular Classicism'. The Doric Order, elaborating and symbolising wooden construction, is the ideal. We can see the point here, and no doubt Botta as well as Spanish designers Miguel Garay and Rafael Moneo illustrate this morality. Porphyrios, as well as others, may see this as the alternative to kitsch and representational architecture. Indeed the much publicised 'Great Debate: Modernists versus the Rest', which took place at the Royal Institute of British Architects in London in 1982, often touched on this opposition.[81] For many ex-Modernists the only way forward is via constructional logic, and the corollary of this: for strong defenders of Modernism, such as Kenneth Frampton, any use of symbolic or decorative detail is kitsch. This is, of course. an absurd position, but it does help explain the passion with which Neo-Rationalism, or the New Tuscanism, is promoted. Its defenders believe it will further an authentic architecture in an era of commerce.

In fact, the approach is also a style like any other and quite defensible as a genre. 196   It has all the beauties of simple prose. For instance, Takefumi Aida's Toy Block

195 *Casa Rotonda*, Stabio, 1979-81. The cylinder is ordered as a Palladian nine-square solution oriented to the view. The masonry is violently torn apart to dramatise the view and light. Every constructional block is drawn and understood. The primitive column unites earth and sky. The austere New Tuscan Style is impersonal, dignified, inexpensive, and appropriately used on modest houses. (Mario Botta)

Houses are as easy to understand conceptually as the child-like blocks from which they are built. Basic constructional elements, forming a thick wall pattern in various hues, are stacked and surmounted by Platonic solids – pyramids or extended pediments. The result is inevitably temple-like, a Free-Style Classicism that recalls the unadorned Tuscan style as well as Shinto temples. When analysed further they reveal complex spatial and formal asymmetries reminiscent of De Stijl and Modernist aesthetics. Thus the typical Post-Modern hybrid: the constructional element is simple and Classical, while the composition is complex and has the overlapping spaces of Modernism.

Many Japanese designers work in the New Tuscan Style because it is so basic and close, by analogy, to the Shinto aesthetic. Among the most convincing designers who have combined it with a Minimalist High-Tech are Toyo Ito and Minoru Takeyama. Although different in other ways, they share a similar commitment to using pristine industrial materials formed into Platonic shapes – the inevitable semi-circular arch, the archetypal pediment and the window-wall of gridded squares. At first glance it seems surprising that so many Japanese architects should embrace a primitive Western Classicism. Arata Isozaki, as we'll see, even develops a sophisticated Mannerism. But, on reflection, the causes seem obvious. Japan is quick to pick up and transform foreign influences and has been doing this for literally thousands of years; also the universal and archetypal nature of the Classical language lends itself to cultural borrowing. In the hands of one Japanese architect, Toyokazu Watanabe, the Classical language takes on an almost demonic aspect. His concrete houses look like frightening graves, monumental bunkers that have been burnt out leaving stark shells with gruesome black voids. Only on second glance does the beauty and logic of this architecture overcome its fearsome quality. Solid Tuscan wall and window void create the expression in a very logical way. Floors are stepped back like a ziggurat for the artists' studio above, and in order to let in light from many sources the clerestory windows are doubled. Here and in other Watanabe buildings, this doubling of small panes makes the space appear twice its size. Like Adolf Loos' work, which Watanabe has studied, the simple logic of Classicism can lead to some beautiful and humorous propositions. Loos stacked his black and white cubes into ziggurats of housing and amplified a Doric column into a skyscraper. Watanabe has columns hanging in space – necessary for formal logic, unnecessary for support. Both Loos and Watanabe get a wry pleasure from the paradox inherent in Classicism.

The New Tuscanism, to summarise, is now a dominant genre in parts of Europe such as Italy and Spain, and is used as one of several modes by Post-Modern Classicists. It is, as Serlio prescribed, most suitable on impersonal, rough and functional buildings – today the hospital, factory and street arcade. It may not stop kitsch commercialism as some of its adherents hope, but it does amount to an aristocratically restrained mode. Understatement and cool probity are its virtues, brutalism and shoddy detailing are its occasional vices. Several American architects such as Batey and Mack or Mangurian and Hodgetts use it as a calculating 'Primitivism' to counter an over-elaborate sophistication. It can have constructional purity and thereby moral virtue, when handled by someone like Mario Botta. But as

196 TAKEFUMI AIDA, *Toy Block House III*, Tokyo 1980-81. Large elemental blocks – both construction and structure like Froebel Blocks – are stacked sometimes as bricks, sometimes as post and lintel. This basic Classical compositional method is then contrasted with De Stijl asymmetries and overlapping units of space. The decoration results from the joining of blocks as it often does in the Tuscan Style. (T Aida)

197 MINORU TAKEYAMA, *Nakamura Memorial Hospital*, Sapporo, 1978-80. Platonic shapes, High-Tech materials and a planar architecture of minimalist decorative surface, all appropriate to the hospital function of studied neutrality and expertise. (Taisuke Ogawa)

198 TOYOKAZU WATANABE, *Sugiyama House*, Osaka, 1980-81. For Adolf Loos, who influenced Watanabe, architecture resided in the monument and the grave. Nothing is more powerful than these monumentally haunting images, made more fearsome by the tricks in scale. Whether it is appropriate for housing – even an artist's house as here, is debatable. But it is certainly sublime and logical. (Hitoshi Kawamoto)

the universal or majority style as proposed by the Neo-Rationalists, it is much too limited in scope: no symbolism, or ornament, little polychromy and almost never sculpture.

The example where a figural sculpture has been introduced – Rob Krier's Ritterstrasse apartments – remains the exception, and the sculpture remains 199 primitive. Although the intention to use art in a symbolic and urban way is exemplary, its meaning here is still esoteric rather than fully public. This is not to argue in favour of a facile populist aesthetic, but rather to demand the same clarity in expression that Rob Krier attains in his urban design. If his statements, drawings and city schemes propose a partial return to a world of urbane rooms – streets, squares, arcades – then his use of art remains, by contrast, inarticulate. The problem of the New Tuscanism, if it has one, is too much primitivism.

The New Representation – The Communicational Mode
Post-Modern Classicism is still very young; it has only been defined since 1980,[82] and we ought to make severe demands on its practitioners. Virtually the only criticism of it is dismissive, and this in turn is dismissed by its creators. Sympathetic criticism, the growth of a critical meta-language, is needed so that the young tradition will start to develop a more sophisticated language. As it is, the ornament, polychromy, symbolism and use of sculpture and painting remain somewhat cursory. This can be seen with those who base their building on theories of communication, those who practise what I have called the New Representation.[83] Robert Venturi, as we have seen, is one of the leaders of this movement with his many writings, exhibitions and buildings. He has developed a language to communicate with different 'taste-cultures' that is not only based on the rhetorical types of 'complexity and contradiction' but 'ugly and ordinary' elements, and ones geared to a commercial society – Las Vegas in the extreme. They don't support this society, but criticise it ironically with mannered and distorted shapes – the demi-forms we have analysed above.[84] More recently, Venturi and Scott Brown have put forward arguments for an appliquéd ornament, based on symbolism, of course, but also on cheap, quick construction:

> In the progression of our ideas about appliqué, first as spatial layerings, then signboard, and then ornament, we came to appliqué as representation in architecture . . . manifestations of this approach to symbolism in architecture are essentially two-dimensional and pictorial . . . In our time, economy and industial standardisation, on the one hand, and lack of craftsmanship, on the other, justify this simplified, repetitive and depictive approach to ornament.[85]

Critics of this would say the generalisations are untrue and the resultant architecture is pastiche. They would argue that there are plenty of craftsmen still around, that one can manufacture curved shapes quite cheaply and that, in any case, industrialisation can now produce variation, not just repetition. There is certainly much to be said for each side of such arguments, ones that have been used by the Modernists as well as Post-Modernists. In the event, however, Venturi's flat ornament is both original and enjoyable for its flatness, while stereotyped at the same time. For instance, his Gordon Wu Dining Hall uses Early Renaissance 200

199 ROB KRIER, *Ritterstrasse Apartments*, Berlin-Kreuzberg, 1977-81. The eroded figure marks the public doorway as a Classical caryatid would, but becomes more a comment on the ruins of Berlin than a public figure. The flat Tuscan Style with symmetrical window voids is used in housing here to define urban space and the street. (Gerald Blomeyer)

200 VENTURI, RAUCH and SCOTT-BROWN, *Gordon Wu Dining Hall*, Princeton, New Jersey, 1981-83. Serlian ABA motifs hang symbolically to announce an entrance and contrast strongly with the flat ribbon window. The billboard approach of the sixties is still being used ironically on a campus with other Free-Style Classical revivals, but these are of a more naive kind. (Venturi, Rauch and Scott-Brown)

stereotypes on a Princeton campus where such revivalist architecture was produced in a straight way – and Venturi does it in a crooked way. The flat forms are cut off, slit at the top, or guillotined at the base. All this would be more acceptable if the irony were signalled more explicitly: people, or many of the taste-cultures for whom Venturi so thoughtfully designs, tend to read architecture straightforwardly, not in quotation marks. Thus they tend to see his work as pastiche, not as acceptable 'pastiche'. Secondly, the flat stereotypes might have gained greater force by contrast with a few beautifully crafted and sculpted details. It is no use justifying a fast-food architecture as inevitable and then producing quick clichés: that only worsens a deplorable situation.

On the other hand, and this is what I mean by sympathetic criticism, we might agree that flat, cut-out patterns have their own inherent strengths of rhythmical opposition. Strong dark and light areas give a striking steady beat like cut-out silhouettes. The visual logic of paper-dolls and stencilled patterns is to be supported if time and creativity have gone into their invention. For instance, the 201 Ionic colonnade on the porch of the Brant House is paper-thin, the flatness indicating the non-structural role while the Order indicates the major view over the Bermuda Sea. Here, real structure and applied ornament are in clear opposition. Elsewhere in the house, craftsmanship and careful detailing are evident. Finally, the white silhouette rhythms of the cut-out forms make a delightful foamy dance against the dark blue sea. Thus flat appliqué is vindicated by contrast and a successful use of ornamental symbolism.

The handling of ornament has grown around the world in volume if not in understanding. America is no doubt the country that is leading the rush to decorate and it's produced a lot of colourful results of varying success. There have been exhibitions and commercial competitions on ornament, and a slick book, packaging *Ornamentalism* as a movement, was given its intellectual launch by Paul Goldberger.[86] A host of West Coast architects, influenced by Venturi and by Moore, produced a highly iconic decoration. Thomas Gordon Smith, a group called ACE, the San Francisco architect Hans Kainz, all mixed Classical, vernacular and decorative motifs in a free-style way. Inevitably, Robert Stern summarises many of these tendencies in 202 his design for a Pool House. It is full of dazzling colours that enhance the delight of bathing: glistening bronze and stainless steel 'palm columns' based on those of Hans Hollein provide wet-look decor. A staccato beat of ornamental tiles represent foam splashing: columns and quoins represent bathers. It's all slightly heavy, like an overblown Lutyens fireplace, on which it may be based. The Secessionist and other quotes are a bit obvious. But, as a hedonist temple for bodily pleasure and regeneration, the flash detailing is perfectly suited.

Suitability, appropriateness, decorum – these were the catchwords for the Classically correct, or Vitruvian canon of ornament. It's true that Stern's proportions are noncanonic: the Tuscan Columns are squat. And the obvious display, the explicit reference, would be faulted by the straight Classicist. But if some would criticise the emphasis on private wealth they would still have to applaud the appropriate fit between form and meaning.

What is an acceptable face to a building in the city street and in the public eye?

201 VENTURI, RAUCH and SCOTT-BROWN, *Brant House*, Tuckers Town, Bermuda, 1976-80. View of cut-out Ionic columns which give a rhythmical white dance over the dark blue sea, a rhythm which is syncopated in the arches below and beam ends above. (Venturi, Rauch and Scott-Brown)

202 ROBERT STERN, *Cohn Pool House*, Llewelyn Park, New Jersey, 1981-82. Palm columns glisten, Secessionist tiles bubble, fat women dance as quoins on the side, while the shades of blue and gold shimmer with the utmost luxuriant pleasure. (Norman McGrath)

This sort of issue was raised by the 1980 Venice Biennale, as noted, and the many modest additions to urban streets which followed it. Harry Cobb, for his Museum in Portland, Maine, produced, in 1982, a well-mannered Classicism with large voids cut out at the top, and understated brick and stone piers at the base. This sort of Post-Modern Classicism became the hallmark of large firms and was used in what are euphemistically called prestige commissions. Edward Larrabee Barnes, like Cobb a recent convert to Free-Style Classicism, uses the restrained symbolic manner in his Asia House. And IM Pei, another Modernist trained under Walter Gropius, produced a restrained mixture of Chinese and Renaissance design for his hotel on the edge of Peking, also finished in 1982.

For Pei the experience was quite significant because it was the first time he used tradition in a representational manner. Appropriately enough, his Post-Modernism 203, 204 was prompted by a return to his home country, something that really engaged his architectural commitment. Of all his buildings it is the most rooted in culture, with the strongest sense of place. Although still committed to Modernism, Pei has acknowledged the necessity of ornament and symbolism in this building. Perhaps he will see their legitimacy in other cultures, although in his large volume of international work they have yet to appear. Like Kevin Roche, who is also taking tentative steps in this direction, he remains fundamentally committed to abstraction and seeing architectural problems in terms of the large sculptural gesture. Like SOM, who have actually held seminars on Post-Modern design, he is aware of the shift in architecture and will probably make use of the change in a small percentage of his commissions. The question facing all these large offices, some with multinational work in the Near East and places like Singapore, is how to ornament? If the tradition had died, and if a deep philosophy of ornament has not developed, can the results be anything but hesitant?

Books like *Ornamentalism* don't give that much aid, beyond a selection of largely American examples. The only philosophical treatise to appear, and I believe it to be

203, 204 IM PEI, *Hotel in the Fragrant Hills*, Peking, 1979-83. The large interior lobby is a grand Modernist space with a stylised decoration midway between Early Renaissance and stylised Chinese patterns. The courtyards and wall architecture are also extensions to the Chinese vernacular tradition. (IM Pei)

the most profound writing on the subject, is EH Gombrich's, *The Sense of Order*.[87] This elucidates ornament, or more generally pattern-making, from a psychological, historical and constructive viewpoint. It could well provide just the sort of grounding that is needed, if architects will take the trouble to study it thoroughly. Ornament, or ordering patterns, are seen as a fundamental way of making sense of a building. They give it visual logic and musical life. They lead the eye and mind forward to look for certain expectancies – a change in rhythm, a culminating theme, a beginning and end to an architectural idea. Perhaps the multinational designers will buy the time from their multimillion dollar practice to study this new science. As it is now, the first impetuous steps are being made by the smaller firms.

Kazuhiro Ishii, who has studied with Venturi and Moore, makes use of his American training in the Gable Building, an inexpensive office building in Tokyo. Here several ornamental motifs order the tall profile. The stepped gable culminates the vertical movement set up by the side edges and central balconies. These last white elements lead the eye upwards towards a broken semi-circle and split pediment – Venturian motifs – and thus the impression of a thin tower is created within the overall tower. This visual movement is rather Baroque and rhythmical since arches at the base are broken and the balconies are given slightly different articulation: the eye is kept moving up and down to where one expects a strong resolution. The expected Classical theme – base, shaft and capital – is partly fulfilled and yet partly denied since the usual Platonic forms are present, but eroded by dark voids. The stilted arches at the base are each cut on their inside edge to hang in space, a visual joke with a functional reason since they allow two entrances. But there is a perceptual logic to this joke as well, for it takes the cliché of the stilted arches and turns it into a new figure, a conjoined U-shape, which also reinforces the vertical movement. Thus a Free-Style Classicism revives one of the oldest stereotypes of the skyscraper, the tripartite elevation, in a fresh way.

Vertical movement has often been represented in the skyscraper, whose metaphysical purpose, after all, is to touch, scrape or pierce the heavens.[88] And this raises a major architectural point: besides representing ideas extraneous to building, architecture also represents itself. This tautology it shares with other arts. They are all concerned with their own language, their own possibilities *sui generis*. Thus if one asks about architectural representation, there will always be a double answer. The medium tells a story about society and pure architectural possibility. Two Post-Modern Classical skyscrapers, one in New York, the other in Houston, bring this out. Philip Johnson's AT&T tops the monumental slab form in a very effective way with an up-reaching split pediment. This crown is a dignified, indeed almost grave-like, culmination to all the verticals that shoot up around it and through it. The further one is away from the building, the better is the upturned profile. Unfortunately, when one gets too close, the kitsch detail and Golden Boy of AT&T, placed on the High Altar of this Pazzi Chapel, become not funny enough. Kitsch for commerce, pediment for skyscraping – this is the double formula.

This not very subtle argument and building show one of the undeniable characteristics of the New Representation: it has a tendency, like Pop Art, to be brash and obvious, hallmarks of a commercial society. At least one American

205 KAZUHIRO ISHII, *Gable Building*, Tokyo, 1978-80. The Dutch gable and Japanese Minka roof are mixed here, as Ishii states in a tablet inscribed for the passer-by. The entrance to the offices and Sushi bar are announced by the eroded arches. (Katsuaki Furudate)

206 PHILIP JOHNSON and JOHN BURGEE, *AT&T, Building*, New York, 1978-83. This media-event of Post-Modernism has become, in the event, a wonderful urban landmark when seen from a distance. The pink granite sheathing is also a welcome change from its repetitive neighbours. (Johnson and Burgee)

142, 143   architect, Stanley Tigerman, has developed this tendency as the subject-matter of his work. Many people, not surprisingly, find his explicit representation vulgar and exploitive. His Anti-Cruelty Society, for instance, represents a dog's face with part

209   of a false pediment, the stray dogs involved either being adopted or unceremoniously extinguished. Some people find this black humour upsetting, although it has to be said the building is ambiguous and quite friendly. Tigerman's Pensacola Place Apartments also use Classicist elements – balconies which form the shaft of an Ionic column, a top cornice which hides mechanical equipment – because they lend themselves to this layout. There is no reason housing has to look like an Ionic temple any more than a machine, and in that sense the imagery is arbitrary. But Tigerman, like Bofill, is arguing that Classical references are less odious for mass housing than Le Corbusier's *machine à habiter*.

Flat, brash, repetitive ornament – stylised and distorted – the formula that, as we've seen, Venturi proposes for an industrial society is perhaps one of the new rules, or canons of Free-Style Classicism. The Houston group called Taft have

207, 208   extended its use in all sorts of inexpensive buildings, and Terry Farrell in England has manipulated it with High-Tech details, again with ingeniously cheap methods of building. His television studios, TV-AM, manages to symbolise the exotic glamour of the medium – Japan, Mesopotamia and Hollywood – with thin, industrial materials. Perhaps the content of the symbolism is a bit trite – breakfast-egg decorations are turned into gigantic finials, because this is a breakfast television station. But then the content of TV programmes is often like a runny egg. And if the detailing looks cheap and expedient that's because it is: realism in a fast-moving industrial society means a quick, deft reaction to immediate possibilities. Farrell, like Norman Foster, knows how to exploit available techniques on the site.

There are, however, other attitudes towards Free-Style Classicism and new technology which result in a different kind of ornament. A group in Hungary called

207, 208 TERRY FARRELL, *TV-AM*, London, 1980-82. The central, public space culminates in a sunburst stair which acts as the focus of studio life. Eastern and Western images, Shinto Shrine and ziggurat, are set off against Hollywood. On the exterior, shades of industrial grey are used ornamentally with a cool sophistication. Farrell's exploitation of current technology on a decorative level is always fresh and pragmatic. (Richard Bryant)

209 STANLEY TIGERMAN, *Pensacola Place Apartments*, Chicago, 1978-81. Ionic silhouettes and flared cornice form the slab block into a gigantic hexastyle temple. The black window grid is reminiscent of Tigerman's Modernist slab block just behind this one. Compare with Bofill's more articulated Classicist housing. (Howard N Kaplan (c) HNK Architectural Photography)

210 GYORGY CSETE and JENO DULANSZKY, *Cave Research Station*, Pécs-Orfu Hungary, 1971-78. A geodesic dome is supported by a floral 'petal' in wood and a concrete base: the metaphorical equivalent of nature research is thus symbolised in the volume and stylised volutes and trefoils. A mixture of modern fabrication and hand-crafted ornament, nationalist and Celtic decorative motif. (Group Pécs)

211 ARATA ISOZAKI, *Tsukuba Civic Centre*, 1980-83. Flat steel frame and grid versus articulated masonry, Western Classical motifs versus High-Tech imagery, all of this disciplined within well-mannered surfaces. Certain literal borrowings from Ledoux and Michelangelo make some of the details rather notional, but their translation into a new scale and medium give them a certain life.

Pécs (from that city) mixes materials and genres in a decorative way. They have produced several hybrids of concrete, wood and steel, mixing traditional domes 210 and geodesic lanterns. Their work is highly suggestive of regional craft and local symbolism, such as the trefoil taken from wooden Hungarian grave markers. But they combine this national expression with both metaphorical forms – the flowering blossom – and the latest technology. They have followed the development of Post-Modernism in the West, and perhaps been influenced by the metaphorical work of Tigerman and Goff. Indeed, in Hungary as in Yugoslavia, Romania and Poland, Post-Modern developments are closely followed through the magazines and it wouldn't be surprising to see some more interesting developments coming from these countries in the near future.

Another approach to inventing a relevant ornament is to re-think the production methods and design elements that already have an order, or Classical Order, in them. In this case the ornament can be constructive and three-dimensional, much like Classical masonry of the past except usually at larger scale and in unmalleable material such as reinforced concrete. Arata Isozaki has mixed flat metallic surfaces with heavy quoins turned on the diagonal – sculptural masses 211 meant to recall Ledoux. Although Michelangelo is recalled in floor patterns, no sculptor has spent his angst-ridden time chipping away at blocks of stone. An academic Classicist, or an Italian, might be perturbed: how dare this motif be borrowed so brazenly? Looked at from Japan, however, the same theft can have a liberating effect because it is being absorbed into a new language of form, being combined with the syntax of rounded plastic forms and metallic sheets.

The most extraordinary invention of mass-produced ornament, or constructional ornament, is by Ricardo Bofill and his Taller de Arquitectura. Their scheme near Versailles called Les Arcades du Lac (because it borders an artificial lake) mass-produces arcades, window-walls, broken pediments at triple the usual scale, that is, about one storey high. New functions are poured into old forms – an end 212 column might be a stairway, or bathroom core. And a positive urban space is formed with this new constructional means – a pedestrian circus, or circular centre. The return to the notion of the 'heart of the city' is, as we've seen, a Post-Modern leitmotif. This new town area is well-scaled, successfully rented and as far as we can tell after a year's inhabitation, enjoyed by the user.

Much more controversial, and questionable because of its scale, is the Taller's Palace of Abraxas, also on the outskirts of Paris. Here again modern concrete is 213 used to do heavy Baroque tricks; again urban space is nicely moulded to form an enclosed 'theatre' that steps down to a large 'arch' and densely planted 'arbre'. But the handling of the Classical language and technology is more sure. Nine-storey fluted glass columns alternate with pilasters of masonry and carry a triple capital of planting surmounted by a cypress tree! Is it the New Corinthian Order? Will giant, hormone-injected acanthus leaves shoot out of the six-foot high planters? In case these surreal, inhabitable glass columns are not enough, Bofill has provided a ten-storey, live-in Arc de Triomphe (in fluted Doric concrete) and a nineteen-storey Palace of Abraxas (named after that magician who gives us the celebrated nonsense known as abracadabraca). It's a stimulating paradox, fitting for an architect who comes from the land of Don Quixote. Like Salvador Dali and Buñuel, from whom Bofill also learned, there's a great deal of realism involved in these fantasies. They appeal to almost everybody (whom they don't repulse); they remind Frenchmen that their Classicism is the most proud, hard-edged and militaristic version of this universal style; they lend drama to everyday life and above all give an interesting image that isn't just another dull Modernist machine.

Herein lies the revolutionary message. Bofill and the Taller have shown that mass-production is not necessarily tied to any language of form – the machine aesthetic, as has been argued this century. The greatest orthodoxy of our time, that the fabrication process leads to an inevitable industrial style, is shown to be false. There must be several possible languages of mass-production and, as the Egyptians discovered, Free-Style Classicism is one of them. The Taller is not only mass-producing new towns in a monumental Classical style, but also small individual villas, the popular house. They have made links with the large French construction company, Phoenix, who will churn out industrialised Palladian temples by the thousands. This 'Technological Classicism', as Peter Hodgkinson calls it, is quite different from some of the historicism we have looked at: as he says, 'Much of Post-Modern Classical revivalism is a fad pretending to relate to the past. The Marne-la-Vallée complex relates to the future. It is the Cape Canaveral of the Classical space age, the return to a people's ritual.'[89] It seems the people who live in and visit these monuments do prefer them to other mass-housing. They may be a trifle bombastic and over-dense in certain places, they may suffer from too much architecture, they may not be perfect in detail, but like the Brighton Pavilion, it's nice to have them around. For they show Post-Modern Classicism can have a three-dimensional, constructed ornament, that it can be put together with harmonic proportions and above all it can form positive urban space. We'll have to wait for five years and the sociological research before we can say it is either the Cape Kennedy of mass-housing, or an aborted space venture.

212 RICARDO BOFILL and the TALLER DE ARQUITECTURA, *Les Arcades du Lac*, St-Quentin-en-Yvelines, 1974-81. The heart of the scheme is a circular pedestrian piazza focusing on this enigmatic temple, another example of the Taller's mass-produced urban furniture in a Free-Style Baroque. The surrounding arcades are actually very small, while the end tower/columns are huge. The scale of pedestrian space is very pleasing and when the trees grow, the urban space should be quite sensual and public.

213 TALLER BOFILL, *Theatre of the Palace of Abraxas*, Marne-la-Vallée, 1978-82. A ten-storey amphitheatre is evenly divided into three visual storeys. Tuscan columns shoot up three storeys and are paired, giving a pleasing rhythm between windows; vertical circulation is behind fluted 'Art Deco' engaged columns throughout the ten storeys. The large vs small Order was a Michelangelesque motif and Bofill has been known to compare himself, modestly, to this character.

Abstract Representation – The Expressive Mode

While direct communication with its users remains the primary goal of Post-Modern Classicism, there is a more subtle and related one: architecture, as a poetic art, has levels of communication that are more powerfully suggested than specified. An architecture cannot afford to name everything, spell out all its messages in a clear, denotative language. To insist that it do so would be to reduce it to a revivalist genre: building rather than architecture. Among the practitioners of the 'New Classicism',[90] three develop it as a time-consuming art: Michael Graves, James Stirling and Hans Hollein. They also practise an expressive form of Classicism I have termed Abstract Representation, because it abstracts certain representational themes and uses them both in a stylised and recognisable way.[91] A series of pavilions I have designed with Buzz Yudell, The Elemental House, may make this concept clear.

The Elemental House is made from many rustic pavilions, or aediculae, organised loosely on a wooded site of a place called Rustic Canyon. These Classical 'temples' constitute the abstraction of a village, and one that is vaguely recognisable because it is pulled together by a colonnade of wooden piers. These in turn have plants growing up them – abstracted ornament – and their 'capitals' form an abstracted L and A (Rustic Canyon is part of Los Angeles). The pavilions are labelled *Terra, Aqua,* **214** *Aer* and have somewhat conventional sculpture in their pediments symbolising these elements, but the representations are again stylised to the point of abstraction. Finally, the swimming pool is in the abstracted shape of California with the pool lights marking the major cities. All of this representation is kept multivalent, ambiguous and suggestive. It is sometimes explicitly named in the rustic lettering but only enough to prompt the viewer to discover further meanings. The ornamental stencilling, for instance, abstracts signs of the Four Elements which are used in different ways throughout the site. Thus a theme and variation is used to create a narrative drama, a game of Hunt the Symbol.[92]

Nineteenth-century designers such as Owen Jones developed sophisticated theories of ornament which placed emphasis on a similar stylisation of historical patterns. Once abstracted from their source these patterns could be endlessly transformed like a musical theme and its variations, giving the ornament a dynamic life of its own. For Michael Graves, as for so many other Post-Modernists, this method of transformation has proved a fruitful way of using familiar themes without lapsing into cliché. For instance, at the Environmental Education Center, or what Graves calls less pompously the 'Frog Museum', he abstracts the square **215** window, the aedicule or temple form, the square pier and round capital ornament and then these shapes are constructed with very primitive and inexpensive means. The result, reminiscent of Leon Krier's designs, also recalls both vernacular and Classical architecture, but the proportions and flat construction are very much Graves' own trademark. They stem from the realities of modern construction (hence their taut simplicity), and the designer's admiration for heavy Egyptian architecture and particularly the nineteenth-century work of Peter Speeth. The Frog Museum, as an abstract representation of these various sources, is more effective than a literal recollection, because the memory is engaged in an active

214 CHARLES JENCKS and BUZZ YUDELL, *The Elemental House,* Rustic Canyon, Los Angeles, 1980-82. The Aer Pavilion is to the left, with Timothy Woodman's sculpture personification of Aer flying in its pediment; The Aqua Pavilion is to the right with Charles Moore's personification of Water; the California Pool is below, while all around are rough eucalyptus trees and rustic wood – the impetus for the Elemental style.

manner: it is forced to work over the material until its latent meanings are revealed. For instance, the strange entrance arch, or 'trellis-pediment', relates to bridge construction, a site-specific meaning since the museum is located overlooking the stretch of water near lower Manhattan. And the primitive nature of the forms is obviously meant to relate to the function of a wildlife centre located in a marsh.

For a library in San Juan Capistrano, Graves has abstracted a related grammar, this time one based on the Spanish Mission Style since that is the local vernacular. And here again the forms are heavy, reminiscent of Egyptian proportions and such things as obelisks, but in a general, not literal, way. Partly this is due to the fact that two related grammars are being consciously crossed, the Spanish Mission Style and the Hispanic architecture of South America, in particular the semi-curves of the former and 'light monitors' of the latter. The delightful village quality of this building springs from such crossings, a quality which is very playful without being trite, and one quite appropriate for dividing up a municipal library into semi-private places for reading.

No doubt Graves' ability to transform sources springs from his ability to draw. His notebooks are filled with many quick sketches, referential drawings of historic and vernacular buildings, which are abstracted and then combined in new ways. In a sense, he creates by elaborating pre-existing motifs until they look fresh and fitting to the new context, but they always carry over some memories of the past. This dual nature is what gives his work such a wide reference – it can call up the historical and the familiar without seeming hackneyed. This is particularly true of the Humana Headquarters Building, one of the most provocative skyscrapers built in recent years and a seminal work of Post-Modern Classicism, much more accomplished than the Portland Building because Graves was given a free hand and an adequate budget. The twenty-seven storey structure relates both to its Modern and nineteenth-century neighbours, quite a feat since they are so different in scale and appearance. The older street scale is held to one side with a lower frontage

215 MICHAEL GRAVES. *Environmental Education Center*, New Jersey, 1980-83. Vernacular forms of wood and stucco construction are abstracted and given a monumental form: the square piers have an almost Egyptian stateliness to them. Note also the entrance truss, a transformed arch and pediment. (Proto Acme Photo)

216 MICHAEL GRAVES, *San Juan Capistrano Public Library*, 1981-83. The Spanish Mission style of the area is alluded to with the pantiles, high light hoods, flat walls and heavy curves, but these signs of context are merged with other Classical ones to become more general. (Proto Acme Photo)

217, 218 while the huge, black Miesian box is acknowledged in material and abstraction on the other side. Abstract representations of several local structures are suggested – not explicitly named: the bridges of the Ohio River are recalled by the cantilevered trusses on the twentieth floor, the 1930s Louisville dam is recalled in the topmost semi-circular crown and the pervasive industrial Classicism is generalised in the square windows, large mouldings and tiny temples that mark the four horizons.

Such bold contrast of Classical shapes has been taken up by many large firms, such as Kohn Pedersen Fox, and now it has become a Post-Modern formula; but no one to date plays with these contrasts as forcefully as does Graves. His sculptural work is based on Corbusian composition – 'architecture as the masterly, correct and magnificent play of volumes in sunlight' – but now these violently juxtaposed volumes are given an urbane elegance. They also suggest, when looked at frontally, a symmetrical body or anthropomorphic figure. In the Louisville building this human presence confronts the river, giving scale and dynamism to what is actually inert material. The Humana Corporation is thus an abstract representation of the Classical humanist figure with its tripartite divisions – legs, torso, head – and a metaphor of the healing process with its emphasis on sun rooms, views over the river and water. Fountains, in particular, are used to suggest purification rites (and again the nearby Louisville dam). All in all it's a multivalent building which resolves into a tense whole the building task, anthropomorphism and urban landscape of the past and present.

James Stirling has, since about 1975, turned to a very understated form of Free-Style Classicism. His first schemes in this genre, for Germany, were low-key versions of a Schinkel grammar used on urbanistic schemes that both fitted in and contrasted with their surroundings. Since then, he has continued to elaborate this grammar very slowly and carefully. Indeed, if there is one thing that sets his and Hans Hollein's work apart from American Post-Modernism it is this patient thought: the opposite of 'fast-food architecture' – three or four buildings finished per year – is, I suppose, 'slow-food architecture'. It has taken both Stirling and Hollein at least seven years to finish their museums, and these were virtually the only moderate size buildings they were working on. Their quality of detail and thought stand out in this era of architectural inflation. If they pay a price for their lack of work and speed, it is the inability to test a lot of new ideas quickly, and use current imagery. High quality more than makes up for these drawbacks.[93]

The Stuttgart Museum, we have seen, is also a careful and low insertion into an urban fabric. Stirling reflects the Schinkelesque Classical plan to the left of his Museum by mirroring its U-shape. And he adopts many Classical motifs, including a rusticated base and Egyptian cornice. The rustication in layers of travertine and sandstone roots the building on the ground and in the Stuttgart fabric. But, whereas this handling of masonry is traditional – even Romanesque, the sudden imposition of a brightly painted metal awning is anything but Neo-Classical. It is decidedly Post-Modern, as harsh a collage as anything Le Corbusier might have done, and similar to the way Mario Botta confronts tradition and modern technology, giving neither a supreme role. It's probably for the same reason. They both feel the present condition of culture – and the Stuttgart buildings are cultural institutions –

217, 218 MICHAEL GRAVES, *Humana Corporation Medical Headquarters*, Louisville, Kentucky, 1982-86, model and view from Main Street. The building mediates between the large Modernist block to the left and nineteenth-century building to the right, using a basic tripartite division, setbacks and square windows. Anthropomorphic elements – head, shoulder and body – can be seen on all the elevations. (Paschall/Taylor)

demands a juxtaposition of conflicting ideologies, not a resolution.

Hence the vibrant De Stijl awnings (violent red, blue and yellow set in angst-ridden dissonance) seem to be from another world-view than the serene Classical background. Like Graves, Stirling uses the tiny square windows high up on his vernacular 'barn', the rendered blank walls. These serve again like Graves', as a white canvas, a breathing space between ornamented entrance and edges. This carefully detailed background finds dynamic contrasts throughout: the green undulating entrance lobby, the steel temple-gate, the yellow mushroom column. Dissonance has always been an aesthetic strategy with Stirling and we can see his urban reasons for it. It represents, again in an abstract way, the palimpsest that is any historic city, the collisions of Rowe's Collage City.

The central rotunda, an outdoor sculpture gallery, is one of the most successful public spaces created in the last twenty years, a well-scaled place that mixes sacred and profane meanings in equal measure. Here Stirling's skill at manipulating historical precedent in a new way is used to great purpose. Each formal element carries a wide range of associations and solves a functional problem. Echoes of the Pantheon Rotunda are combined with the ruin of Hadrian's villa to contain a beautifully scaled space open to the sky as a paradoxical 'domeless dome'. Contrasts of meaning and time further the delightful ambiguity: an eighteenth-century portico after Weinbrenner is the focus of a modern stairway. All of this 219 eclecticism feels quite inevitable and fresh, a suitable outdoor room protected from the noise and traffic of a modern metropolis. The quality of the urbanism and symbolic use of high-tech ornament make the Stuttgart Museum, along with Humana, a paradigm of Post-Modernism, just as the Bauhaus and Villa Savoye were exemplars for the previous movement.

The Museum has now become the significant building type of the eighties, the most suitable place for architectural expression and symbolism. Stirling's Clore Gallery, an extension to the Tate Museum in London, takes some of his previous urban ideas to an extreme, changing its facade five times to relate to adjacent buildings. This exaggerated contextualism, and discontinuity, has the virtue of 220 showing a Post-Modern idea in its ultimate form, the idea that different taste-cultures and functional requirements should have priority over an homogeneous expression and over-simple unity. In this cheerful building, an order of square motifs, used at different scales, pulls the variety together. Unfortunately, an unusual choice of colours, and the beige background for the Turner paintings, dominated all journalistic comment on the building and its very real virtues have gone unremarked. But the building is likely to 'settle down' as Stirling has said and, when the vegetation has grown over the pergola and trellis, become the modest kind of garden pavilion he intended.

Hans Hollein, a friend of Stirling, has spent a considerable time shaping and detailing his museum at Mönchengladbach. Originally designed in 1972, it was constructed from 1976 to 1982 and this time-lag shows in the lack of explicit ornament and symbolism. But in other respect, it's as fine a space and museum as one will find today. No doubt this is due to the patience with which Hollein, a designer of furniture and interiors, has detailed it. And yet, conceptually too, it's a

219 JAMES STIRLING, MICHAEL WILFORD and ASSOCIATES, *Neue Staatsgalerie*, Stuttgart, 1977-84. A wandering path culminates in an outdoor room, the sculpture gallery, a rotunda space with its 'domeless dome' created by the illusion of the sky being held by curved walls. A sunken portico, after Weinbrenner, and other historicist quotes are given new uses and meaning in this *res publica* isolated from urban traffic and noise. (Richard Bryant)

220 JAMES STIRLING, MICHAEL WILFORD and ASSOCIATES, *Clore Gallery*, London, 1982-86. This 'garden building' with its pergola, pool and trellis, adapts the Classical grammar of the Tate and brick vernacular of an adjacent building to become a complex mediation of its context. Mannerist touches can be seen in the 'hanging brick' (right) and the fact that the building changes material and rhythm not on the corners, as expected, but half way down one facade and on the diagonal! (Richard Bryant)

complex masterpiece. Fundamentally the scheme is an acropolis,[94] a group of temples and warehouses of art, set on a hill enclosed by a public terrace – almost a *temenos*. Undulating brick forms spill down the hill, conceptually vineyards in front of the acropolis, but holding luscious plants. On top of this is the main propylaeum in marble with its honorific column in stainless steel; then behind is the main administration building – less of a temple and more of an office building with eroded undulations which echo the brick walls. Further buildings to left and right are a lecture hall and galleries. These are in still other forms and materials, so the effect of a complex collage is, as in Stirling's work, omnipresent. And the abstraction of themes is so great, or subtle, that they are occasionally missed. But, what is being represented here is an acropolis of related but different 'temples'. They may not have pediments, but their material and treatment mark them as special. The grid of sandstone and polished aluminium facing, especially the way the mirror-plate window catches the reflection of the cathedral opposite, all mark the intention. It is a celebration of art, the local context and the significance of building types.

If, on the outside, the Museum is being equated with the Acropolis and set as the twentieth-century equivalent of the adjacent church, then, on the inside, the meaning of art is given a different significance. For here a complex Post-Modern space allows the viewer to travel through the collection of Modern Art in four or five ways. The implication is that there are various ways to interpret the destiny of Modernism: not one *Zeitgeist* and story, as it used to be taught, but a plurality of meanings. But, this again is only a suggestion of the plan and space. It is abstracted, not given a single label marked 'pluralism'.

Arata Isozaki, who has written on Hollein and Stirling, quite naturally follows a similar paradigm in his museum buildings. His temple for Modern Art in Los Angeles, MOCA, is as one would guess an eclectic mixture of western sources with hidden eastern references, all abstracted to the point of extreme ambiguity. Pyramidal galleries, a Renaissance garden, a diagonal trellis motif in steel (shades of Michael Graves), and the Palladian motif above the entrance gate are clearly western, while the sunken courtyard entrance, Indian sandstone and yin/yang circulation patterns are not so evidently eastern. There may be no great logic in the choice of languages or imagery, but the juxtapositions of styles and motifs again signify a generalised pluralism and the notion that art must today reflect this heterogeneity.

More single-minded is Gae Aulenti's conversion, along with French architects, of an old railroad station into a museum of nineteenth-century art. Here Egyptian motifs and proportions are abstracted to produce, where the trains used to arrive, very heavy walls and tight spaces that one might find in a Nile temple. The Egyptian style is only present as an abstract representation – there are no solar discs or lotus columns – and it is fairly suitable as a stable background for viewing sculpture and paintings. It also contrasts effectively with the ornate Beaux-Arts architecture and filigree of structure and top lighting. Like her conversions of the Pompidou Centre, the new Musée d'Orsay abstracts a generalised Classicism to calm down a voluble, indeed highly argumentative, structure. Unfortunately, her interventions have been

221

222

223

221 HANS HOLLEIN, *Stäedtiches Museum Abteiberg*, Mönchengladbach, 1976-82. The enclosed piazza in the air, or 'temenos', connects the 'propylaeum' left, with the city. The administration and galleries are to the right.

222 ARATA ISOZAKI, *Museum of Contemporary Art (MOCA)*, Los Angeles, 1982-86. A curved 'Palladian' window surmounts the library, while a diagonal pattern on green sheet steel indicates the administrative block. Indian red sandstone unifies most of the museum in this understated use of Western Classical sources. These subtle forms are used to create a constantly changing route full of gentle surprises, something that does not overpower the art.

criticised for being too reminiscent of Michael Graves and Egyptian precedent, and for competing with the nineteenth-century building: but this criticism might well be inverted, because the impressive fact is that Post-Modern conventions have finally been used with great skill and sensitivity.

Countless framed views through tight apertures reveal many interesting contrasts of the nineteenth century. The avant-garde is given its sequence of rooms, the Academy its parallel set of *petits salons* and every now and then the space opens upon a surprising set-piece which forces one to confront the horrific and contradictory beauty of the previous century. One end of the train shed/nave focuses on Charles Garnier's Paris Opera House, which now can be walked over because Aulenti has sunk a model underneath a glass floor. On one side of the major transept are two, somewhat kitsch, products of academia which are used as commentary on the role of the museum today. The placement of *The Romans of* 224 *the Decadence*, by Thomas Couture (*sic*), is the supreme piece of curatorial wit and the way it is framed and set up by the architectural promenade vindicates the design as well. For it is the quality and liveliness of the spaces which here heighten our perception of meaning. Small-scaled spaces, contained like closed rooms, are punched apart to reveal parallel movements and contrasts. As in Hollein's museum there is the possibility of both linear and comparative history, a sequence of schools and opposition of movements. I can't think of any museum which handles such contradiction any better, and particularly that between small, domestic art and large-scale public works. By adapting the conventions of Post-Modern space – its layering, surprise and historical associations – Aulenti has been able to control, even perfect, her medium. The subtle colour contrasts and skilful handling of different materials show the kind of high quality which can only be reached when one works within a tradition.

223 GAE AULENTI and ACT, *Musée d'Orsay* conversion, Paris, 1980-86. A gently rising nave space contains nineteenth-century sculpture while different schools of painting are located behind the abstracted Egyptian forms in small spaces which are delicately layered, beautifully lit and subtly detailed in related forms of masonry. (Justin Jencks)

224 *Musée d'Orsay*. Sculpture, painting, train shed and interior architecture placed in meaningful contrast. Jean-Baptiste Carpeaux's *Ugolin*, Thomas Couture's *Les Romains de la Decadence*, Victor Laloux's coffers and arches, and Gae Aulenti's masonry walls and frames – in ironic but respectful conversation with each other. (Justin Jencks)

Post-Modernism Becomes A Tradition, Fifth Edition, 1987

Post-Modernism has become a widespread tradition in the 1980s with many large offices producing huge works at great speed: Philip Johnson, SOM (when they eschew Modernism) and KPF (Kohn Pedersen Fox). This situation produces its problems: as the reader will remember, Modernism suffered from over-production and the vulgarisation of its language, and there is no reason to suppose the new tradition will not ultimately succumb to these same pressures. Already there is enough kitsch Post-Modernism for some to declare the movement middle-aged, if not moribund; so the few large-scale buildings which have managed to evade this death sentence are especially relevant. They survive not because of their innovations or personality, but for the quality of their construction and the thoughtfulness with which they carry through the new conventions.

KPF, the most commercially successful Post-Modern firm, have produced thirty or more skyscrapers using the contextualist arguments of the tradition. For the
226 Procter & Gamble Headquarters in Cincinnati, they have abstracted an Art Deco language of truncated pyramids and stepped octagons. These forms are placed at a key juncture of the city where the expressway meets downtown. To mark this urban gateway, they have designed two rather squat towers sheathed in white and grey masonry. This language continues that of the pre-existing building, then subtly bends it towards more urban ends, forming a park-like setting on the city side. The interior carries through the grammar of octagons, white marble and stainless steel with a precision and consistency that is rare in a large building. Predictably there are no surprises and little individuality here – it *is* Procter & Gamble after all – yet the sheer professionalism commands respect. Who else but a large integrated firm could achieve a consistent quality at such a scale and down to such detail?

For the most part KPF adopts an Art Deco Classicism, coloured by modern
225 production methods and a Gravesian manner, but occasionally they aim at a more revivalist mode and produce an almost canonic Classicism. Such is their New York skyscraper of residences on the upper East Side, a building in brick with white mouldings top and bottom. This could have been built at any time from 1900 to 1935 except that its Classical details are blown up in scale and abstracted. Again the detailing is commendable and the contextualism makes sense: the street front mounts straight up to a crown of three arches while the side cascades down to acknowledge an adjacent skyscraper with related stepped forms.

Contextualism has provided the most acceptable public excuse for the return to historical forms and thus it has emerged as a major argument for those former Modernists committed, as they were, to a rationalist aesthetic. Cesar Pelli and Tom Beeby are the most skilful of these recent converts and the excellence of their architecture reminds us, once again, that the best Post-Modernists still keep one eye firmly focused on their former training and belief. Pelli, whose office is nearly as productive as KPF, will adapt practically any visual grammar based on the local context, but he always treats it as a thin curtain wall that reveals – for those who care to look – the reality of the steel construction underneath. Thus his work on the Rice campus in Texas takes the pre-existing Romanesque Style – rendered in red brick and white masonry – and gives it a contemporary jazz rhythm of staccato

225 KOHN PEDERSEN FOX ASSOCIATES, *Condominium 70th St*, New York, 1984-87. A Classical skyscraper, with base, middle and top, holds the street front while also cascading down to an adjacent stepped building. KPF have emerged as the professionals of contextualism. (Jock Pottle)

226 KOHN PEDERSEN FOX ASSOCIATES, *Procter and Gamble Headquarters*, Cincinnati, 1982-86. Two truncated towers mark the city gateway to one side and contain an urban park on the other side. An octagonal geometry rendered in white, silver and grey ties the old building with the new.

227 CESAR PELLI & ASSOCIATES, *Rice Jones School*, Houston, Texas, 1983-85. A contextual skin is hung on a steel frame in such a way that the underlying construction is revealed. Both the diaper pattern of bricks and the lines of the thin walls are emphasised and thus the historical language is given new rhythms and meaning. (Paul Hester)

228 CESAR PELLI & ASSOCIATES, *Proposed Carnegie Hall Extension*, New York, 1986. The familiar Post-Modern treatment of a skyscraper, in colour and articulation, is enlivened by the rigorous use of a thin skin and the re-interpretation of traditional motifs, such as the cornice, in terms of new functions – for window cleaning equipment. (Cesar Pelli)

229 KISHO KUROKAWA, *Wacoal Building*, Tokyo, 1982-85. Kurokawa's eclecticism resolves an unusual array of styles and motifs within a grey aesthetic. The scale of this large headquarters is broken down by a tartan of small grids which are punctuated by advertisement and signs of the Edo Period, absorbed into a totality without conflict or irony. (K Kurokawa)

horizontals and ribbon windows. The rhythms of shape are emphasised by a change in material, from brick to steel to glass, and are underlined by a change in colour, from pink to Burgundy red. On the ends of the two long wings is a diaper pattern of bricks punctuated at random and with side walls sliding by and visually separated. This punctuation and immaculate separation underline the rationalist 227 point that the cladding is a thin veneer, not a real Romanesque structure of stone. So the truth of construction is expressed. Furthermore, it becomes a pretext for inventing new rhythms and proportions in an old language. Thus while the context provides the rationale for the chosen grammar, the structure and construction provide the cues to how it is articulated. This keeps almost all of Pelli's buildings fresh and honest and, it must be admitted, slightly flat-chested and awkward, like adolescent girls.

Pelli, like James Stirling, takes particular pleasure in showing the logic of construction and this may result in a truncated top, as at Rice, or a brittle surface that accentuates flatness. Most of his Modernist work achieved an extraordinary tense quality – like the Blue Whale – because it developed the thin skin that elided glass wall and mullion. This 'membrane aesthetic' has now been pushed in a Post-Modern direction with the introduction of complex ornamental patterns and polychromy. The resultant mixture is unusual enough to deserve a new name – High-Tech Contextualism – and it can be seen in the proposed addition to Carnegie Hall in New York. Here the pre-existing Renaissance grammar is shot 228 upwards to sixty storeys and flattened out in a crisp grid of well-proportioned rectangles and areas of contrasting colours. The spiky structure at the top, which carries window cleaning equipment, becomes the contemporary equivalent of a cornice. Pelli, the typical Post-Modernist here, is looking for new uses and proportions for old forms.

Kisho Kurokawa, the Japanese architect, often achieves a similar mixture, what he calls an 'architecture of symbiosis'. Past, present and future are consciously synthesised into an ambiguous whole and the results are beautifully enigmatic. One is never quite sure whether the synthesis is, in the end, incongruous or limpid. In either case, it is masterfully done, harmonious and just a bit facile. Whereas Stirling will confront past, present and future as if there were no question of peaceful coexistence between them, Kurokawa will blend them together into a seamless web. His Wacoal building, for a major lingerie manufacturer, looks directly at the Emperor's Palace in the heart of Tokyo. Here is a potentially fraught and ironic situation – the eye of fashion, women's panty girdles and so forth, focused directly on the centre of Japanese tradition and power. Commerce confronts culture, the 229 ephemeral dominates the permanent, at least in scale and visibility. Kurokawa is intensely conscious of such oppositions, but unlike a Westerner he chooses to smooth over the differences. Thus, in the Wacoal Building, the emblematic 'eye of fashion' is both a telescope looking into the future of *haute couture* and a somewhat traditional rising sun, with signs from the Edo Period, looking at the Emperor and the past. A Roman barrel vault is rendered in a newly-invented glass material which emphasises the slickness and sensuality of the surface. Indeed Kurokawa describes the structure as a 'pleasure machine' and one can find many parallels between the

inherent sensuality of the product — skin-hugging lingerie — and the quality of the finish. In one place an artist has impressed the nude female body onto the glistening steel facade. On the ninth floor, in a reception room, polished and reflective surfaces in various shades of grey again convey the hedonistic mood of luxuriant sensuality. But this space is more than an up-market boutique, much more. It's an integrated kaleidoscope of heterogeneous meaning.   230

The doorway is adapted from the work of the Renaissance architect Giacomo della Porta, the walls have Japanese brackets and sliding screens and the columns are a new Order with mirrors top and bottom that dissolve their weight. This mixture, to distinguish it from Pelli's, might be called High-Tech Eclecticism, yet the synthesis, or 'symbiosis', is so complete that one might well overlook the differences in language, mood and meaning. In this way Kurokawa comes closest to conveying the homogenised variety of an information society, the way it will incorporate all contradictions into a total ideology or life-style. Some will damn this as consumerist and argue that it suppresses experience and dissent, much as did Modernism. But like the Baroque style, with which it shares totalising motives, it can actually enhance experience and choice if it is done well enough.

There have been many calls for a synthesis of technology and cultural expression, which amount more to statements of intent than announcements of success. Cesar Pelli, Kisho Kurokawa, Helmut Jahn, Mario Botta and others are trying to reach this middle ground. The desire for synthesis is a very real one and it is not just confined to architects; but it still remains on the horizon. Through the abstract representation of themes, the opposite poles of technology, on the one hand, and history, context and anthropomorphism, on the other hand, are brought into a tenuous form of union. The Taft group from Houston, for instance, redirects technical requirements within a Palladian solution so that what were previously chimneys in the eighteenth century now become complex service ducts, handling the electrical, mechanical and plumbing runs. Their River Crest Country Club in   231
Fort Worth Texas, has four massive stacks which orient the building to the four horizons. The Palladian image, clad mostly in banded brick, is directly based on traditional American prototypes such as Stratford Hall in Virginia. But at certain points — in the concrete base and metal windows — there is a hint of the steel reality which holds the whole thing up. Such contradictions between image and reality are played down by Taft, and one may well ask whether this sublimation is not closer to traditional architecture than it is to Post-Modernism. Clearly the latter type of building must express the difference between truth and illusion as well as their occasional correspondence, and the conventional aspect of artifice as well as its occasional naturalness.

The London buildings of Terry Farrell are in this respect more self-conscious than those of the Taft group, the artifice of Classicism is more clearly played against the current conventions of fabrication. Farrell inevitably adopts the tripartite elevation for these city buildings, using ·the normal repertoire of rustication, abstracted pediments and rotunda, but he also features the bolted-together construction, the stainless steel washers and bands, so there is no doubt about how thin the masonry really is and how it is clipped on. These bolts and clips recall Otto

230 *Wacoal Building*, executive reception room in shades of grey mixes traditional sliding screens and brackets with a Free Style Classical Order, in the centre, which has a dissolving capital and weightless mirror base. The 'symbiosis' of east and west, high-tech and tradition. (K Kurokawa)

231 TAFT, *River Crest Country Club*, Fort Worth, Texas, 1983-86. The members asked for a Classical building and received this Palladian, nine-square solution with its banded base of concrete and tile, and its synthesis of steel and brick. The upraised chimneys mark the four horizons with a monumental presence. (Taft Architects)

Wagner's Post Office Savings Bank, just as the general massing, flared cornices and
232 abstract representation of themes recall Michael Graves. Thus, the Fenchurch
Street building gains its presence more through the sensible way it fills out the site
than through its originality, and Farrell's particular virtue is in making his contextual
interventions seem pleasingly inevitable. Here on a corner triangular site he has
taken the two street facades of either side, continued their cornice lines and
rhythms and turned the corner with the customary 'hinge' – a rotunda surmounted
by a huge abstracted column. The banded masonry and steel ornament have a
crisply detailed look, a precisionist quality which emphasises their flatness. In
contrast to other such work, the effect is neither insubstantial nor gratuitous, as the
various themes are incorporated into an overall geometrical abstraction.

Tom Beeby, previously in the Miesian tradition like so many other Chicago
architects, also attempts a synthesis of opposite qualities through an abstract
representation of structure and historical imagery. His American Academy of
Pediatrics again shows a Post-Modern Classical formula of banded masonry
contrasted with steel structure, closed and permanent forms set off by more open
and light-hearted ones. Basically, on the lakeside elevation, it's an octastyle temple
front crowned by the white outline of a steel pediment (which is cleverly the half-
233 conic section of an atrium in the back), with palazzo book-ends and a rusticated
base. The plan shows the same free-style mixture of Classical precedents which call
on Mies and Palladio equally. The restrained gravitas of the whole building might
have appealed to both of Beeby's exemplars – except for the robust colouring.
With this building, Post-Modernism returns to the knowing game of constructional
representation where brick pilasters divide up the surface into well-proportioned
rhythms and every other one signifies the actual steel construction inside. But,
whereas Palladio or Mies would have confined himself to the use of homogeneous
materials and structure, Beeby uses brick cladding, limestone trim and steel plate
columns and cornice – the last two painted in strong colours. As a result the
building manages to be both serious and lively, background and foreground. It takes
on a series of 'both-and' antinomies, just as Venturi recommended, which mediate

232 TERRY FARRELL PARTNERSHIP, *Fenchurch Street* bank and
offices, London, 1984-87. This contextualist building fills its
corner site with the customary tripartite elevation which is
given a nicely layered articulation as the three parts are subtly
independent. (Justin Jencks)

233 HAMMOND, BEEBY AND BABKA, *American Academy of
Pediatrics*, Elk Grove Village, Illinois, 1984-85. A set of Classical
types is cleverly combined and hung on a steel frame which is
symbolised in the brick pilasters and illusionistic pediment.
The robust colouring recalls nineteenth-century theories of
Classic polychromy. (Tom Beeby)

between the extremes of technical necessity and cultural expression.

Even more thoroughly dualistic than Beeby is the Belgian Charles Vandenhove, an architect who also departed from an earlier Miesian approach based on constructional purity. His work has developed patiently in a direction which uniquely combines technical and semantic aspects, using constructional elements such as the precast column to carry specific contextual meaning. These virtually constitute a new Order of architecture, something which ties Vandenhove to the Western tradition in a much more direct way than either, for instance, Robert Venturi or Quinlan Terry. Where the former will parody Classicism and the latter copy it, Vandenhove will imitate its spirit using the current technology. Furthermore, he gives artists a primary role in articulating a building or urban space. One of his most convincing works is the reconstruction of a small part of Liège, Hors-Château, which consists of single-family dwellings grouped around a tiny pedestrian square. For this he has invented the 'Liège Order', a post and beam system in concrete, that articulates the most significant entries with an amusing but beautiful 234 version of the Ionic Order, with its bull's-eye volutes. In the background he uses the more appropriate and understated version of the Doric, with T-capitals and stepped architraves. Cast-iron window boxes repeat the steps in a different key, and the sculpture, by Anne and Patrick Poirier, which gives the new square its name, rings yet another change on the motif, turning it into a totem-like ziggurat. The texture of this rehabilitated *place* recalls that of the past, since the new post 235 and beam structure is comparable in scale to what existed; but because the Order so successfully fuses an ornamental and constructional logic it avoids anachronism.

In his other work, Vandenhove has continued to mix approaches which invariably have remained separate. For the sixteenth-century Hotel Torrentius, where he now lives and works, he has grafted square geometries and a Secessionist 236 vocabulary onto the former Renaissance building to produce an inclusive whole which combines various periods of art as well. For the Opera in Brussels, he has worked with the artists Sol LeWitt, Sam Francis, Daniel Buren, and Giulio Paolini to redesign several key spaces, including a paradoxical marble chamber which reverses expectations. On the ceiling hang sculptural fragments, on the floor are suggestions of wooden beams, while Paolini's sculpture is duplicated in reverse at either end. In such interventions, his control of constructional elements comple- 237 ments the art and the pre-existing building. Classical precedent underlies these structures, but so too does a Modern sensibility. In this way, Vandenhove is something of a missing link between the past and present, a character who would be much more in evidence today if traditional architecture had continued to evolve along with technology and not been displaced by the Modern Movement.

Several Post-Modernists, such as Tom Beeby, Michael Graves, Monta Mozuna and Charles Vandenhove have carried on an inclusive architecture which makes use of the differing building arts as a related totality. Construction, ornament, furniture and works of art are brought into play together in a way that recalls at once the nineteenth-century *Gesamtkunstwerk* and traditional architecture, where these totalities could be expected. Such work, where all the parts are related, produces a resonant whole, something I have termed 'symbolic architecture' to

234 CHARLES VANDENHOVE, *Portico to Place Tikal*, Hors-Château, Liège, 1980. The entryways and important points of Vandenhove's buildings are articulated with invented Orders, both beautiful and technically current, that relate to those of the past. (Ch Bastin & J Evrard)

235 CHARLES VANDENHOVE, *Renovation in Hors-Château*, Liège, 1978-85. Sixteenth-century *hôtels* restored with a new polished concrete Order (left) and apartment building with its prefabricated grid of post and beams and window boxes (right). This new/old fabric contains the Place Tikal, a square with several sculptural monuments including *Tikal* by Anne and Patrick Poirier. (Ch Bastin & J Evrard)

236 CHARLES VANDENHOVE, *Renovation at the Hotel Torrentius*, Liège. The Renaissance grammar has been kept, in part, repainted by Olivier Debre and then extended by Vandenhove's fireplace and columnar mullions in bronze. Fragments of Renaissance murals complete this Post-Modern *Gesamtkunstwerk*. (Charles Vandenhove)

distinguish it from the compilation of elements and signs, or 'signolic architecture'.[95]
Robert Venturi's notion of the 'decorated shed' illustrates the latter approach,
238 while my own work in collaboration with others attempts to be symbolic –
especially when it is designed under the guidance of an iconographic programme.
Here, an overriding theme unifies the building and plastic arts, a sequence or
narrative route is conceived, and signs of all sorts are used – including words and
phrases - to clarify the many types of meaning.

Such integration is obviously easier to achieve in a traditional, slow-changing
building type, such as a church, than in a flexible, often-changing office or
commercial building. This is why Venturi and others support the idea of a functional
shed with signs attached to it. But while Venturi's signolic architecture was important and liberating in 1972 because it reaffirmed the necessity for considering signs,
by the 1980s it had led to many dissociated buildings with caricatured motifs stuck
all over them. The reaction against this shoddy building (*not* of the Venturis, it
should be emphasised) was both professional and public, and the Post-Modernism
that has grown as a result is more tied to the integration of the building arts with
construction and geometry than their gratuitous collage. The fundamentalist
239 Classicism of Mario Botta is typical of this reaction as it mixes primitive stepped
forms with brick construction, a primary shape grammar (circles and squares) with
vestigial mouldings, and the extreme mannerist contrast of interior technology
erupting through an exterior envelope that looked permanent.

The Mississauga City Hall, by Ed Jones and Michael Kirkland, is also characteristic
of this trend, a type of proto-symbolic architecture which stops short of an
iconographic programme, but one that nonetheless resolves function, image,
technology and sign. In that sense it becomes a resonant, symbolic architecture.
Although not a seminal work of Post-Modernism, as are Stirling's Stuttgart Museum
240 and Graves' Humana, it does show, like Aulenti's Musée d'Orsay, the virtues of
working within an inclusive tradition. This city hall combines various influences – the
small block composition of Leon Krier, some formal motifs of Aldo Rossi, Rob Krier
and James Stirling – and it makes them fitting for a public building located in
Canadian suburbia, midway between urban Toronto and a farming community.
Hence its mixture of an industrial and civic language, a clock tower held on steel
cross-bracing, and the abstracted pediments and rotunda. The signs are complex
and conventional enough to root the building in the community. Like a medieval
city hall the belfry and palace element dominate the *res publica* in front, an open
square shaded on three sides by colonnades. The basic functions are placed within
Platonic solids so that one can recognise the difference between the bureaucracy
and the assembly, the office tower and cylindrical council chamber. Banded
masonry is used as an ornamental motif and it increases in scale, colour and
emphasis as one walks through the sequence to its final culmination in the rotonda,
the symbolic heart of a downtown that one hopes will come to exist in the future.
All this is carried through in a sober yet dynamic language which can speak
coherently of place, function and history. Perhaps this sobriety and modesty have a
particular virtue now as they show Post-Modern Classicism in its most inclusive
role as a language open to different taste cultures, to an élite, a profession and the

237 CHARLES VANDENHOVE, *Le Salon Royal*, Renovation
in the *Théâtre de la Monnaie*, Brussels, 1986. Guilio Paolini's
sculpture is rotated in opposition, connected by thin bronze
wires and fragmented on the ceiling; the floor stripes are by
Daniel Buren; a running frieze, blank windows and icy marble
complete this surreal installation by Vandenhove. (Charles
Vandenhove)

238 CHARLES JENCKS, *Summer Room* with Sun Table and
Chairs and symbols of summer in the radiators, lights and
overall ambience. Allen Jones' personification of Summer
dancing can be seen reflected in the mirror, and the rest of
the Thematic House, designed with Terry Farrell Partnership,
takes on themes of the seasons, time and the cosmos.
(Richard Bryant)

159

public which will use the building.

One of the attractions of the Civic Center is the way it becomes a variegated fortress set in an open landscape. From a distance the massive solids in wheat-coloured brick contrast with the big sky and flat prairie, rather like a medieval citadel done in Cotswold stone. Cream colours are set against blue and green following a well-proven formula only slightly marred by the eclecticism of the campanile which never makes up its mind whether it is a Romanesque tower, engineering structure or blue *cabanon*. The positive intention, as in Graves' Humana, is to recall local buildings, but here the parts have dominated over the whole. Also there's a tendency for the volumes to be too heavy, especially the office tower and most of all the cylindrical Council Chamber, which surely should have risen above the pediment-building of councillors' suites to announce the priority of politics over administration. The danger courted by all civic structures since the United Nations Building in New York, is that of allowing the image of bureaucracy to triumph over the symbol of democracy. Nonetheless, in Mississauga the basic approach of small block planning and collage of Classical solids is particularly dynamic, especially from the south-east where each volume sets off the next in a sequence of contrasts. Square pavilion, semi-circular amphitheatre, broad pediment, campanile, tower, cylinder and rectangle – a basic typology of urban forms is juxtaposed on an axial plan and 'architectural promenade'.

241   Actually the central axis, north-south, has two minor cross-axes which are divided roughly by the pediment-building, thus forming an important opposition between the public and government. The public is given ceremonial assembly
242 space either in an amphitheatre, or between the colonnades, the 'embracing arms'. These focus in one direction on a central column and 'rostrum' (shades of both Leon and Rob Krier) and in the other, on the endless prairie void. No doubt all this owes much to the Post-Modern tradition, but it also extends the tradition in an important way. The *raison d'être* of a democratic architecture is the agora, the general assembly of citizens, and even if this usually has a ritualistic function in a television democracy, there is the opportunity here for it to be something more.

239 MARIO BOTTA, *Office Building*, Lugano, Switzerland, 1981-85. A Platonic geometry, with brick used in ornamental patterns, is eroded to reveal a stern, high-tech interior. Botta achieves many Mannerist contrasts including an overall 'big/ smallness', here realised by adopting a simple, small figure and using it at gigantic scale. (A Flammer)

240 ED JONES AND MICHAEL KIRKLAND, *Mississauga Civic Center*, 1982-87. The view from the southeast reveals the opposition of primary building types: colonnade, amphitheatre, pediment building, campanile, tower and rotonda – an object lesson in small block composition reminiscent of Leon Krier's School for 500 Children. (Robert Burley)

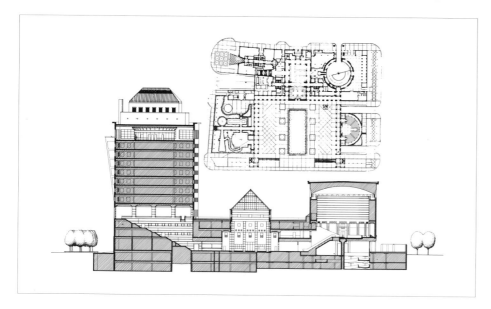

241 *The plan* reveals the architectural promenade from the south public area to the north governmental area, and the two secondary cross-axes. The section shows the sequence through high and low volumes connected by The Great Hall; the office tower and Council Chamber are both connected by forced perspectives.

The pediment forms the background for these assemblies, the porous 'arms' hold the space which opens up appropriately into the landscape. Thus, the notion of the people's government is effectively symbolised as prior to and distinct from representational government.

244   One enters the representational institution from the north through a Great Hall surmounted by a glass pyramid. This building type developed from Ed Jones' former scheme for the Northampton County Hall, 1973, and it amounts to one more giant northern atrium, a protective space for the long winters. The bands of black and green marble now play the exterior theme in a more sensual key, an appropriate intensification – except that it makes the culminating bands of the Council Chamber look rather bland by comparison. The atrium again repeats the motif of the rostrum over an arch and the small square window in different rhythms, a formula of many Post-Modern Classicists.

    From this point the architectural promenade forks, one way up a perspectival
243 stair to the office tower, the other way up an escalator to the rotunda. Here one reaches the Holy of Holies, the Pantheon with its dark blue ceiling of constellations and child-book Indian legends, its Gravesian-Roman mixture of paired columns, sconces, lettering and rusticated bands. This space looks reduced in height from eleven to seven bands and, as mentioned, it might well be bigger on the outside. The exterior and interior of the rotonda in the Asplund-Gravesian manner are a bit of an anti-climax to this promenade, which is due in no small measure to the competence of what has occurred before. For the overall planning is a tightly organised sequence of axes and cross-axes, forced perspectives and culminating halls, low spaces set against high, square against circle, and one building type against another. It always holds our interest while at the same time, dividing government into a village of workable blocks. The building thus represents many of the most cogent ideas and motifs developed by Post-Modern Classicists over the last ten years, and shows the level at which they have jelled into a paradigm for a developing tradition.

    This tradition will undoubtedly continue to deepen and spread out as it becomes still more popular. And the pressures of mass production and consumption will clearly take their toll as tons of work in this mode, without thought or quality, is dumped on the environment. In this ambivalent situation, as Post-Modernism becomes just as commercial as its Modern and Late-Modern competitors, we might pause to remember the fate of every successful movement launched on the industrial world since 1800. Under their aegis, masses of shoddy work was produced until each movement in turn lost its leaders and direction. This commercialisation of all successful styles – consumed, discredited and exhausted – helps to explain their continual obsolescence. The situation today is only different in degree, since there are many more approaches and these are commercialised faster. The cycles of change are much quicker. If this is true we might focus less on the change in style, the way one supersedes another, and concentrate more on the few individual buildings and urban groups of worth, for they are being created, relatively speaking, as fast as the junk. Post-Modern masterpieces exist amid Post-Modern and much other trash, and we mustn't let the latter obscure the former.

242 *Mississauga Civic Center,* 1982-87. The public realm is embraced by two 'arms' which open onto the flat prairie landscape. The pediment-building forms an effective monumental background for the *res publica,* and marks a place and event in suburban sprawl. (Robert Burley)

243 *The Council Chamber* rotunda with its paired Tuscan Doric columns and a frieze of sconces and townships has a dark blue fresco by Sharon McCann which combines the constellations with images of Indian legends. (Robert Burley)

244 *The Great Hall,* an indoor assembly area, transforms the motifs of the exterior assembly including the rostrum and banded masonry, here finished in green and black marble. (Robert Burley)

Post-Modernism Between Kitsch and Culture, Sixth Edition, 1991

The last edition of this book, written in 1987, ends on a disturbing note – the commercialisation of Post-Modernism. Today an architectural movement may find it easier to survive persecution than success. Widespread acceptance not only diffuses the aims of a tradition – because so many followers get them partially wrong – but it also confuses the leaders. Single-minded and strong in opposition, they lose direction when they become the focus for mass culture and adulation. They may confuse their own success with a deeper change in society or the profession of architecture; or their message may be co-opted by large firms in a way that betrays its essential meaning. Such things had happened to the tradition of Post-Modern architecture by the late 1980s as it became successful, middle-aged, part of the Establishment and taught in the academies.

Conceived as a wide language which cuts across high and low taste cultures with a double coding that still holds the integrity of each voice, it can result in crude compromise. In the 1950s Dwight MacDonald and other literary critics damned such mixed gruel as Mid-Cult – neither high nor low culture but a parody of both. This is the constant danger for Post-Modernists in every area, especially the most commercial ones: film, TV, music, the popular novel and architecture. Always trying to reach a wider and more varied audience than that which John Barth (following Thomas Mann) calls 'the Early Christians: professional devotees of high art', Post-Modernists may be constantly tempted to simplify their message, edit out its irony and double coding, and appeal to the largest group with the falsely consoling idea of an integrated culture.[96]

This oversimplification betrays the basic goal of the movement, which is to enhance pluralism and cultural difference. Totalisation, by contrast, was often the goal of traditional culture and Modernism, especially in the latter's Heroic Period and the 1930s. Then Walter Gropius, Mies van der Rohe, Giuseppe Terragni and Le Corbusier, among many other Modernists, made their placating overtures to the centralising states of the time – the Nazis, Fascists and Petain's government.[97] Modernists today might prefer to forget these revealing slips into compromise, especially since their movement is often portrayed as anti-Establishment and pure. But these lapses, and Nikolaus Pevsner's defense of the new architecture as 'totalitarian' (in the 1936, but *not later* editions of his *The Pioneers of the Modern Movement*) should make them look again. Their halo has always been a bit tarnished. The 'universalist' tendency of Modernism was always an inducement to compromise with power, and remains so today. Post-Modernists, with their theories of pluralism, have produced a new form of compromise – sending different groups or taste cultures different messages – and not trying to resolve the implications for society as a whole. To repeat: there's a downside to all traditions, especially evident when they are most successful.

Disney Gives PM the Kiss

In 1985 Michael Eisner, head of the Walt Disney empire, set up the Disney Development Corporation and decided to develop theme parks, resorts and convention hotels as an integrated package. In this he was enormously enterprising,

245 MICHAEL GRAVES, *Newark Museum refurbishment and construction*, New Jersey, 1982-89. The atrium is the culmination of a sequence through a Post-Modern Classical background that is punctuated by subtle changes in colour, skylights and room shape. (William Taylor)

165

transforming a $1 billion per year turnover into $5 billion – revenue which was mostly dependent on parks and resorts, not films.[98] Euro-Disneyland, opening in 1992 outside Paris, is a $2.3 billion, 4,800 acre resort/theme-park and what-have-you (with Grid Building by Frank Gehry, the Happy Trails Motel by Antoine Predock and other themoids by Antoine Grumbach, Michael Graves and Robert Stern). Disney World in Florida, on 28,000 acres, is already a mega-park of specialised fun. This is perplexing. Why millions of people like to congregate together in one fantasy ghetto to undergo a strict regime of entertainment escapes me, but it's a secret on which the Disney corporation has thrived for years. The formula of controlled ride-through parks, 'theming', ersatz and mechanised experience appeals to the masses as much as it does to the multinationals, and, as I pointed out at the beginning of this book, it led to the 'crisis of Modern architecture'. Fifteen years later it struck Post-Modernism.

Robert Stern designed Michael Eisner's parents' Manhattan apartment in the early 1970s so it was perhaps predictable that Eisner would consult Stern for architectural advice. This led to a meeting with Michael Graves and the transformation of Disney, as Paul Goldberger put it, into 'the IBM of the post-modern age'.[99] Not only did this conglomerate commission well over a billion dollars of work from Post-Modern architects, but Eisner asked Graves and Stern for strategic advice in transforming his empire from what was a mass-cult enterprise – when Walt Disney died – into something more up-market. It is too soon to judge the results of this policy, which in the end will take ten years, focusing on three cities, but one can estimate the outlines through the two hotels by Michael Graves in Florida: there will be something like eighteen more of these leviathans including some office buildings in the future.

The first conclusion may seem too obvious to mention, but from it everything follows: Graves' structures are big. The Swan Hotel, with its twenty eight-ton 248 turquoise birds, has 758 bedrooms, the Dolphin Hotel has 1,510 and together these artificial mountains cost more than a third of a billion – $375,000,000. The average huge hotel built during the London boom in the early seventies had 500 bedrooms and, as I also point out in the first chapter, 'creates a disruption in scale and city life which amounts to the occupation of an invading army – a role tourists tend to fulfil'. Here, in the reclaimed swamps of Florida, it is ironically the hotels the tourists will come to see: they are far more interesting and culturally challenging than anything to be found in the ride-through parks.

This 'entertainment architecture', as Eisner has christened the fruits of his new policy, has more references to European culture than a PhD source-spotter can find in all the Magic Kingdom. Some of it is a bit heavy, like Bernini's swans inflated nine times in volume from then old perches by the Palazzo Barberini, now to loom forty-seven feet above the awed hordes. The other exterior sources are more allusive – water cascade from the Villa Lante, sailboat bridge and central pyramid from Ledoux, stepped massing from Zoser's famous pyramid, and the layout from 246 the nineteenth-century Ecole des Beaux-Arts. Such Euro-delights rev one up for more sourcery on the inside (thirteen restaurants, one themed as a fish, the next as the Palio race-course, etc). The ride-through park has now become the walk-

246 MICHAEL GRAVES, *The Dolphin and Swan Hotels,* model from the north, 1987. The volumes have a flat monumental quality like Boullée's diagrammatic drawings of the Scaleless Sublime. (W Taylor)

through cafeteria with menu by Sir Bannister Fletcher: comparative Western architecture on the digestive method.

Most of these delights were run up in a year or two when Graves, like Disney, had an enormous boom. In April 1990, his office had just completed eight major projects – such as the Newark Museum Renovation at $17 million, or the Crown American Corporate Headquarters at $27 million – and had sixty-four more under way. Most were hotels, offices and commercial buildings, but others included five large private houses and five museums, bringing the total amount of work to over a billion dollars. Such figures may be misleading, but it is still of interest to compare them with those of Philip Johnson who, at the height of his professional success in 1985, had thirteen mega-projects in hand and $2.5 billion worth of work.[100]

Perhaps with a hint of competitive spleen Robert Stern dubbed Graves 'the Paul Rudolph of PM', because so much of the work was signature-stamped rather than context-specific: it said more about who designed it than where it was. But closer to the mark would be 'the SOM of PM', because like this large firm, Graves churns out architecture of a generally high standard. The question then might be – 'Isn't it all really *Modern*'?

Mechanisation, quick speed of production, massive scale of building, stereotyping are all hallmarks of the Modern Movement, especially in its latest alienating phase – as I point out above in 'The Death of Modern Architecture'. But the related question also has to be asked, when it comes to designing entertainment architecture: 'How big is too big?' Here one finds divergent answers. As functioning hotels my view is that the Swan and Dolphin are not much better or worse than the average, gargantuan Sheraton which is their equal in cost and type: impersonal, efficient and bland in service. But as stage sets, which is the more proper comparison, they are on the scale of Cecil B DeMille and quite appropriate for circuses and the slaughter of the Christians. The critique might thus be one that Reyner Benham levels at the Getty Museum: 'no blood was spilled here'. Blood is no more likely to flow at the Swan or Dolphin, given the super-controlled Disney atmosphere. The problem then is less that the hotels are too big than that the everyday activity is too small. One needs grand functions for the grandiosity to feel right – something like the naval battles staged on false lakes, as the Romans and Florentines used to put on behind their similarly Herculean palazzi.

All the problems of scale, size, detailing and conception are well symbolised by the sweet little predatory birds which dominate the swamps for miles. The swans give the hotel its name, and are repeated resonantly throughout the interior. But they are so predictable in every fibreglass inch of smile and arch of neck that one has trouble seeing them as they almost disappear in a quack of banality. Worse yet, underneath the oleaginous skin there are two extraordinary realities – a steel frame, and the plywood ribs on which the fibreglass is stuck. Here are two unpredictable and elegant deep structures which the typical Post-Modernist – Venturi, Stirling, Hollein to name the three obvious ones – would have partly revealed. This would have made the emblems both literal swans *and* beautiful diagrams which showed their internal workings. If ever there were a case for producing a multivalent symbol that would work on many levels of perception and

247

247 MICHAEL GRAVES, *Swan Hotel,* Lake Buena Vista, Florida, 1987-90. If one overlooks the diagrammatic tents and underlooks the clichéd emblems, there is some rather sophisticated ornament and architecture in between. Lapping turquoise waves play a nice game of camouflage with the window patterns, and the long sweeping curve of the roof is a fresh gestural shape that Graves has added to his repertoire. (Steven Brooke)

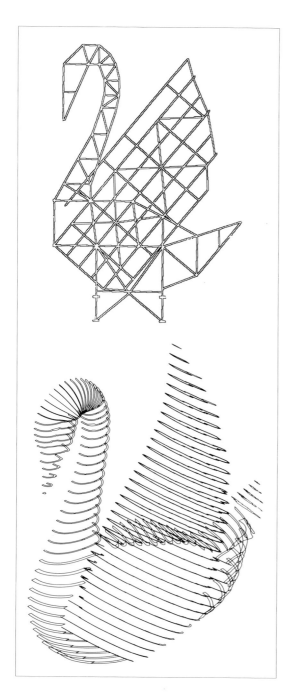

taste, it was here with these multi-layered, but hidden structures. At forty-seven feet they might even have been used as habitable rooms.

Aside from their size and a few other infelicitous blotations like the turquoise sea-shells, the buildings are quite imaginative and praiseworthy. The interiors show a lighter touch than the outside, and an interesting handling of what could be called colour-field architecture. Especially successful is the long lobby of the Swan which creates a vibrating pattern of floral lights, cut-out palms and parrot chandeliers – all against a red, white and blue backdrop. It's the kind of cheap, but convincing all-over pattern which Robert Venturi and others have been attempting for years, but never achieved so successfully. Furthermore, the drama is sustained over a series of public spaces right through the corridors and into the bedrooms. The pictorial effects look as if one crossed a David Hockney with a Paul Cézanne – the Pop images of trees and beach umbrellas with the more subtle tonalities of a Provençal landscape. What one is bound to miss in photographs, but is apparent from the plans, is that Graves has become adept at pacing the sequence of Classical rooms that vary in shape and size. He has understood the Beaux-Arts promenade for which he is here finding a new use and mood.

This is even more true of his renovations for the Newark Museum in New Jersey, a laborious job of shoe-horning a fine collection of mostly American art into a converted YWCA and other old buildings. Graves started talking about the project in 1967 and then designed it from 1982 to 1990, so in terms of scale and speed of production it is the opposite of his Disney work. Here the earlier small houses and the showrooms for the Sunar Corporation have paid dividends: Graves has produced one of the few really convincing buildings of Post-Modern Classicism. From the stuccoed entrance through the round, square and rectangular spaces the visitor proceeds both understanding the logic and anticipating surprise. Low and high spaces are set in subtle contrast, drawing one forward. Every so often the sudden reappearance of a dramatic skylight punctuates the sequence, reminiscent

248 MICHAEL GRAVES, *Swan Statue*, deep structure in steel and plywood. The 46-foot birds have plywood ribs fastened to a steel frame on which a fibreglass skin is fixed. These beautiful underlying structures might have been partly revealed by a Post-Modernist such as James Stirling or Robert Venturi, and the giant swan could have become a real fantasy room from which to view the monuments in the swamp.

249 MICHAEL GRAVES, *Swan Hotel Lobby*, with its tent-like ceiling, floral lights hung from parrots, swan seats, papyrus bundled columns and stylised palms which explode into the space. The all-over colour and lush tropical imagery are transformed in other rooms. (Steven Brooke)

of the John Soane museum – and it's a measure of Graves' success that his building can stand up to the comparison. The Soane Museum and Soane's Dulwich Museum and Art Gallery as well as Graves' buildings are all in a restrained Classicism of wall planes, skylights and slight articulations that create an ever-varying backdrop to the art. The proportion of flat surface to void reaches an optimum for a museum, and I can think of no better ratio in recent architecture, unless it is the Picasso Museum in Paris. In any case, the relation of the background building to the foreground art is as satisfying as I've found.

A consequence of the understated Classicism – close to the Tuscan mode – is that it can seem an inevitable partner to the existing brick vernacular, the old YWCA, and also accept the new synthetic vernacular: the vinyl floor tiles, municipal EXIT signs and industrial sprinkling system. Such are the realities for any but the most expensive museum. In accommodating their presence in an abstract way Graves produces a double coding that convinces one it is possible to refer both to the Age of Plastic and the ancient Greeks. Much of the collection is Yankee Neo-Classical and thus also relates to this cultural gap. The culminating space of the museum intensifies the same duality: the 'atrium', which shoots up four storeys and unites all levels in a single view, is at once spartan and grand. Industrial glazing is set against a yellowish *faux-marbre,* while the abstract pattern created by punched-out window voids has a bi-axial symmetry. The whole space has the dignity of a present-day Pantheon, created with minimalist means. The particular virtue of the space is that it affords glimpsed and framed views of what is to come, increasing the anticipation of further pleasures. In this way it is rather like the central space of the Guggenheim Museum, except that here, rectangular and semi-enclosing walls form a stable backdrop for the art.

What conclusions can one draw from this stage of Graves' career and its intersection with the fortunes of Disney? Some of his work is produced slowly and remains well-controlled, like the Newark conversion, whereas an equal amount is

250-51 MICHAEL GRAVES, *Newark Museum,* New Jersey, 1982-89. The atrium skylight punctuates the sequence of restrained Classical spaces – a satisfying environment in which to view the art.

252 *Inside south entrance.* A sequential hierarchy of move-ment allows the visitor to feel orientated within this large complex. (Steven Brooke)

produced quickly, like the Momochi apartment building in Japan, a caricature of his style. Perhaps another third is both creatively integral and yet still flawed in parts, like the Youngstown Museum. This has an interesting massing that is ultimately dissatisfying because of its heavily proportioned backside and notional details. Looked at from the angle of fast-build, the sixty-four projects under way are noteworthy because of their high average quality. This is, oddly enough, a point the Modernist Aldo van Eyck would appreciate: although the self-confessed enemy of Gravesian Post-Modernism, he does preach the 'quality of quantity' rather than the much easier quality of small-scale production. However, judged solely in these last terms, those of pre-industrial handcraft, the buildings are diagrammatic.

The balance of contending judgements could continue endlessly, culminating in the Disney work itself. Looked at in terms of the corporation's past, the new 'entertainment architecture' is obviously one giant step better than Cinderella's Castle (a sugary pastiche of Ludwig II of Bavaria's pastiche of *Les Très Riches Heures'* exaggeration of a real Gothic castle); but seen in terms of the developing Post-Modern tradition of ornament and symbolism, some of the work is regressive. This is particularly true of the Seven Dwarfs facade of the headquarters building for Disney in Burbank, California. This phase in Graves' work has been called 'hokey-tecture' because its tongue-in-cheek fakery is so knowing.[101] The attempt, as in kitsch, is to succeed through excess; but when it is this calculating and obvious, one wonders. 'I've tried to walk the line between the whimsical and the jokey', Graves has said, 'or to navigate between the chasm of the cute and the abyss of easy irony'. The question is, what positive terrain exists between these four trifles?   253

One thinks of Mannerist and Baroque fantasies, those of Giuliano da Romano and the fountains of Rome, which had an equally explicit imagery; or the papal symbolism dominating Catholic structures; or even iconic roadside architecture, the Hot-Dog stand. Each of these, in different ways, is equally literal with its signs – so what is it that makes them more acceptable? Perhaps craftsmanship in the first case, the actual content in the second, and the surreal brazenness of the third. In three hundred years' time, might the Seven Dwarfs turn into mysterious icons?

As it is, Dopey, the central dwarf caryatid – a mere nineteen-foot midget – looks for the moment only like Dopey. Unlike Michael Graves' earlier sketches for sculpture – notably 'Portlandia' for the Portland Building – there is no ambiguity, abstraction and transformation of the content and image. The whole facade becomes a 'signolic', not symbolic architecture.[102] Just as the circular tempietto which surmounts the scheme is a one-liner, so too are the dwarfs – which unfortunately set the opening theme. This stereotyping is a pity because it makes one overlook the strengths of the plan and the back elevation: the latter, for instance, fully absorbs one of the hallmarks of the new Disney architecture –   254
Mickey Mouse ears – into an interesting bay rhythm that, at the same time, turns the corner very well. The building, at these points, becomes more resonant and symbolic.

Robert Stern's work for the corporation varies more widely, from the revivalist beach resort hotel to the crazy decorated shed that is the Casting Center for Disney, in Orlando, Florida. This latter confection has the real spirit and vulgarity of

253 MICHAEL GRAVES, *Walt Disney Headquarters*, Burbank, California, 1988-90. This Tuscan style palazzo has seven 19-foot dwarfs – 133 feet of midget – holding its front door. Michael Eisner, who commissioned it, said: 'When I come to work I want to smile', and the dwarf's leader, Dopey, smiles back. Above all this is a round tempietto, a Hadrianic 'hinge' that is just as notional. (Maureen Sajbel)

254 MICHAEL GRAVES, *Disney Headquarters* from street intersection. Red sandstone and cream stucco divide the building, while the four executive pavilions are marked by the large Ledoux/Mickey curves and a dignified symmetry of massed elements.

roadside architecture, it is definitely aiming at what Herbert Gans – a major theorist of Post-Modernism – would call the 'lower middle taste culture', those suburbanites who cruise the edges of Houston and Los Angeles looking for cheap real estate which still has royal pretensions. Bald-faced deceit which is this brazen is sublime. The diaper pattern meant to evoke the Doge's Palace and the Grand Canal has, indeed, Gothicesque windows, but like the airfoil entrance canopy [sic], it belongs very much in The Age of Metal. Two little golden peaked finials (gratis Aldo Rossi) hold this airplane wing in place, while a truly grotesque lantern giggles between them.

Just so no one could possibly take any of this seriously, the images are collaged out of phase and their flat insubstantiality is exaggerated by paper-thin layering. Blue Mickey Mouse ears further punctuate the pretence, and Mickey Mouse's head is, appropriately enough, empty – the perfect visual void. (One is reminded here of Stern's masterful satire of the Best discount store and its caryatids with their empty heads shaped like TV sets.)

The view from the roadside spells C A S T I N G in giant gilt letters. One goes into this decorated shed to get a job as an imagineer, or some other engineer of fantasy, and is delighted to find the Disney icons played with as well as put on pedestals. Through his shifts in scale and violent confrontations of good and bad taste, through his collage of genres, Stern, of all the architects, has come closest to re-using the Disney iconography for his own whimsical purposes.

At this stage of incompletion, the Disney work still cannot be judged as a whole, nor can its effects on Post-Modernism be gauged. Some Post-Modernists such as James Stirling have declined Disney commissions because, as he said: 'To me [the theme idea] seems demeaning and trivial and somehow not profound or important. It's overly commercial. In England, we're subjected to it in a gross way – the parading of the guards, the dressing up at the Tower of London, and Madame Tussaud's. Maybe we invented the bloody thing.'[103] Robert Venturi, Charles Moore, Aldo Rossi, Hans Hollein have all been considered for jobs, and may still get them; Arata Isozaki is producing the 'Time Building' in Florida – what looks to be the most dignified and abstractly themed structure so far. Many more Post-Modern architects are at work, so the tradition is now deeply involved with, and implicated in, the fortunes of Disney. Michael Graves and Robert Stern contend, as do others who are at work here, that entertainment architecture should not be judged by the same canons as serious work, but rather on a populist level: whether people like it; whether, in Stern's laconic, Warholian words, 'Disney is fun'.[104]

So far their schemes are successful in these restricted terms – no small endeavour – but questionable on more ambitious levels. If so many Post-Modernists had not been commissioned at once, for so many expensive and visible jobs; if the Disney empire had not turned their change of style into a media event and dominated the Sunday supplements; if Post-Modernism were not at the same time so concerned with the incorporation of high and low tastes and symbolism, then I wouldn't waste my time writing about it, and would accept Stern's singular canon of judgement. As it is, by historic accident the Walt Disney world happened to be changing its look and market niche just at the moment when Post-

255 ROBERT STERN, Casting Center, Walt Disney World, Lake Buena Vista, Florida, 1987-89. Venetian Gothic diaper pattern blown up and played against an airfoil door held in tension, some baby-blue Mickey Mouse scuppers, and a couple of clown hats à la Rossi. Never has the decorated shed been so clearly decorated, and shed-like. (Peter Aaron, ESTO)

Modernism was most fashionable and vulnerable, and so their fortunes crossed. Whether in the end this will be seen as the kiss of life, or death, for the PM movement remains open, but kiss it is: ambiguous, ambitious and expensive to both parties.

Urbane Mega-Build

Just as mixed in quality are the results of Post-Modern urbanism as interpreted by large developers and civic authorities. The early 1980s saw the widespread acceptance of Jane Jacobs' critique of Modern planning and the great sense of her primary message: mixed uses, mixed ages of building, mixed social groups. Mixture and pluralism – two central tenets of Post-Modernism in all fields – replaced functional zoning and the *tabula rasa* approach to the city. Most cities in the West adopted a version of Jacobite planning lore, but unfortunately scaled it up to huge size, thus in a sense cancelling one of her chief points: piecemeal growth. The reason for this inversion, as might be expected, was quick profit. In London the Covent Garden district, Broadgate in the City and the massive Canary Wharf area of the Docklands received the Post-Modern formula, often distorted by large size: 'urbane mega-build' was the oxymoronic result.

In America the Rouse Corporation carried out a slightly more yuppified version of the genre, notably in New York, Baltimore and – to my mind the most successful application of the formula – Boston's Faneuil Hall marketplace area. Here they were aided in urban place-making by the considerable experience of Ben Thompson and the infill buildings and towers of Graham Gund and Adrian Smith of SOM. The mixture of functions and new and old structures, the carving out of positive public space, the contextualism and ornament of the architecture are all of a generally high standard. A certain debt in pleasing the crowds is, ironically, owed to Disneyland where corporate street theatre was first formulated, but of course Disney himself learned this Main Street formula, in turn, from successful European cities.

Furthermore, like the mega-developments of Battery Park City in New York and Canary Wharf in London, there was even a positive social policy introduced which supported the visual pluralism. Hiring a minority workforce, reserving a certain percentage of employment for the black community, women and the disadvantaged, and encouraging small businesses have led to a social diversity that is the essence of urbanity. Enlightened planning everywhere in the eighties was based on a similar mixture of public and private co-operation which transcended the either/ or categories of socialism or capitalism. A central planning authority might lay down the ground rules, supposedly provide most of the infrastructure and then let different private developers build and reap the profits. Such a Post-Modern mixture might be called 'socitalist' to underscore its hybridisation as socialised capitalism, a fusion the Japanese have perfected.[105]

Name it what you will, this synergetic enterprise was responsible for the most successful urbanism. Particularly important was the IBA (International Building Exhibition) in Berlin, a project of town building that continued over a decade, from the late 1970s to the late 1980s. In addition to the aforementioned Post-Modern

256 GRAHAM GUND & ADRIAN SMITH (SOM), *75 State Street*, Boston, Mass, 1987-89. A 31-storey tower surmounts an urban ensemble created by Gund and other architects in the refurbished Faneuil Hall Marketplace. Adopting the Post-Modern formulae of Jane Jacobs, the Rouse Corporation has turned this area into one of the most urbane places in America.

257 ADRIAN SMITH (SOM), *Rowes Wharf*, Boston, Mass, 1985-87. Urbane city building that provides several semi-public spaces and a magnificent transition point for commuters from the sea. (Steve Rosenthal)

256

257

formulae there was a particular emphasis in Berlin on perimeter block planning – that is, pushing the building right up to the street edge on four sides of a city block to allow maximum shelter for the backyards and the recreation of city street life. As Jane Jacobs pointed out, this life is essential to the functioning of a city, and as Leon Krier added, it provides the basic visual and circulation logic. Also the policy of choosing several architects for a site was emphasised, so that the city might once again have the visual variety and typological diversity that has always been its strength. Broadgate and Canary Wharf in London and Battery Park City in New York followed IBA's example in carrying out these principles, albeit with less sensitivity.

Another significant strategy the authorities adopted, under the guidance of Josef Paul Kleiheus and Rob Krier among others, was to set up a competition system that selected some of the most creative international architects. This resulted, negatively, in a certain number of signature-buildings and, positively, in an equal number of well-designed housing layouts – perhaps as much as thirty per cent of all the schemes over ten years. Two of the best projects were designed by the California-based team of Charles Moore and the Italian-based team of Aldo Rossi, 258 and in both cases the architects were spurred to perform above their average for 259 the natural reason that they were placed on the centre stage of a major city along with their international peers. Moore, Ruble and Yudell's housing was Schinkelesque in front and picturesque on the garden side, whereas Rossi's was industrial Classicism on both sides of the perimeter wall. General guide-lines did not mandate a variable Post-Modern Classicism everywhere – and by the end of IBA development the competition system was favouring the Deconstructive approach of Daniel Libeskind – but in general, new versions of a traditional grammar and street layout were preferred.

In many ways IBA represented the high point of Post-Modern urbanism and it has become the model for other cities such as Frankfurt (where a central district has been developed) and Odense in Denmark (where the various types of new 260 housing are even being evaluated by sociologists). This is all very worthy and enlightened. If the projects have an obvious fault, however, it is that housing alone cannot make a city either functional or urbane. Planning authorities in Europe do not appear to have the power or political will to commission a really rich mixture of public, commercial and domestic building. Paris, of course, is the notable exception where its *grands projets* are predictably all civic, public and imperial in scope. No doubt these were realised only for the last reason: because French presidents, in the manner of Louis XIV, have a tradition of leaving behind large objects that mark their reign. Is it a surprise that this memorialising urge has resulted for the most part in Late- rather than Post-Modernism? Could it be that monuments on this scale, without any great social idealism, *have* to be abstract?

Be that as it may, a really balanced urbanism has eluded all countries. In America and Britain, where the political orientation favours market-led solutions, the developer has played a larger role than the planning authority. When the conditions are right, when there is an economic boom and a street-wise entrepreneur, this can lead to whole tracts of a city undergoing immediate urban

258 MOORE, RUBLE & YUDELL, *Tegel Housing,* IBA, Berlin, West Germany, 1980-88. The perimeter block is Classical on the front and picturesque here, on the enclosed garden side (which has a view to the river in back). This housing is popular with the residents and unpopular with the Modernists in Berlin.

259 ALDO ROSSI (with G BRAGHIERI), *Social Housing,* South Friedrichstadt, Berlin, West Germany, 1981-88. The street side of this perimeter block shows a strong industrial Classical facade of Jaguar-green steel, banded brick and curious, steep-pitched roofs – all of which gives great character to mass housing.

transformation. The Los Angeles-based Jon Jerde partnership characteristically finds itself simultaneously re-designing twenty or thirty 'hearts' of a city that had suffered cardiac arrest in the sixties and seventies as the combined result of Modernist planning and the flight to the suburbs. Jerde regenerates these old centres, again with the Jacobite remedy of mixed uses, mixed ages and mixed types of buildings: but his injection of public space, street theatre and commerce make it work economically. Whenever a central district needs regeneration, such as downtown San Diego, or whenever a sixties sprawl needs tying together, such as the suburban shopping mall, Jerde provides his medicine: shopping arcades, pedestrian space, and lots of street activity *à la* Rouse and Disney. As architecture the results are dayglo 261 Michael Graves; as urbanism they are sensible versions of street planning. The missing factor is, again, the public realm of real civic buildings: commerce, as the single urban generator, is only marginally more effective in creating the city than housing.

The most ambitious urbane mega-build in America is no doubt Battery Park City, a 'city within the city' in downtown New York near Wall Street and next to the World Trade Center. Here on a 92-acre landfill site on the Hudson River, a state agency teamed up with several developers including the largest in the world, the Canadian group Olympia and York, to produce urbanity at a massive and, it has to be added, lumpish scale. Planned again on Jacobite and Post-Modern principles by Cooper, Eckstut Associates, the scheme consists of two major residential areas north and south of the World Financial Centre (WFC).

This complex of four squat skyscrapers contains seven and a half million square feet (the equivalent of three Empire State Buildings), six million of which will house office workers beavering away for giant corporations (inside are the headquarters of American Express, Merrill Lynch and Dow Jones). Surrounding these 30,000 workers there will be by 1993, 40,000 upper-income residents. The figures, like some of the repetitive architecture, can be fatiguing.

The WFC cost over $1.5 billion while the whole scheme is reckoned to finally cost $4.5 – although these figures were 1986 estimates and may work out higher.[106] Even greater sums are being spent by Olympia and York and others in the London Docklands and, when one thinks of the figures in the context of Disney, Graves, Philip Johnson *et al* the conclusion is reached that the billion dollar development has become as common to Post-Modernists as it was to the Modernists (even if a billion isn't what it used to be). One doesn't have to be a Marxist to believe that *all* this development has enough in common to make its stylistic and philosophical differences marginal. Too big is too big, whatever the approach.

Nevertheless for Paul Goldberger and many astute critics 'Battery Park City is a Triumph of Urban Design', because it mixes public and private values in about equal measure.[107] The public amenities include a riverside esplanade, lots of open space filled with art works commissioned for a specific site, and Rector Park – what Goldberger calls the best of its kind in New York since Gramercy Park. Also it 262 follows the general aesthetic guide-lines concerning massing, cornice lines, masonry materials and tripartition (most buildings have a defined base, middle and top). This

260 POUL INGEMANN, *Social Housing*, Odense, Denmark, 1987-88. Concrete and aluminium Classicism in the northern Scandinavian mode defines, in a very loose way, the street and garden sides with three forms: a tower, temple and terrace.

261 JON JERDE, *Westside Pavilion*, Los Angeles, 1985-86. The shopping centre and retail, in Jerde's hands, becomes the means to re-create a convivial urbanism. Dayglo-pastel-Michael Graves-ism holds the street line very effectively and shields it from the parking lot in back, thus overcoming the bane of Los Angeles.

262 CESAR PELLI, *World Financial Center Towers*, 1982-87 and (left) CHARLES MOORE, *Housing*, Battery Park City, New York, 1985-87. A Classical urbanism set the guidelines and enforced street patterns, squares, similar cornice lines, tripartition and a common masonry base-line. The urbanity would be more urbane if it weren't so dense.

263 CESAR PELLI, *World Financial Center Tower*, 1982-87. The building peels back as it rises to its stepped copper pyramid, changing its granite/glass ratio to become lighter and enigmatic. Is this a geode, or a thin building trying to get out of a fat one?

creates the unity with variety that is the hallmark of urbanity. As for the private sector and contribution, this includes not only the housing as a function, but the fact that more than fifteen developers own the properties – so public and private values do interact synergetically in many ways.

Architecturally the results are impressive but flawed, and like Graves' work for Disney they lead me to reassert the Ivan Illich Law of Diminishing Architecture. Since no one paid the slightest attention when I divulged this hypothesis in these pages fifteen years ago, and since it now looks true beyond reasonable doubt, I will ask the reader's indulgence for repeating it: 'for any building type there is an upper limit to the number of people who can be served before the quality of an environment falls'. QED 40,000 inhabitants plus 30,000 workers placed in an environment run up in ten years results in, well, wallpaper architecture.

Given these limitations Cesar Pelli has produced very intelligent, sensuous and creative wallpaper. For one thing his towers set back, thin out and change their window/wall ratio as they rise – some up to fifty storeys – thus reducing the visual bulk. For another thing the granite at the base decreases in quantum jumps just as the reflective glass increases, thus creating the interesting illusion of a building within a building within a building – or else another new idea, 'the peeling building'. 263 These squat-scrapers also share similar granite bottoms and related copper tops. It's true the distinctive hats – stepped, pyramidal and domed – do not symbolise anything other than 'unity in variety' and are thus only a superior form of wallpaper, but at least they *are* visual culminations.

On the inside of these office labyrinths Pelli has designed extremely elegant domed spaces which transform the wallpaper into flat repetitive patterns which are cut across to accentuate their applied thinness. At these points the Post- 264 Modernism is explicit and masterful: we know that he intends the sign of insubstantiality to be an essential part of the morality and aesthetic because the cuts are so abrupt. The centre of the whole scheme, indeed Battery Park City's 'heart', is the vaulted Winter Garden which now wraps the theme of the exterior skin into a series of telescopic folds. These repeat in section the stepped layering of the towers and thus conceptually bring the whole scheme into focus. But the 265 Winter Garden is again a flawed masterpiece, a battle between economy and gesture with no clear winner. As an interior space it is extremely urbane and pleasant, especially in the cold season when the sixteen palm trees and warmth are most welcome. Equally positive are the views to all sides: down the thin end of the telescope towards the World Trade Center towers, down the other end towards the Hudson River. Only the awkward shapes of the exterior look unfortunate and mean, as if the developer had cut back the money. This of course reminds us of the four towers, which look as if the planners had shortened and fattened them.

If Battery Park City is the best of urbane mega-build, then it shows this genre still has a way to go before it constitutes an entirely balanced fabric. No city hall or church graces this city within the city. There is just the typical over-concentration of offices and housing, the over-specialisation which distorted Modernism and still plagues its offspring. We have become so accustomed to this situation, it is so ubiquitous, that it now escapes comment, and there seems little political will to do anything about it. Thus if we are to continue with 'fast-food mega-build' – a horrible phrase and an unfortunate reality – then it is progress of a kind when it reflects Jane Jacobs' principles and is carried out with the skill of a Pelli. This is of course no substitute for real urbanity.

Village Planning as Model

The big cities of the world have expanded into huge regional megalopoli relatively recently, mostly in the last thirty years. The growth of the Boston to Washington megalopolis ('Bosh-Wash' as it was called in the late sixties) is typical and has its counterpart in Europe, Japan, Mexico and the Greater London region. Like all these communicational sprawls, it has too many interlinked causes to analyse here. But one thing can be said quickly. No society is politically or economically equipped to deal with this inflation on the macro-scale, and so imbalances in fabric will continue to occur. Lucky is the city that can just keep its transportation system up to date, never mind its overall plan, or balance in structure.

Chaos theory and self-organising theory derived from the Nobel laureate Ilya Prigogine are being put forward as proper ways to conceive of, and perhaps contain, this runaway growth – for instance the anarchic beauty of Tokyo.[108] But architects who must, perforce, deal with the micro-scale of city fabric need more explicitly formal models, and for this the idea of small block design, or village planning, has recently come to the fore. It constitutes one of the ways Post-Modern precepts overlap with, but don't quite match, traditional ones.

Designing a city of small blocks is a goal that has appealed to three entirely different urban theorists – Jane Jacobs, Leon Krier and Christopher Alexander – no doubt for completely different reasons. But the three agree on its suitability because of one point: it allows a piecemeal growth which is economically and aesthetically desirable. Small block planning lets feedback work, whether it concerns an investment, or a visual decision. For this model of the Italian hill town, or 'organic village' as it is also known, is a stereotype appreciated now by everyone, thanks to tourism and the media. The force of the idea gains further weight, not only because of this popular and variegated acceptance – by three different schools of design – but also because of a recent fourth and fifth. Some Deconstructionists, particularly Frank Gehry, have now added their weight to the bandwagon, Prince Charles has climbed aboard and soon, no doubt, President Bush will agree it's a good thing. It is, especially when compared with the superblocks of Le Corbusier, or those of the mega-builders.

Interestingly enough the village model has been applied where one might least expect it: to the huge office building and multinational bank. The probability was that these leviathans would continue in the Modern corporate mould, building highly visible tributes to their might as they have done since the 1870s, with one freestanding monument trumping the previous one: the Woolworth Tower, the Chrysler Building, the AT&T, the Hongkong Bank and, needless to say, the Trump Tower. One doesn't have to be Freud to know what is going on here. But lo, there is now a feminine response to all these upright members – the groundscraper and undulating body building that hugs the earth, and tries to be 'green'.

264 CESAR PELLI, *WFC*, interior circulation rotunda. Corporate executives hurtle through these Classical spaces like the punched-card imagery of the dome – randomised, anonymous, beautiful and cut-up, where necessary.

265 CESAR PELLI, *WFC*, Winter Garden. Down the end of the telescoped space one sees, above, the outside World Trade Center and, below, a grand staircase cascading into the marbled and palmed court. The tough detailing is good industrial Classicism.

In Holland the architect Ton Alberts has broken up the mammoth NMB Bank – with its 2,400 employees – into a cluster of ten brick 'blobs'. These chunky 'pavilions', as they are also known, snake around the site in an irregular, choppy S- 266 curve thus providing a unique set of profiles from any one place. Gone is the image of the bank as a stiff Classical ramrod, or pompous mirrored erection; gone too are the images of bureaucracy and monotony; and back is the image of a medieval village, taller than usual, covered all over with perhaps too many 'Dutch' bricks (3.5 million of them) and full of odd animal and organic metaphors. The architects are dedicated followers of Rudolf Steiner and his anthroposophical method of design, one that stresses ecological sense, passive solar heating and all sorts of humane qualities. While the NMB Bank is not notable as high architecture, it is certainly popular and sensible, especially because it breaks up a large volume and introduces the notion of the street and square into the building (which does, of course, take them from the outside world where they belong).

A few other large corporations have attempted a related concept – the Centraal Beheer in Appeldorn and the Colonia Building in Cologne – and we could say the 'office as village' may soon become an accepted model for the future. After all, sixty percent of the work-force in the First World is destined to spend their lives in these post-industrial factories, and each year this population demands more and more amenities just to keep on the job. If the corporation doesn't provide acceptable spaces and services then, as in Los Angeles, the 'electronic cottage' may start to become a more pressing challenge to the central office – at least for a few days each week. In 1990 the London Telecom system estimated that perhaps twenty per cent of the population would soon be telecommuting.

In Tokyo the architect Hiroshi Hara has designed an exquisite High-Tech office as village for the international fashion company Yamato. This has a 'big/smallness' that is uncanny, a big volume that is broken up into so many small parts that it looks like a bubbly Italian hill-town of the future: one can't tell quite how large it really is. 268 The room-size forms are layered back and stepped to the right as they rise, as if tiny buildings were clinging to the face of a canyon. The reality is as charming as the photographs suggest, creating, for a change, a corporate world that is pleasantly subdivided and semi-private in parts.

One approaches under a large gate/bridge into a piazza with a flat reflecting pool and polished paving-stones – so highly polished that one can't see the transition between water and masonry. Lighting standards here and elsewhere vary between 269 the abstract and representational. Throughout the stacked village a series of abstracted themes repeat in a transformed way – clouds, shore-lines, geodesic structures, birds and trees – to create a very consistent ornamental programme. These images are not insistent one-liners, as they are in the Disney Kingdom, but much more subtle variations on a set of natural and cultural signs. They are often made of an industrial material – sheet metal, etched glass – and layered in flat, 267 horizontal planes like the building itself. This correspondence between parts and whole gives both a delightful resonance. Because of one repeated fractal pattern it also makes one see the entire metallic building as a wafting cloud. In the end this office as village is so successful because the architect has adopted a mixed grammar

266 ANTON ALBERTS and VAN HUUT BV, *NMB Bank*, Amsterdam, The Netherlands, 1984. Ten brick pavilions snake around the side providing various anthropomorphic and animal images – horses' heads. Pentagonal sun collectors surmount each horse and provide light to the interior court and street.

267 HIROSHI HARA, *Yamato International*, Tokyo, 1984-87, exterior light. Cut metal clouds and computerised ornament ring changes on natural and geometric themes.

268 HIROSHI HARA. *Aluminium forms* step up and billow to the right. Not only does the architecture resemble cloud forms (which are also stylised in the ornament), but a village hung from a rock face. The small block architecture manages to house the production and distribution functions of a fashion company.

269 HIROSHI HARA, *plaza entrance*. The water imitates the highly polished stones; also note the Secessionist lighting standards.

270 ALBRECHT JOURDAN MULLER and BERGHOF LANDES RANG, *Rooftop of Landeszentralbank*, Frankfurt, 1982-88. The greening of the post-industrial landscape. During lunchtime the employees come out on to this roofscape which is a sensuous, herbal garden framed — Mondrian-like — by window cleaning tracks.

271 AJM and BLR, *'Houses'* grouped around a hanging garden combines French topiary, diagonals and computer imagery.

272 AJM and BLR, *The fabric* is layered and stepped making an ornament from the construction, which features the difference between hung stone and load-bearing steel.

273 AJM and BLR, *Landeszentralbank*, the garden 'face' or 'tree' trellis. Steel, stone and nature are carefully intermeshed in an architecture that tries to overcome contradictions of period, material and style. (Waltraud Krase)

of curves and straight lines and played them at such an intricate scale that he has managed to symbolise the interpenetration of nature and culture. We begin to believe a giant fashion company can work like an organic community: all the functions from design to manufacture and distribution are housed here, and the image of interdependence is so convincing. One wonders if it is a real community?

The most convincing Western example of a corporate village is the recently completed Landeszentralbank in Frankfurt. It nestles so effectively into the urban fabric that many people would overlook its presence altogether. But when they ascend to one of the many surrounding towers — the typical Modern shafts of corporate potency — and look down, they will discover an exception to the tough urban roofscape. There below is not the usual collection of mechanical boxes, but a wild garden of hardy plants — herbs, junipers, polychromatic heather and cacti — 270 all held within a discipline of grey steel tracks, the window cleaning equipment. Here is the typical double coding of Post-Modernism, and the greening of the industrial landscape.

The Landeszentralbank actually has six 'hanging gardens' as well as the growing roofscape, and all six are in a unique style. Some are modifications of the traditional French garden and set dark green topiary against a flat white pebble background. 271 Others combine the English romantic garden with wandering patterns based on the computer circuit-board. But the point is that each of the six gardens, one floor above ground level, acts as a focus for the cluster of offices which surround it on three sides. These are conceived as 'houses' grouped around a common green court.

Thus the huge corporation, a central bank for others in the region, is broken down into units at a village scale. Instead of these units being stacked vertically as they are in Norman Foster's Hongkong Bank, or scattered about rather wastefully as in the NMB Bank, they are grouped in an urbanistic pattern that visually welcomes in the rest of the city and reinforces the existing street grid.

The building is convincing not only because of its layout and gardens, but also because of its symbolism and structure. The difference between the underlying steel structure and the visible surface of stone blocks becomes the pretext for the 272 characteristic Post-Modern type of symbolic ornament. Instead of the load-bearing construction of traditionalists, or the curtain wall of Modernists, we find the 'hung and peeled' facade of stone slabs, which are exaggerated in their layering to emphasise their non-structural, but urban role. The intermediate layers of construction are shown because of the peeling process, and the fact that the stone is non-structural is revealed by the cracks between them and their bevelled edges. Thus the ornament derives directly from revealing the truth of construction, as it does in Stirling's work at Stuttgart and elsewhere.

A steel motif in the shape of a T, or tree, or face is repeated in several ways 273 throughout the building, changing its shape to suit the particular context. When the T-shape is on the outside it works as a giant trellis so that growing plants can shield the hanging gardens: here it is surmounted by a delicate, tapering curve appropriately creating the profile of the crown of a tree. On the inside the T-shape is painted in shades of green and the natural imagery is made even more explicit in

the piazza where the T-piers are accompanied by potted trees.

If a large corporation is to embody the true urbanity of a village, then it must instantly fabricate the variety of spaces and moods that the urban realm creates over time. This the bank does by employing different designers, artists and craftsmen to work on a set of related themes, many of which concern, inevitably, the making and losing of money. By the entrance lobby, where the myth of Dr Faustus is portrayed in murals, and just as one is ascending into the grand, enclosed piazza, are three large golden balls suffering various kinds of distress. The cleanest of these sculptures is the *Deutschmark* as the bank would like it, whereas the other two, with their erosions and protrusions, perhaps represent deflation and inflation. Throughout this five-storey village artworks point up the space or the banking function. The accent on variety extends also into the boardrooms, each of which is given a different character. For instance the breakfast room from John Soane's   274 house in London, or the Café Aubette of Theo van Doesburg are slightly transformed by the architects into the grammar of layered planes; but still the image is distinctive and recognisable, the mood made *different*. If we must build large chunks of the environment quickly, then it is only right that they incorporate a heterogeneity of taste and represent the pluralism of time.

The most impressive space in the building, and the culmination of the route, is the grand central piazza: this forms a spine of circulation that connects the six   275 'houses of the village'. Here would be a true public realm, if only the bank were open to outsiders with one end of this space actually opened to the city. The irony is that the Landeszentralbank has created such a good simulacrum of urban architecture that they should sell it to the authorities to make it actually work. The better the spaces and art and architecture, the more one wants them given over to the public.

Towards a Subtle Urbanism

If a few enlightened corporations are resisting the pressure to create architectural one-liners and instead are concentrating on producing varied urban fabric, then so too are a few museums and art centres. Again this shift towards village planning may not represent much yet in terms of construction, but it does indicate a very real change in paradigm which ought, soon enough, to be followed by building. Three, loosely termed, cultural centres built in the late 1980s show the way, by James Stirling, Kisho Kurokawa and Antoine Predock. Each is a multi-use art centre, or part of one, and a convincing piece of urbanism in its own right. Each heralds the development of Post-Modernism towards a more subtle elaboration of symbolism and historical reference than has been seen in the recent past. All three once again make a virtue of small block planning. They may not be great buildings, but they're good ones, and they point Post-Modernism in the right direction.

Stirling and Wilford's Center for the Performing Arts at Cornell University divides up a very complex mixture of functions into nine chunky blocks and then crashes them together very tightly because of a crowded and precipitous site – teetering on the edge of Cascadilla Gorge. The scheme is in a fragmented Classical   276 style for several reasons. One might be its location in a quasi-Mediterranean

274 AJM and BLR, *Boardroom* that interlaces Gravesian Post-Modernism and the Café Aubette of Van Doesburg. The pastiche is done so well that the room looks better than the originals. (Dieter Leistner)

275 AJM and BLR, *Central Piazza*, again with the steel trees and masonry skin placed in rhythmical alternation. (Dieter Leistner)

context: 'Cascadilla' is Spanish for 'little cascade' which is in 'Ithaca' and on a historicising campus where there are many faint memories of the arcadian tradition. A second reason is the architect's previous use of this language, but there is yet another and surprising source for their grammar. It harkens back to Stirling and Gowan's Leicester Engineering Building of 1963, where small volumes were also juxtaposed and elided in a very compact way. They may not have been given the kind of Classicising ornament that the architects use today, but their deep structure is the same. It relates to the small grammatical units that can be found in any Classical hill town, or urban settlement in the ancient world, a comprehensible way of handling lots of space. Stirling has continued this method of articulation throughout his career, even if, from time to time, he has resorted to the Modernist device of the megastructure. In a sense his whole oeuvre is a complex dialogue of the method of compaction composition with Modern requirements.

At Cornell the volumes of the performing arts building huddle around a central 'campanile' rather the way they do in any *ville perchée* in the Mediterranean, and this has led many visitors to a first quick reaction – 'Ah, an Italian hill town, I can see the gable-end of the church, the octagonal baptistry and the adjacent loggia.'[109] But as always with Stirling, there is much more to it than historical allusion, and as usual the old forms turn out to mean new things. In this sense the Center for Theatre Arts is an artful piece of theatre, and a supreme example of second-glance architecture. If you think you've understood it, you haven't. The 'baptistry' is really at the base a public bus shelter, and above a private office, while as a whole urban form it is a gateway to the spectacular gorge and the main element which defines the 'piazza' on the public front of the complex. One volume thus equals one historical reference – baptistry – but in addition, four different meanings.

Next, the 'campanile' indeed has a melancholic Romanesque quality because of its lone, dark arch on each face, as if it had survived as a ruin from some abandoned village – but it's not a bell tower. It actually works as a lift shaft (though, it has to be said, its central position clearly plays a visual role, anchoring the very restless forms). The pitched roof 'nave' of the 'church'? Actually this shelters both a theatre and a dance studio, the latter jumping through the gable end to proclaim itself with a diagonal window – which also shows the dancers off to the street. Two functions are compressed into one volume, which has, on second glance, subtle articulations that express this combination. But if you approach the centre from the public piazza side you expect not only an ecclesiastical function, but a single nave interior. There is thus a certain pleasure in discovering that the two readings of the form – a historical allusion and real function – are each carried through with determination, producing, for instance, a dancer where a rose window might have been.

This expectation and surprise continue around the site and into the details. The stone and steel loggia is, as you'd imagine, a doubly-coded sign of the past and present – meeting each other halfway in a cultural stalemate as it were – but it's also a sign of another duality: the fact that there are two, parallel loggias under one roof. One is glass-enclosed for the winter and the other is open to the view over the gorge. The mixed meanings of the rugged setting are also articulated in this dual structure, since the rock outcrops and landscape are at once violent and

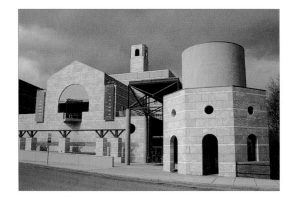

276 JAMES STIRLING and MICHAEL WILFORD, *Center for the Performing Arts*, model, Cornell University, Ithaca, New York, 1984-89. Nine small-block volumes are tightly packed on the edge of a gorge. The magnificent view is framed by steel and masonry piers whose cut signals a floor line, among other things.

277 JAMES STIRLING and MICHAEL WILFORD, *Center* seen from the street side and 'piazza'. Highly edible marble, in grey and white bands, is juxtaposed with stucco and industrial concrete. Octagonal 'baptistry' and gabled 'church' are juxtaposed with neutral, functional elements – an architecture of two languages battling, conversing, laughing.

278 JAMES STIRLING and MICHAEL WILFORD, *The Loggia* overlooking the gorge. The marble is cut in an industrial manner and the crisp black voids not only symbolise this, but also the fact that it is hung from steel.

domesticated.

Finally, close up, the effect of grey and white Vermont marble recalls the rusticated bands of Siennese buildings. But if you get very close and examine the cracks you find the, by now, standard Post-Modern non-joint joint, the sharp black void that tells you these are stones which do not 'stand' on each other, but 'hang' from a steel frame.

In effect Stirling and Wilford are interweaving two separate languages to see how they may mutually enhance each other, and they are doing this with enough subtlety to keep one step ahead of the viewer. Of course their use of a relatively popular code is appropriate – 'cultural centre = Mediterranean hill town' – and it allows the visitor to take in the overall use quickly. Furthermore the typology allows the mass to be broken up into small, grammatical blocks. But then there is the second, contemporary reading of realistic functions, which are allowed to speak in their utilitarian and economic language, their stucco surface and box-like shape. These form dignified but tight spaces for performers and an audience who are there as much to see the gorge as the drama. The Classical and functional languages are given equal weight, suggesting that neither has the sufficiency to dominate today.

Kisho Kurokawa's Museum of Contemporary Art on a hill overlooking Hiroshima has a similar taut ambiguity between several languages. At first glance we might think this is a Modern or Neo-Modern complex because of its glistening metallic surfaces, and it is only on second glance that we discover the historical subtext. Thus it inverts the emphasis Stirling gives his two texts and adds a third one, the future. Past, present and future are very clearly interwoven in this, yet another 'village on a hill'. From afar one sees only the mute, pitched outlines of the museum – sixty percent of the mass is sunk out of sight into the small mountain – and these roofs are proportioned like traditional sixteenth-century Edo storehouses.

Would anyone grasp this? Perhaps not at first, because the shapes might be understood as simply ubiquitous, the common pitched forms. But after a while, as one sees the same shape used in profile again and again – twelve times – it begins 279 to play an iconic role, haunting the memory like an old tune that won't go away. In some cases the pitched form is played straight, in others with a little ornamental flourish, and in the heart of the museum – the entrance – it is curved in a circle and 280 sliced apart with a silver flash. Does this refer to the A-bomb? Or is it simply a consequence of cutting the circle to signify entry? Further cues just increase the controlled ambiguity.

If one imagines the entry space as seen from the air, it takes on the shape of that very ominous and familiar image, the mushroom cloud; this interpretation is further suggested by the discovery of stones scorched by the blast which are set by the entry-way. Everyone in Hiroshima is, of course, constantly reminded of the catastrophe in their city's history, as indeed is every visitor; so the references to the blast are bound to be assumed in any building as significant as a museum. On the other hand, the wrapped circular form on columns is also the sign of community, a veiled reference to the embracing arms of St Peter's in Rome and a natural sign of unity, of coming together. And the framed void from its centre, the view of the sky,

279 KISHO KUROKAWA, *Museum of Contemporary Art*, Hiroshima, 1988. This museum will form part of a huge 'cultural centre as village', but already the small-block planning is clear. The tripartite code is established here with a base symbolising the past, Edo construction; the middle in white tile representing the present; and the top, in aluminium, signifying the future.

280 KISHO KUROKAWA, *Entrance Rotunda*. A flash is created by cutting the cross-section of the Edo storehouse motif.

281 KISHO KUROKAWA, *Sculpture Court*. The references to different cultures and periods are lurking, masterfully, below the surface to keep peace in this magical space.

is a sign of the cosmos, as it is in the oculus of the Pantheon. So we are free to read this circular form in at least four ways: as a functional entrance, a mushroom cloud, a sign of community and the conventional view of the heavens. Like Stirling's 'baptistry' it is coherently multivalent.

Throughout the museum one meets more explicit signs of East and West, for instance the crackling stone patterns of the traditional Edo castle and the 'light canons' of Le Corbusier. But these are just incidents which punctuate a more general language of past (masonry base), present (tiled middle section) and future (metallic top). This codification of time is carried through with consistency and subtlety. The most magical space, where all three ages mesh in a seamless manner, is the sculpture court. This reminds one at once of the raked pebble garden of 281 Ryoanji, the airfoil door of Le Corbusier's Garches, the Post-Modern columns and keystones of Michael Graves and the sleek aluminium fuselage of a long UFO. None of these images is explicit, and for me to name them is to betray their ambiguity and understatement. Their aura comes from being only suggested.

Here we return to an idea broached in the second section of this book, the power of suggested metaphor to capture the imagination and send it off, running in coherent but divergent ways so that it catches many types of animal, not just the hare or the goose. The example was Le Corbusier's Ronchamp chapel, a building which is over-coded so that it alludes to many things, but abstract enough to avoid reduction to any one of them.

The third 'cultural centre as village', Antoine Predock's Fine Arts Center for Arizona State University, also has this suggestiveness. Like most of his work, it hints at a regional location, the Southwest landscape of rock outcrops, buttes and parched desert, but it never actually names these references. The closest it comes is at the symmetrical entrance-way, where rows of Saguaro cacti transform into freestanding columns cast from a purplish grey concrete which is an actual desert colour. It's appropriate to be explicit about the code here, where people first meet 283

282 ANTOINE PREDOCK, *Fine Arts Center,* Arizona State University, Tempe, Arizona, 1987-89. Night view of the roofscape with the small-block volumes cascading about to create a virtual world set apart from the chaotic city. (Timothy Hursley)

283 ANTOINE PREDOCK, *Entrance.* Saguaro cacti form the ritualised entryway, like sphinxes in front of an Egyptian temple, and then they turn into purple-grey concrete piers, again of an Egyptian muteness. Straight ahead is a trussed bridge and high wall for protecting images. (Timothy Hursley)

284 ANTOINE PREDOCK, *The Roofscape* captures the beauty of an arid climate and makes us believe for a moment that students can inhabit the world of the pueblo. (Timothy Hursley)

the building, but how many of them could decipher it? The complex is understated and ambiguous enough to require patient analysis, even architectural cryptography. If cactus = concrete column = colour of desert stone, then on the roof-top maze one traverses the divided pyramids = mountains, and the terraces = buttes? So much for the murmurs and hints of a desert landscape, they are no more than this. 286

Other meanings, lurking well below the surface, are the two high points, a trussed gateway to the main entrance side and a blank concrete wall facing it. Functionally these serve all sorts of minor uses such as a bridge, projection booth and large screen on which images are cast at night. This wall also marks the fly- 282 tower of the auditorium. But what do these rhetorical shapes mean? They certainly suggest more than their relatively unimportant uses. Here, perhaps, we can borrow another code Predock established in a previous building, the Fuller House. In this desert complex or *faux* village as Kurt Anderson has called it, there are two enigmatic shapes that also book-end a pyramid.[110]

At the east end is a pavilion for watching the sunrise, while on the west there's a slightly different one for watching it set. While the two dominating forms of the art centre do not entail an activity as specific as this, they certainly evoke it. In mood the roofscape is a cross between a Mayan temple of sacrifice and an eighteenth- 284 century Indian astronomical observatory; and here one feels part of some brooding cosmic spectacle where the planets and stars must be consulted to ward off feelings of existential angst. Perhaps all that is rather a heavy load to drop on to these austere concrete forms – their emptiness does suggest a slight melancholia – but this portentous note is never finally struck: the architecture just manages to avoid slipping into the bathos it so clearly tempts, the New Age, sci-fi 'altered atmospheres' that the architect mentions as a motive for his work. 285

Partly this is because it is so abstract and tough as to discourage explicit interpretation and sentiment. And partly it is because there are other allusions to some of the forms – the very small windows, the metalwork railing and the red

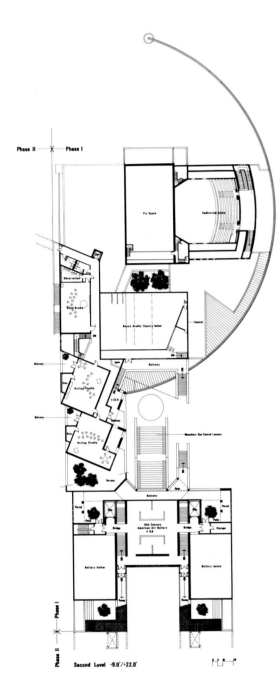

285 ANTOINE PREDOCK, *Plan of the Center.* A symmetrical entrance leads up and down to skewed studios and then the culmination, an auditorium set at right angles to the movement pattern.

286 ANTOINE PREDOCK, *The Roof forms* – pyramid, tower, bridge, void and a space full of promise. (Timothy Hursley)

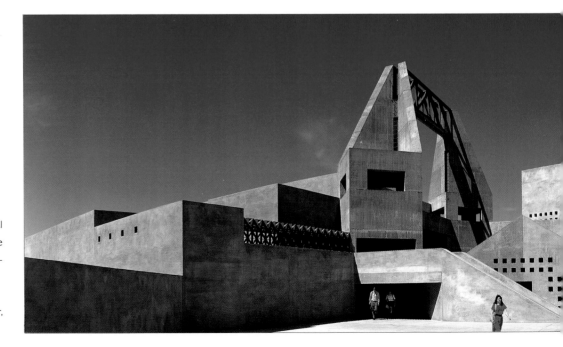

arcades. These last, for instance, relate to the red curves of the adjacent building and strike an entirely new note: that of a pergola and refined European gallery. Without such occasional divergent signs the building would sink back into that mute Modern abstraction from which it is perhaps derived – the wall architecture of Luis Baragan.

There is no question that as a Post-Modernist Predock is a minimalist who confines himself to one or two materials from which he constructs his virtual all-over world, his lunar landscape. The purple-grey concrete follows one almost everywhere, from the art gallery lobby to the dance theatre and auditorium, although it is punctuated by slight articulations and details which define different parts of the area with a specific character. This is place-making of an allusive sort, like Ronchamp an enigmatic building with no specific interpretation that unlocks its secret, but many different keys that work on parts.

During the late eighties when much Post-Modernism was becoming too literal, that work re-confirmed the truth that the most effective architecture is one which communicates as much indirectly as it expresses literally. Like Stirling and Kurokawa, Predock handles his symbolism with a benign restraint – lets it grow from the site and function, and like them, produces an articulated world of small-scaled parts set in tense opposition. Whether these three cultural centres and the offices as village constitute a major paradigm for the 1990s remains to be seen. The urban and economic forces of concentration make this problematic, but not impossible. The traditions of Late- and Neo-Modernism which favour huge scale, repetition and abstraction go against it. But if it is unlikely to dominate the whole profession in this age of welcome pluralism, at least it will concern that minority who care for an intimate and convivial urbanism. After the orgy of success, and after being declared dead because of it, a leaner, tougher, more chastened tradition has emerged.

ARATA ISOZAKI, *Art Tower Mito*, Mito, Ibaragi, Japan, 1986-90 (Yasuhiro Ishimoto)

Notes

1 See my *The New Moderns*, Academy Editions, London, 1990.

2 See Mies van der Rohe, 'Industrialized Building', originally printed in the magazine *G*, Berlin, 1924, and reprinted in Ulrich Conrad's, *Programmes and Manifestos on 20th-Century Architecture*, London, 1970, p 81.

3 See Manfredo Tafuri, 'L'Architecture dans le boudoir', *Oppositions 3*, New York, 1974, p 45 and note p 60. Tafuri claims that the 'accusations of fascism hurled at Rossi mean little, since his attempt at the recovery of an ahistoricising form excludes verbalisations of its content and any compromise with the real'. This escape clause is, of course, impossible; all form will be looked at historically and have conventional associations tied to it, and Rossi's work cannot escape this 'compromise with the real' any more than all other architecture.

4 Peter and Alison Smithson, *Architectural Design*, October 1969, p 560.

5 P Smithson, *AD*, May 1975, p 272.

6 A and P Smithson, 'Gentle Cultural Accommodation', *L'Architecture d' Aujourd'hui*, Janvier/Fevrier 1975, pp 4-13, quote from page 9. The Smithsons contend that they didn't write this, although it is typical of their ideas. See *Architectural Design 7*, 1977 and my answer.

7 See Tom Wolfe, *The New Journalism*, Picador, London, 1975, pp 54-56, and my article 'The Rise of Post-Modern Architecture', *Architectural Association Quarterly*, London, Summer 1976, pp 7-14.

8 For the call to morality see Sigfried Giedion, *Space, Time and Architecture*, Cambridge, Mass, 1971, pp 214, 291-308. For the 'Heroic Period', see Peter and Alison Smithson, issue of *Architectural Design*, December 1965.

9 Sant'Elia's 'Manifesto', July 11, 1914, is quoted from *Futurismo 1909-1919*, exhibition of Italian Futurism organised by Northern Arts and the Scottish Arts Council, catalogue, 1972, p 49.

10 A more rigorous comparison of architecture to language is made by architectural semioticians who substitute technical terms for these imprecise analogies. For our general purpose however, the analogies will suffice, as long as we don't take them too literally.

11 A point made by Umberto Eco in 'Function and Sign: Semiotics and Architecture', published in *Structures Implicit and Explicit*, Graduate School of Fine Arts, University of Pennsylvania, Vol 2, 1973. Republished in our anthology edited by Geoffrey Broadbent, Dick Bunt and myself, *Signs, Symbols and Architecture*, Wiley, 1980.

12 See Umberto Eco, 'A Componential Analysis of the Architectural Sign/Column', in *Semiotica 5*, Number 2, 1972, Mouton, The Hague, pp 97-117.

13 See for instance Herbert Gans' description of the five major 'taste cultures' in his *Popular Culture and High Culture*, Basic Books, New York, 1974, pp 69-103.

14 See G L Hersey, 'J C Loudon and Architectural Associationism', *The Architectural Review*, August, 1968, pp 89-92.

15 E H Gombrich, *Art and Illusion*, London, 1960, pp 316-317.

16 Nikolaus Pevsner, *An Outline of European Architecture*, Harmondsworth, 1964, p 374.

17 I've discussed these debates in *Modern Movements in Architecture*, Harmondsworth, New York, 1973, pp 318-28, and footnotes for references. The Italian press took up the controversy and applied the metaphors of 'refrigeration' in English criticism (if my memory serves me).

18 Philip Johnson, 'The Seven Crutches of Modern Architecture', *Perspecta III*, New Haven, 1955; 'Whence and Whither, The Processional Element in Architecture', *Perspecta 9/10*, New Haven, 1965.

19 See John Jacobus, *Philip Johnson*, George Braziller, New York, 1962.

20 Letter to Jurgen Joedicke, 6/12/1961 reprinted in Jacobus, *op cit*.

21 See Robin Boyd, *New Directions in Japanese Architecture*, New York and London, 1968, p 102.

22 See *CIAM '59 in Otterlo*, ed Jurgen Joedicke, London, 1961, p 182.

23 A fairly complete bibliography of these writings and comment on the Venturi Team can be seen in *Learning from Las Vegas*, revised edition by Robert Venturi, Denise Scott Brown and Steven Izenour, Cambridge, 1977. For criticism see my review, 'Venturi *et al* are Almost All Right', in *Architectural Design, 7*, 1977.

24 See *Learning from Las Vegas, op cit*, pp 130 and 149.

25 They have often pointed this out. Robert Venturi for instance said at a conference at Art Net, London, July 1976: 'I apologise for all these Rich Men's houses, but I'll take anything we can get.' Their projects are often for more social tasks, sometimes minority groups and the under-serviced.

26 See A+U, 74:11 devoted to their work from 1970-74, p 43.

27 See my 'MBM and the Barcelona School', The Architectural Review, March 1977, pp 159-165, and Arquitectura Bis, 13 and 14, Barcelona, May-June, 1976.

28 I've discussed this 'threat' of pluralism and eclecticism in 'Isozaki and Radical Eclecticism', Architectural Design, January, 1977, pp 42-48. In this article I try to distinguish between a radical eclecticism which is semantically based and multivalent, and the nineteenth-century weak eclecticism which was an easy-going shuffling of styles.

29 I have investigated this in an unpublished work on ersatz.

30 See Aldo Rossi, L'Archittetura della Città, Padua, 1966; Arquitectura Bis, No 12, pp 25-31. Gijon is a monumental form of Classicism with Venturi-like juxtapositions.

31 See L'Architecture d'Aujourd'hui, the issue devoted to Formalisme-Realisme, 190, April, 1977, p 101.

32 I'm sure there will be misunderstandings on this score as I seem to be having it both ways, arguing in favour of 'the spirit of the age' and against it; but the distinctions between 'climate of opinion' and 'Zeitgeist' concern the former's basis in convention not necessity, choice not force, change not permanence, and morality not behaviour.

33 Henry-Russell Hitchcock, Architecture Nineteenth and Twentieth Centuries, Penguin edition, Harmondsworth, 1971, p 533.

34 Quinlan Terry, 'Architectural Renaissance', Building Design, Sept 17, 1976, p 18. Terry gave a lecture in a series on Post-Modernism at the AA in 1976.

35 For an excellent discussion of this trend, see Chris Fawcett, 'An Anarchist's Guide to Modern Architecture', AAQ, No 7, Vol 3, 1975, pp 37-57. The 'guide' is not so much about anarchism as parody.

36 Conrad Jameson's writings have mostly been published in England, in various journals. Among the sources are: 'Social Research in Architecture', The Architect's Journal, 27 October, 1971, and following controversy; 'Architect's Error', New Society, 8 May, 1975, and following controversy; 'Enter Pattern Books, Exit Public Housing Architects: a friendly sermon', The Architect's Journal, 11 February, 1976, and following controversy; 'British Architecture: Thirty Wasted Years', The Sunday Times, February, 1977, and following controversy. Jameson, unlike other polemicists, really knows how to fire the nerve-ends of Modern architects. His book, Notes for a Revolution in Urban Planning, was published by Penguin and Harper and Row, 1978.

37 Maurice Culot, one leader of ARAU in Brussels, spent ten days at Port Grimaud discussing its implications with the architect François Spoerry. In conversation, June 1977, he told me he was convinced this was the type of housing for the people, but that his local Communist leaders, some attuned to 1930s models, might not accept this.

38 David Gebhardt, 'Getty's Museum', Architecture Plus, Sept/Oct, 1974, pp 57-60, 122. See also Reyner Banham, 'The Lair of the Looter', New Society, 5 May, 1977, p 238; Building Design, September 13, 1974; in England, The Observer and The Times ran articles on the building.

39 James Stirling, letter in Oppositions, 1976, Summer, p 130. But some part of Stirling's recent work is definitely Post-Modern in its contextualism, for example his Düsseldorf and Cologne projects, see below.

40 Colin Amery and Lance Wright, 'Lifting the Witches' Curse', The Architecture of Darbourne and Darke, RIBA Publications, 17 May-29 July, 1977, exhibition handbook, pp 7-8.

41 Andrew Derbyshire, 'Building the Welfare State', RIBA Conference 1976, RIBA Publications, op cit, p 29.

42 Ibid, p 50.

43 Aldo Van Eyck, 'In Search of Labyrinthian Clarity', L'Architecture d' Aujourd'hui, Jan / Feb, 1975, p 18.

44 RIBA Conference, op cit, p 62.

45 The 1968 Skeffington Report recommended greater public participation in planning, but so far this has led only to increased consultation, or the minimum choice about room layout, location of partitions, etc, as in the PSSHAK project, or to the development of plans, as in the Swinbrook project of North Kensington.

46 'Signification and richness' in architecture are assumed as ultimate values in my argument, and not justified here; arguments for pluralism in politics are given by Karl Popper, and for richness in art by I A Richards. For my misgivings concerning the Neo-Rationalists, see 'The Irrational Rationalists', A+U, April and May, 1977, published in The Rationalists, edited by Dennis Sharp, Architectural Press, London 1978.

47 See Architectural Design, 3, 1977, p 191, the issue devoted to Culot, Krier and Tafuri.

48 Hannah Arendt has written about the public realm at length in The Human Condition, Chicago, 1958, and On Revolution, New York, 1963. Her ideas have influenced George Baird, Kenneth Frampton, Conrad Jameson and Nikolaus Habraken among others in the field of architecture.

49 Leon Krier, 'A City within a City', Architectural Design, 3, 1977, p 207.

50 See Graham Shane, 'Contextualism', Architectural Design, No 11, 1976, pp 676-9, for a discussion and bibliography.

51 Colin Rowe, 'Collage City', *The Architectural Review*, August, 1975, p 80.

52 *Ibid*, pp 80-81.

53 See Nathan Silver's letter to *The Architectural Review*, September, 1975, and following exchanges.

54 See T S Eliot, *After Strange Gods*, London, 1934.

55 Kent C Bloomer and Charles W Moore, *Body, Memory and Architecture*, Yale University Press, New Haven, 1977, pp 41-2.

56 Carl G Jung et al, *Man and his Symbols*, Aldus Books, London, 1964, p 78.

57 See Rudolf Wittkower, *Studies in the Italian Baroque*, London and New York, 1975, p 63.

58 For the notions of layering see Colin Rowe and Robert Slutsky, 'Literal and Phenomenal Transparency', *Perspecta 8*, 13-14; for 'compaction composition' see my *Le Corbusier and the Tragic View of Architecture*, London and Cambridge, 1973.

59 Robert Stern has written on Post-Modernism in various journals, among them *Architectural Design*, 4, 1977, and has defined three aspects to it: contextualism, historical allusion and applied ornament. In America the social and participatory aspects of Post-Modernism are considered unimportant as the argument is conducted more on the stylistic and semantic levels. Stern has discussed 'inclusivism' in his *New Directions in American Architecture*, New York and London, 1969, re-edited with a postscript on Post-Modern, 1977.

60 C Ray Smith 'Supermannerism', *New Attitudes in Post-Modern Architecture*, E P Dutton, New York, 1977, pp 91-99.

61 See Maggie Keswick, *Chinese Gardens*, New York and London, 1978. The last chapter, which I wrote, discusses the notion of this kind of liminal, religious space, a notion which I adapted from Edmund Leach's concepts. See his *Culture and Communication*, Cambridge, 1976,

pp 6-7, 14, 51, 71-75.

62 See Charles Moore, 'Hadrian's Villa', *Perspecta 6*, 1958, 'You have to Pay for the Public Life', *Perspecta 9/10*, 1975, both reprinted in *Dimensions*, with Gerald Allen, New York, 1977. See also the issue of *Architecture d'Aujourd'hui*, March/April, 1976.

63 *Architecture d'Aujourd'hui, ibid,* p 60.

64 The idea has not been developed here, but see, for instance, Juan Pablo Bonta, 'Notes for a Theory of Design', in *Versus, 6*, Milan, 1974. If meaning consists in relation then a restricted as well as rich palette can articulate it. My general favouring of rich over restricted systems is partly due to our Miesian age, and partly due to the fact that élites and specialists are better at decoding restricted systems than the general public.

65 See Basil Bernstein, *Class, Codes and Control*, Vols I and II, London, 1971-3 and Linda Clarke, 'Explorations into the Nature of Environmental Codes', *The Journal of Architectural Research*, Vol 3, No 1, 1974.

66 The studies are admittedly very fragmentary and made with students in England, Norway and California, although several interviews at buildings were conducted in England and Holland. One study has been published, 'A Semantic Analysis of Stirling's Olivetti Centre Wing', in *AAQ*, Vol 6, No 2, 1974, and part of another is included in my 'Architectural Signs' published in *Signs, Symbols and Architecture, op cit*. Supporting evidence can be found in B Bernstein, *op cit* and Philip Boudon, *Lived-in Architecture, Le Corbusier's Pessac Revisited*, London 1972, pp 46, 65, 112.

67 See chapter 3, *Late-Modern Architecture*, Selected Essays, Academy Editions, London and Rizzoli, New York, 1980.

68 The Chicago Seven were formed in 1976 partly in response to other city groupings. By the time of the Townhouse competition, March 1978, they included eleven architects: Thomas Beeby, Laurence Booth, Stuart Cohen, James Freed, Gerald Horn, Helmut Jahn,

James Nagle, Kenneth Schroeder, Stanley Tigerman, Cynthia Weese and Ben Weese.

69 See 'Roma Interrotta', *Architectural Design*, Vol 49, No 3/4, 1979, p 163.

70 'Hiroshi Hara, an Interview with David Stewart', *AAQ*, Vol 10 No 4, 1978, pp 8, 10.

71 See Stephen Kieran, *VIA II*, 'On Ornament', Pennsylvania, 1977; a symposium at the Architectural Association in December 1978 on 'The Question of Ornament' (unpublished), Boyd Auger, 'A Return to Ornament', *The Architectural Review*, 1976, and subsequent correspondence; an exhibition at the Cooper-Hewitt Museum organised by Richard Oliver, 1978; E H Gombrich, *The Sense of Order*, A Study in the Psychology of Decorative Art, Phaidon, Oxford, 1979.

72 Several of these meanings were pointed out to me by Charles Moore in a discussion, March 1979; others can be found in Martin Filler's excellent article on the Piazza in *Progressive Architecture*, Nov 1978, pp 81-7.

73 See pages 79, 88, 128, 130, 146 and also note 62.

74 See for instance Peter Davey's issue of *The Architectural Review*, September 1983 on 'Romantic Pragmatism'.

75 For a discussion of the politics behind the Biennale see my article 'Free Style Classicism', *Architectural Design* 1/2, 1982, pp 4-7.

76 See my 'Mario Botta and the New Tuscanism', in *Architectural Design*, 9/10, 1983, pages 82-85 and 'The New Abstraction' by OM Ungers, 'Abstract Representation', *Architectural Design*, 7/8, 1983, pp 23-58.

77 *Op cit*, p 37.

78 *Op cit*, note 74.

79 Tom Wolfe, *From Bauhaus to Our House*, Farrar, Straus and Giroux, New York, 1981. Wolfe bases large parts of his satire, without acknowledgement, on earlier editions of this

book. His amusing invention of Modernism as fear of the bourgeoisie is, however, entirely his own. See my 'Wolfe Bites Wolfe', *AD News Supplement*, No 1, 1982, pp 1-5.

80 Demetri Porphyrios, 'Classicism is Not a Style', *Architectural Design*, 5/6, 1982.

81 'The Great Debate: Modernism versus the Rest' is now available in part in *Transactions III*, RIBA Publications, London, 1983. My own article 'Post-Modern Architecture, the True Inheritor of Modernism' and Kenneth Frampton's 'Modern Architecture and Critical Regionalism' are one set of opposites, but there are others who join the debate: Will Alsop, Peter Hodgkinson, Richard McCormac and Jules Lubbock.

82 The term and concept were coined by me in February 1980 and published as a profile and as 'Post-Modern Classicism – The New Synthesis', *Architectural Design*, 5/6, 1980.

83 For 'The New Representation' and some of its practitioners see 'Abstract Representation', *op cit*, pp 17-19, note 74.

84 See for instance pages 87 and 123.

85 Robert Venturi, 'Diversity, Relevance and Representation in Historicism, or *plus ca change* . . .' *Architectural Record*, June 1982, p 116.

86 *Ornamentalism*, by Robert Jensen and Patricia Conway, Clarkson N Potter Inc, New York and Allen Lane, London, 1982.

87 E H Gombrich, *The Sense of Order*, Phaidon Press, Oxford, 1979.

88 See my *Skyscrapers-Skycities*, Academy Editions, London, 1980, Rizzoli, New York, for a discussion of these metaphors.

89 See *The Architectural Review*, June 1982, largely devoted to the Classicism of the Taller Bofill: quote from p 32.

90 A substituted name for Post-Modern Classicism: see the exhibition catalogue by

Helen Searing, *Speaking A New Classicism: American Architecture Now*, with an essay by Henry Hope Reed, Smith College Museum of Art, Northampton, Mass, 1981.

91 See my issue of *Architectural Design*, 'Abstract Representation', 7/8, 1983, pp 4-22.

92 For an abbreviated description see my article on 'The Elemental House', *Architectural Digest*, November 1983, pp 107-113, 122.

93 Buildings designed six or seven years before they are completed inevitably look, in our world village, old-hat when they are finished; often the more influential they are the older they look, because the fast-food architects beat them by many years to publication. This is sad because it takes the edge off some of the innovations.

94 For this interpretation, see my 'The Museum as Acropolis' in 'Abstract Representation', *op cit*, note 74, pp 110-119.

95 See my 'Symbolic or Signolic Architecture', *Art and Design*, London, October 1985, pp 14-17, 48, and *Symbolic Architecture*, Academy Editions, London, Rizzoli, New York, 1985.

96 John Barth discusses the search for a wider audience in 'The Literature of Replenishment, Postmodernist Fiction', *The Atlantic*, January 1980, pp 65-71; quote, page 70.

97 For some of these compromises see B M Lane, *Architecture and Politics in Germany, 1918-45*, Harvard University Press, 1968, p 181; Sibyl Moholy-Nagy, *Journal of the Society of Architectural Historians*, March 1965, p 84; my own *Le Corbusier and the Tragic View of Architecture*, Penguin and Harvard, 1974; *Modern Movements in Architecture*, Penguin, Harmondsworth, 1973, pp 45-51, and much literature on the subject published since then.

98 See Patricia Leigh Brown, 'Disney Deco', *The New York Times Magazine*, April 8, 1990, pp 18-24, 42-49, 68.

99 *Ibid*, p 24.

100 See my *Post-Modernism, The New Classicism in Art and Architecture*, Academy Editions, London, *1987*, 'Wrestling with Mega-Build', pp 228-237, and references there.

101 See Leon Whiteson, 'Disney Design', *The Los Angeles Times*, January 25, 1990, section E1 for 'hokey-tecture' and quotation from Michael Graves.

102 Applied signs are 'signolic', multivalent relations between signs, space, function, etc, are 'symbolic'; see my *Architecture Today*, chapter entitled 'Symbolic and Signolic Architecture', Academy Edtions and Abrams, 1988, pp 316-322.

103 See reference note 96, p 49 for James Stirling quote.

104 Robert Stern is quoted in Paul M Sachner, 'Entertainment Architecture', *Architectural Record*, September, 1989, p 66.

105 'Socitalism', socialised capitalism rather than the Eastern European capitalised socialism, is a concept and phrase I am developing to explain Post-Modern economics in a work to appear later.

106 See Michael de Courcy Hinds, 'Vast Project Heads for '93 Finish', *The New York Times*, Section 8, March 23, 1986, pp 1, 18, *ff*.

107 Paul Goldberger, 'Battery Park City is a Triumph of Urban Design', *The New York Times*, August 31, 1986, Arts Section.

108 For the application of Chaos theory and Ilya Prigogine's ideas to Japanese urban development see Kazuo Shinohara, quoted in my *The New Moderns, op cit*, chapter one.

109 For these characteristic reactions see Brendan Gill, 'In the Classic Vein', *The New Yorker*, August 14, 1989; Robert Maxwell, 'Compact at Ithaca', *The Architectural Review*, November 1989, p 38.

110 K Andersen, 'An Architect for the New Age', *Time Magazine*, April 11, 1988, p 40.

Index